Sexual Harassment in the Workplace

Sexual Harassment in the Workplace

*A Guide to the Law
and a Research Overview
for Employers and Employees*

Titus E. Aaron

with Judith A. Isaksen

McFarland & Company, Inc., Publishers
Jefferson, North Carolina, and London

British Library Cataloguing-in-Publication data are available

Library of Congress Cataloguing-in-Publication Data

Aaron, Titus E., 1957–
    Sexual harassment in the workplace : a guide to the law and a
research overview for employers and employees / by Titus E. Aaron,
with Judy A. Isaksen.
      p. cm.
    Includes bibliographical references and index.
    ISBN 0-89950-763-8 (sewn softcover : 50# alk. paper) ∞
    1. Sexual harassment of women – Law and legislation – United States.
2. Sex discrimination against women – Law and legislation – United
States. I. Isaksen, Judy A. II. Title.
KF3467.A915   1993
344.73′014133 – dc20
[347.30414133]   92-56628
                                                                 CIP

Manufactured in the United States of America

McFarland & Company, Inc., Publishers
 Box 611, Jefferson, North Carolina 28640

To Mom

Acknowledgments

The people who have contributed directly or indirectly to this book are too numerous to thank individually. I do, however, appreciate each one of them. I thank my friends Peter Cubra, Eddie Dry, and Gerald Bloomfield for the support and guidance during the years that brought me to this point. And I greatly appreciate the sacrifices my mother made as this book evolved.

My deepest gratitude goes to Judy Isaksen, my friend, editor, and critic.

Contents

Introduction

American men and women are born into a culture which includes a set of ideas and attitudes relating to sex and gender. Sex stereotypes have traditionally been learned from language, parents, schools, and more recently the mass media, long before people became responsible for supporting themselves or a family (Richardson 1988). Institutions such as religion, the law, and medical and mental health systems have historically reinforced cultural sex stereotypes (Richardson 1988). Americans were for many years socialized to believe that they should get married, and the woman's primary role was perceived by men as homeworker, child-care provider, and sexual partner.

Women have traditionally held certain types of important jobs, often identified as "women's work," as if these jobs were unimportant (e.g., secretaries, waitresses, and nurses, yet men also work as secretaries, waiters, and nurses). The primary role of men in America was for many years perceived as worker and provider for the traditional family. Because men were perceived as the breadwinners, many jobs were male-dominated in both raw numbers of workers and ownership of business interests. It has often been alleged that sex discrimination resulted from this American socialization process, which prevailed for many decades. Today, however, children are likely to be brought up in a single-parent family in which the parent works. Fewer children are being taught that a woman's place is at home while a man supports the family. More men are working with women, and more boys are being raised and supported by women. More children are primarily socialized by day-care centers and public schools. The changes in the socialization process of children will have an effect on the work force of the future.

Some citizens were of the opinion that viewing women as "sex objects" in the workplace created barriers for women. A broad term, *sexual harassment,* was conceived, which included diverse conduct ranging from suggestive looks to rape. The federal Equal Employment Opportunity Commission began to enact guidelines that stated that sexual harassment was a form of sex discrimination prohibited by federal law (Chapter 1).

The U.S. Merit Systems Protection Board conducted several studies which verified that conduct labeled sexual harassment existed in the federal work force (Chapter 2), and the U.S. Supreme Court and Congress subsequently recognized sexual harassment as a form of sex discrimination prohibited by federal law (Chapter 3).

While some assert that sexual harassment is an expression of natural attraction (Chapter 4), others argue that sexual harassment results from one person exercising power over another person (Chapter 5).

The process through which sexual harassment claims are evaluated begins at a personal level and can end in court. As the allegations move through the process, the views of the victim become less important in determining whether the conduct constituted sexual harassment (Chapter 6). Once a lawsuit is filed, the judicial process, with its own set of rules, comes to life (Chapter 7). There are many types of sexual harassment cases filed in the courts (Chapter 8), and the courts are not in agreement whether allegations of sexual harassment must be viewed from the perspective of the victim or a "reasonable person" (Chapter 9). Sexual harassment has been said to include sexual teasing, jokes, gifts, remarks, or questions (Chapter 10); letters, calls, and pressure for dates or sexual favors (Chapter 11); and deliberate touching, assault, and rape or attempted rape (Chapter 12).

Employers have a duty to enact policies and training programs designed to combat sexual harassment (Chapter 13), to promptly investigate allegations of sexual harassment (Chapter 14), and to take prompt disciplinary action where an investigation reveals that harassment occurred (Chapter 15). The costs to employers for combating harassment may exceed the cost of the sexual harassment (Chapter 16).

In addition to federal laws prohibiting sexual harassment, employees in some jurisdictions may sue their employer and the harasser under state law for conduct amounting to sexual harassment (Chapter 17). Those wrongfully accused of harassing may also sue the employer and accuser under state law in some jurisdictions (Chapter 15, Chapter 18).

Sexual harassment is not unique conduct involving employees in a given workplace. For example, civil litigation involving sexual misconduct by church employees has increased during the past decade.[1] In *Milla v. Tamayo,*[2] the California Court of Appeals decided a case in which it was alleged that priests utilized their position and confidential relationship with a 16-year-old girl to entice her to have sex with them and other priests. It was alleged that numerous priests had sex with the girl over a period of several years and that she eventually became pregnant. In numerous other court cases, church officials and employees have been accused of engaging in sexual misconduct with both children and adults.[3]

Since the 1970s, sexual contact between psychiatrists and psychologists and their patients has been explicitly prohibited by the Hippocratic oath, the American Psychiatric Association's code of ethics, and the American Psychological Association's code of ethics (Holroyd and Brodsky 1977; Kardener et al. 1973). Yet "prohibited" sexual relationships between male and female psychiatrists, psychologists, and other therapists and male and female patients exist in alarming numbers (Gartrell et al. 1987; Gartrell et al. 1986; Holroyd and Brodsky 1977; Kardener et al. 1973). Perhaps these sexual relationships result from the therapist's position of power vis-à-vis his or her patient (Kardener 1974) or the extent to which sexual relationships exist in educational programs attended by therapists (Pope et al. 1986; Pope et al. 1979).

Research has established that therapist-client sexual relationships can result in the following destructive consequences for patients: (1) ambivalence, (2) feelings of guilt, (3) feelings of emptiness, (4) sexual confusion, (5) impaired ability to trust (often focused on conflicts about dependence, control, and power), (6) identity, boundary, and role confusion, (7) suppressed anger, (8) emotional dyscontrol, frequently involving severe depressions, (9) increased suicidal risk, (10) cognitive dysfunction (especially in the areas of attention and concentration, frequently involving flashbacks, nightmares, intrusive thoughts, and unbidden images) (Pope 1986: 567). In 1986 Pope (1986: 567) noted that the therapist-patient sex syndrome "bears obvious similarities to various aspects of borderline personality disorder, post-traumatic stress disorder, rape response syndrome, reaction to incest, and reaction to child or spouse battering."

And what about those charged with enforcing the laws against sexual assault and rape? Sexual harassment suits have been filed by city police employees,[4] sheriff's employees,[5] state police employees,[6] city corrections employees,[7] county corrections employees,[8] and state corrections employees.[9] Others seek relief from lawyers and the courts. Not surprisingly, sexual abuse or misconduct with clients by attorneys has become such a problem that some state bar associations are proposing ethical and disciplinary rules to confront this problem (Garwin 1992). And judges are no angels. Numerous cases involving sexual misconduct by judges have been filed during the last decade.

This book is intended to provide an overview of sexual harassment in the workplace, a small part of the much larger issue of sexual misconduct in America.

Chapter 1

The Rise of Sexual Harassment as a Social Issue: 1964-1980

Title VII of the Civil Rights Act of 1964 (Title VII) was enacted when many people in our society were involved in opposing perceived social injustices. In 1964, the prohibition against sex discrimination was added to Title VII at the last minute, with little legislative debate.[1] Title VII provides that it is an unlawful employment practice for an employer with fifteen or more employees

> (1) to fail or refuse to hire or to discharge any individual, or otherwise to discriminate against any individual with respect to his compensation, terms, conditions, or privileges of employment, because of such individual's ... sex ...; or

> (2) to limit, segregate, or classify his employees or applicants for employment in any way which would deprive or tend to deprive any individual of employment opportunities or otherwise adversely affect his status as an employee, because of such individual's ... sex.[2]

Title VII further prohibits an employer[3] from retaliating against an employee for filing a complaint or assisting others in prosecuting complaints alleging discrimination prohibited by its provisions.[4] The Equal Employment Opportunity Act of 1972 made Title VII applicable to state and local government employees.[5] In 1972, Title VII was amended to apply to many employees of the federal government.[6] The Equal Employment Opportunity Commission (EEOC) came to be the federal administrative agency charged with enforcing Title VII.[7]

Prior to the 1970s, most of what is now popularly labeled sexual harassment[8] was considered a personal as opposed to a social problem (Skaine 1990; Gillespie and Leffler 1987). Because sexual harassment was considered a personal problem, it required a personal as opposed to social or institutional solution (Gillespie and Leffler 1987). Interest groups, media attention, the creation of "scientific data," court decisions, and other government action played a part in redefining sexual harassment as a social problem. The transformation of sexual harassment from a personal to a

1

social issue involved bringing the problem to the public's attention, consistently labeling it sexual harassment, and defining it as detrimental in the workplace (Weeks et al. 1986).

Researchers primarily credit feminists and union activists[9] with labeling a broad range of behaviors sexual harassment (Brewer and Berk 1982; Livingston 1982). The definition of sexual harassment used in efforts to portray it as a social problem included conduct ranging from suggestive looks to rape. Ellen Frankel Paul (1991: 5–6) has argued that "categorizing everything from rape to 'looks' as sexual harassment makes us all victims, a state of affairs satisfying to radical feminists, but not very useful for distinguishing serious injuries from the merely trivial. . . . Whether it is useful to call rape 'sexual harassment' is doubtful, for it makes the latter concept overly broad while trivializing the former." But then, including such a broad range of behavior in the definition of sexual harassment increased the number of persons claiming to be the victims of sexual harassment and helped paint the picture that sexual harassment was so widespread it was a social problem worthy of an institutional response.

The "first official interest group to protest sexual harassment," a feminist organization named Working Women United, was formed in New York in 1975 (Weeks et al. 1986: 435–36). The research branch of Working Women United, Working Women's Institute (WWI), generated publicity and research and provided counseling, training, and information relating to sexual harassment (Weeks et al. 1986). The WWI used speakouts as a method of showing victims of sexual harassment that others had shared similar experiences[10] and to attract media attention (Weeks et al. 1986). In 1976, another feminist organization, the Alliance Against Sexual Coercion (AASC), was founded in Boston and began offering "comprehensive services to individuals and providing education and training to work organizations" (Weeks et al. 1986).

The redefinition of sexual harassment as a social problem required that sexual harassment be defined and legitimized as actionable (Weeks et al. 1986). Those interested in redefining sexual harassment as a social issue claimed that (1) the problem was widespread, (2) it caused victims to suffer real harm, (3) the problem was caused by social as opposed to individual characteristics, and (4) institutional remedies would therefore be necessary to remedy the problem (Gillespie and Leffler 1987).[11]

Between Title VII's enactment and 1980, courts reached differing results when confronted with the argument that sexual harassment was a form of sex discrimination prohibited by Title VII. In *Corne v. Bausch and Lomb, Inc.,*[12] two female employees filed suit under Title VII alleging that repeated verbal and sexual advances they and others were subjected to became so onerous that they were forced to resign. Judge Frey of the U.S. District Court for the District of Arizona held:

Nothing in the complaint alleges nor can it be construed that the conduct complained of was company directed policy which deprived women of employment opportunities. A reasonably intelligent reading of the statute demonstrates it can only mean that an unlawful employment practice must be discrimination on the part of the employer, Bausch and Lomb. Further, there is nothing in the Act which could reasonably be construed to have it apply to "verbal and physical sexual advances" by another employee, even though he be in a supervisory capacity where such complained of acts or conduct had no relationship to the nature of the employment.[13]

In *Williams v. Saxbe,*[14] Diane Williams, an employee of the U.S. Department of Justice, alleged that she was terminated in retaliation by a male supervisor because she declined his sexual advances. Williams asserted that after she refused a sexual advance by her immediate supervisor, he "engaged in a continuing pattern and practice of harassment and humiliation of her, including but not limited to, unwarranted reprimands, refusal to inform her of matters for the performance of her responsibilities, refusal to consider her proposals and recommendations, and refusal to recognize her as a competent professional in her field."[15] Her employer alleged that Williams was terminated for "poor work performance."[16]

After the EEOC held that the evidence did not support a charge of discrimination based on sex, Williams filed a lawsuit under Title VII in the U.S. District Court for the District of Columbia. District Court Judge Charles Richey held that "the retaliatory actions of a male supervisor, taken because a female employee declined his sexual advances, constitutes sex discrimination within the definitional parameters of Title VII."[17] Judge Richey held that Congress intended Title VII to be broadly construed to eliminate any discrimination based on "gender." He also held that Title VII "does not require that the discriminatory policy or practice depend upon a characteristic peculiar to one of the genders" because the application of a rule, regulation, practice, or policy "on the basis of gender is alone sufficient for a finding of sex discrimination."[18] Thus it was "sufficient to allege a violation of Title VII to claim that the rule creating an artificial barrier to employment has been applied to one gender and not to the other."[19]

The Department of Justice appealed the case to the Court of Appeals for the District of Columbia after a favorable decision was rendered to Ms. Williams.[20] The court of appeals reversed Judge Richey's decision after finding he had applied the wrong standard of review and remanded the case to the district court for a new trial.

A legal definition of sexual harassment began to develop as courts began recognizing sexual harassment as a form of sex discrimination prohibited by Title VII (Livingston 1982). The courts have recognized two general types of harassment prohibited by Title VII: "quid pro quo" sexual harassment and "hostile work environment" sexual harassment. In quid pro quo sexual harassment cases, it is alleged that the performance of sexual favors is directly linked to a workplace benefit such as hiring, promotion, retention, or transfer.[21] Title VII does not, however, prohibit favoritism toward a person with whom a supervisor is having a consensual sexual relationship.[22] In a hostile work environment case, it is alleged that the sexual conduct is unwelcome and sufficiently severe or pervasive to alter the conditions of employment by creating an intimidating, hostile, or offensive work environment.[23]

Early court cases, even if lost, were important because of the publicity and controversy they generated (Weeks et al. 1986). Media coverage of these early court cases served to inform citizens and pressure unsympathetic judges (Weeks et al. 1986). It has been argued that

> litigation contributes significantly toward the generation of social issues by functioning as a mechanism for developing case law and precedents. Even if the case is lost, the controversy it creates serves as an effective device for public and political consciousness-raising. Also, litigation prods the political process and even the private sector by establishing the seriousness and credibility of an issue. . . . Litigation served all these purposes for sexual harassment. [Weeks et al. 1986: 438]

While neither the WWI nor the AASC focused its primary efforts on litigation, they assisted victims of sexual harassment in locating attorneys willing to help them and assisted in the construction of an informal network of attorneys interested in helping victims of sexual harassment (Weeks et al. 1986). Capturing media attention was a primary goal of the AASC and WWI.[24] The AASC and WWI distributed numerous position papers and pamphlets relating to sexual harassment (Weeks et al. 1986).[25] Numerous newspaper and magazine articles addressing the issue of sexual harassment were published during the 1970s, many were written by persons directly linked to the AASC and WWI (Weeks et al. 1986).

A report of the results of a *Redbook* survey (Safran 1976) was one of the most important articles published in the mid-1970s due to the widespread publicity which followed it and subsequent reliance on the results of the survey by others. Kathy Baldridge and Gary McLean (1980: 294) made the following comments about the *Redbook* survey: "When we consider that the majority of the respondents were married women in their 20's and early 30's, working at white collar jobs, and earning between $5,000 and $10,000 a year, it is obvious that a representative sample of women did not respond. Rather, because of their interest in the subject, it is obvious that the respondents were self-selecting; that is, those who have experienced sexual harassment, or know someone who has, are much more likely to respond than are those further removed from the problem. Thus, the responses would tend to overstate the problem."

Wendy Pollack (1990: 42) has noted that the 1976 *Redbook* "survey's aftermath may be more significant than its particular results. The indication that women perceived sexual harassment as a real problem laid the groundwork for further interest and investigation. Speakouts on sexual harassment were held, more surveys were done, papers were written, and the mass media picked up the issue." In a 1987 *New Mexico Law Review* article, Eleanor Bratton stated, "This survey remains the most comprehensive and widely cited to date." Although the *Redbook* survey was biased (Gillespie and Leffler 1987) and contained flaws rendering its results unreliable, it has been cited in numerous articles and studies.

In the spring of 1980, *Redbook* and the *Harvard Business Review* conducted a joint survey relating to sexual harassment, the results of which were reported in the March–April 1981 issue of the *Harvard Business Review* (HBR) in an article by Eliza G. C. Collins and Timothy B. Blodgett, "Sexual Harassment . . . Some See It . . . Some Won't." *Redbook* published an article in its March 1981 issue. The HBR mailed questionnaires to 7,408 HBR subscribers, of whom 1,846 responded (44% were female, 52% male, and 4% of unknown gender) prior to the cutoff date. Collins and Blodgett noted that where the supervisor makes a sexual advance, people are much more likely to call it harassment than when a coworker does so. The HBR survey also found that upper management considered sexual conduct engaged in by supervisors at work more blameworthy than the same conduct by coworkers. Collins and Blodgett found that 32 percent of women and 66 percent of men agreed or partly agreed with the statement "The amount of sexual harassment at work is greatly exaggerated." A substantial portion of both men and women agreed or partially agreed with the statement "Women can and often do use their sexual attractiveness to their own advantage."

In 1980, Kathy Baldridge and Gary McLean conducted a survey of working women in the Minneapolis–St. Paul area. Of 100 females holding management positions and 100 females holding secretarial positions to whom the survey was sent, only 103 respondents were included in the final sample.[26] Sixty-two percent of the respondents reported being subjected to some form of what was labeled sexual harassment by the researchers. This study is important because an inquiry was made into the sex of the initiator of the harassment. The researchers found that some of the sexual harassment reported by the female respondents was initiated by females.[27]

While 62 percent of the respondents reported being subject to some form of conduct labeled sexual harassment, only eighteen percent of the respondents felt that sexual harassment in the office is a serious problem. However, twenty-four percent felt that it is a moderate problem, twenty-two percent felt it is a minor problem, and thirty-five percent felt that it is not a problem. [Baldridge and McLean 1980: 296]

This research suggests that although sexual harassment exists in the workplace, not all people perceive that conduct as a serious problem. If harassment is not perceived as a serious problem by many of those respondents who admit having been subjected to such conduct, we must pause. We must then ask whether it is reasonable to draw an inference about the importance of incident rates alone in telling us anything about the extent to which serious unwelcome conduct exists in the workplace.

By 1980, sexual harassment was seen by some as a social condition worthy of public-policy action (Weeks et al. 1986). In 1980, the Equal Employment Opportunity Commission enacted rules which specifically recognized *some* of the conduct labeled sexual harassment as legally redressable sexual harassment prohibited by Title VII.[28] As one court stated: "While some sexual harassment can certainly be equated with employment discrimination within the purview of Title VII, not all sexual harassment is actionable."[29] The EEOC regulations currently define *sexual harassment* as follows:

> Unwelcome sexual advances, requests for sexual favors, and other verbal or physical conduct of a sexual nature constitute sexual harassment when (1) submission to such conduct is made either explicitly or implicitly a term or condition of an individual's employment, (2) submission to or rejection of such conduct by an individual is used as the basis for employment decisions affecting such individual, or (3) such conduct has the purpose or effect of unreasonably interfering with an individual's work performance or creating an intimidating, hostile, or offensive working environment.[30]

Soon after the EEOC issued its regulations defining sexual harassment, the courts began applying those guidelines in holding employers liable for some forms of sexual harassment.

Sexual harassment cases must be decided on a case-by-case basis, based on the totality of the circumstances, "such as the nature of the sexual advances and the context in which the alleged incidents occurred."[31] An employer can be held liable for sexual harassment by its supervisors even where the employer has a policy prohibiting sexual harassment.[32] An employer is responsible for sexual harassment by coworkers in the workplace where the employer or its supervisors or agents knew or should have known of the conduct, "unless it can show that it took immediate and appropriate corrective action."[33] And an employer may be held liable for sexual harassment by nonemployees where the employer or the supervisors or agents of the employer knew or should have known of the sexual harassment and the employer "fails to take immediate and appropriate corrective action."[34]

According to the EEOC, "Prevention is the best tool for the elimination of sexual harassment."[35] Thus, the EEOC has announced that employers "should take all steps necessary to prevent harassment from occurring, such as affirmatively raising the subject, expressing strong disapproval, developing appropriate sanctions, informing employees of their right to raise and how to raise the issue of harassment under Title VII, and developing methods to sensitize all concerned."[36]

To be meaningful, a remedy must address the roots of the problem it claims to prohibit or alter. Many researchers and commentators have argued that sexual harassment results from sex-role spillover or the notion that men exercise their power over women, both products of the socialization process. Title VII does not attempt to change the way citizens are socialized in America, at least not until a person enters the workplace, usually after many years of irreversible socialization. Title VII does not require parents or institutions to socialize children in a manner consistent with Title VII's equal rights requirements. And it has been argued that Title VII fails to address adequately issues relating to power distributions in the workplace (Livingston 1982). Until the socialization process is changed, discrimination resulting from the socialization process is not likely to change. Discrimination must be confronted at its roots—in the family, the schools, and the law—if it is to become history.

An employer has no control over the preemployment socialization of its employees, and no evidence supports the proposition that an employer can undo what the socialization process has done on the day the employee begins work. It can be argued that the EEOC's recognition of harassment of working women by coworkers and supervisors acted to penalize employers who hire women to work in jobs that have traditionally been considered men's work. For reasons beyond the employer's control (socialization) women entering nontraditional jobs were more likely to be harassed than women hired to work in positions traditionally held by women. This reality may have worked to deter employers initially from providing women equal employment opportunities in nontraditional jobs.

From a risk-management perspective, it could be argued that it made no sense for an employer to hire a woman to work in a nontraditional job in light of the likelihood of sexual harassment and the civil liability imposed on the employer under the EEOC regulations. The question left for an employer was often whether it would rather find itself in court defending a sex discrimination case (for failure to hire a woman in a nontraditional job) or a claim for sexual harassment. Those employers who felt that the stigma of being sued for failing to hire a woman was less detrimental than the stigma associated with sexual harassment may have been deterred from hiring women. In this light, the recognition of harassment as sex discrimination under Title VII can be seen as an attempt to maintain the status quo by deterring employers from hiring women to work in nontraditional jobs.

Although the EEOC regulations make it clear that an employer is expected to take immediate and appropriate corrective action when it learns of sexual harassment in the workplace, state court decisions may deter an employer from doing so. Prior to the enactment of Title VII, state court decisions provided that an employer could terminate an employee who was without an employment contract for a definite period for any reason. Since Title VII's enactment, courts have determined that an employer is not necessarily free to discharge an employee "at will" (Aaron et al. 1990). For example, one court has held that an employee who had a reasonable expectation that he would be employed on a long-term basis could be discharged only for "good cause"; the employee could not be discharged based on a subjective conclusion that he engaged in sexual harassment of female employees.[37] An employer may also be sued under state law by an employee on the grounds that the investigation of the sexual harassment charge was improperly conducted or was not objectively reasonable.[38] And an employer may be sued for defamation under state law for discharging an employee based on false allegations of sexual harassment.[39]

Title VII was for many years limited in that it did not allow for emotional distress or punitive damages in sexual harassment cases. If a person who had been harassed prevailed under Title VII but did not suffer a tangible economic loss and did not quit because of the harassment, remedies were basically limited to injunctive relief, and no monetary compensation was allowed. An employee who quit a job as a result of legally redressable hostile environment sexual harassment could recover lost wages if the employee prevailed on a "constructive-discharge" theory. Title VII has, however, been amended to allow for increased damage awards against employers.

Chapter 2
U.S. Merit Systems Protection Board Studies

While many important studies were conducted during the 1970s and 1980s, surveys conducted by the Merit Systems Protection Board are of particular importance. In 1979, the Subcommittee on Investigations of the Committee on Post Office and Civil Service of the U.S. House of Representatives conducted preliminary inquiries into the extent and nature of sexual harassment of federal government employees.

These preliminary inquiries resulted in the subcommittee asking the U.S. Merit Systems Protection Board to conduct a major study on the extent and nature of sexual harassment in the federal workplace, using the Office of Personnel Management's (OPM) definition of sexual harassment.[1] The task of conducting the study was assigned to the board's newly formed Office of Merit Systems Review and Studies. In the 1981 report of the Merit Systems Protection Board, the following comments were made regarding the literature and studies that had previously been conducted:

> First, most of the literature has been descriptive in nature with little or no explanation for the underlying social process involved. Second, most of the writers have been feminists who have focused on the behavior almost exclusively as it affects women, and not men, the larger society, or the work organization. Third, there has been no common denominator in the literature about what behaviors constitute sexual harassment. Fourth, much of the literature has drawn upon individual case studies to generalize about the victims of sexual harassment, how the experience affects them and how they have responded.
>
> Most of the studies that did attempt to discern the extent of sexual harassment and to explore other factors such as the characteristics of victims and perpetrators, are not scientifically valid. Therefore they are not useful to measure the actual pervasiveness of sexual harassment in the workplace.
>
> The groups surveyed in most of these studies were small and self-selected. In addition, in none of these studies was sexual harassment defined in the same way, making comparison of results difficult. Another drawback was that most of these studies asked about experiences of

sexual harassment over the respondent's lifetime (relying on their recall ability), rather that [sic] using a conceptually stronger finite and more immediate period of time.

However a few studies have had some degree of scientific control. Although they shed some light on the topic, none have addressed all of the issues covered in the Congressional mandate, none have involved Federal employees, all have been restricted to a particular geographic region and/or work setting, only one has included men as well as women as potential victims, and most have restricted harassment to heterosexual behavior. [USMSPB 1981: 21, footnotes omitted]

The Merit Systems Protection Board set out to conduct a study free of many deficiencies of the previous research. The Merit Systems Protection Board conducted a large survey in 1980, published in 1981, and a large follow-up survey in 1987, published in 1988, relating to the sexual harassment of federal government employees (USMSPB 1981; USMSPB 1988). Due to the size of the 1980 survey, the fact that it included both men and women, and that a follow-up study was conducted seven years after the first survey, these studies are very important.

Incident Rates in 24-Month Period

The May 1980 survey of 23,964 employees of the federal government, in which 20,314 usable questionnaires were returned, found that 42 percent of female respondents and 15 percent of male respondents reported being sexually harassed in the preceding 24-month period (USMSPB 1981).[2] The Merit Systems Protection Board's 1987 follow-up study was published in 1988, and reported that the March 1987 survey of 13,000 full-time federal employees, in which 8,523 employees responded, found 21 percent of the men at the Veterans Administration reported being subjected to sexual harassment in the preceding 24-month period. The 1987 survey reflected that of the total number of respondents from all federal agencies surveyed, "42 percent of women and 14 percent of men employed by the Federal Government said they experienced some form of uninvited and unwanted sexual attention; i.e., sexual harassment" (USMSPB 1988: 11).[3]

The nature of the specific conduct to which respondents reported being subjected in the 1980 and 1987 surveys changed very little (see Table 2.1). The number of self-identified victims who reported experiencing a form of harassment more than once in the 1980 survey was substantially higher than the percentage of respondents who reported being subjected to the conduct only once (see Table 2.2). These results suggest that victims of sexual harassment are either more sensitive than the average person[4] and therefore perceive more incidents as sexual harassment or that some

Table 2.1
Percentage of Respondents Who Claimed
They Experienced This Form of Conduct

CONDUCT DESCRIPTION	Female		Male	
	1987	1980	1987	1980
Uninvited Sexual Remarks	35%	33%	12%	10%
Uninvited Suggestive Looks	28%	28%	9%	8%
Uninvited Pressure for Dates	15%	26%	4%	7%
Uninvited Deliberate Touching	26%	15%	8%	3%
Uninvited Pressure for Sexual Favors	9%	9%	3%	2%
Uninvited Letters and Calls	12%	9%	4%	3%
Uninvited Actual or Attempted Rape or Assault	.8%	1%	.3%	.3%

Source: USMSPB 1988: 16–17.

characteristic of these respondents makes them more likely to be subjected to sexual harassment than the 58 percent of women and 85 percent of men respondents who reported not being subjected to sexual harassment in the 1980 survey. When evaluating the incident rates found in the Merit Systems Protection Board studies, it is important to remember that most of the respondents' supervisors were male. It is also important to remember that not all of the sexual harassment reported by respondents involved hetero-sexual conduct (*see* Table 2.3).[5]

Opinions About What Can Constitute Sexual Harassment

The Merit Systems Protection Board studies reflect that men and women are in close agreement about what *can* constitute sexual harassment. The Merit Systems Protection Board surveys reflect that the majority of both male and female respondents were of the opinion that sexual remarks, suggestive looks, pressure for sexual favors and dates, letters and calls, and deliberate touching can constitute sexual harassment when that conduct is uninvited or unwelcome (*see* Table 2.4). The literature and

Table 2.2
Percentage of Victims of Each Form of
Harassment Who Reported Being Subjected
to That Form of Sexual Harassment More Than Once

CONDUCT	MEN	WOMEN
Sexual remarks	71%	77%
Suggestive looks	61%	73%
Pressure for dates	45%	55%
Deliberate touching	54%	62%
Pressure for sexual favors	40%	52%
Letters and calls	38%	42%
Actual or attempted rape or assault	55%	20%

Source: USMSPB 1981: 39.

Table 2.3
Percentage of Narrator Victims Who Indicated the
Sex of the Person(s) Who Bothered Them Sexually

SEX OF HARASSER	MEN	WOMEN
Male	18%	79%
Two or more males	4%	16%
Both males and females	6%	2%
Female	60%	2%
Two or more females	12%	1%
Unknown	.3%	1%

Source: USMSPB 1981: 58.

court cases asserting that hostile work environment sexual harassment claims must be viewed from the perspective of the victim because men and women hold different opinions about the types of conduct which can constitute sexual harassment are in conflict with the results of the Merit Systems Protection Board studies. Men and women may, however, hold very different views about when conduct which can constitute sexual harassment is in fact sexual harassment.

Some of the respondents to the 1980 survey believed they were expected to engage in behavior which could be labeled sexual harassment (*see* Table 2.5). Victims reported being expected to engage in such behavior more often than nonvictims. It may be that those who flirt and make sexual comments about the opposite sex are more often victims because others do not perceive that engaging in like behavior is sexual harassment or unwelcome conduct.

While more federal employees agreed that specific types of conduct can constitute sexual harassment in 1987 than in 1980, this increased awareness did not result in a significant decrease in the number of employees reporting they had been subjected to sexual harassment. These results suggest that training programs designed to inform employees of types of conduct which can constitute sexual harassment are not an effective preventive measure.

Opinions About When Conduct Constitutes Sexual Harassment

Fewer respondents in the 1980 survey reported that unwelcome sexual attention is a problem for employees where they work than the number of employees who reported being subjected to conduct labeled sexual harassment (compare Tables 2.1 and Table 2.5).[6] Both male and female respondents to the 1980 survey were of the opinion that people should not have to put up with unwanted sexual attention on the job (*see* Table 2.6). When sexual attention is considered unwanted cannot be determined from the Merit Systems Protection Board studies.

Some federal employees in the 1980 survey agreed or strongly agreed that those who complain about sexual harassment have either asked for it or are trying to get the accused into trouble (*see* Table 2.6). This suggests many federal employees are of the opinion that conduct constituting sexual harassment is not always "unwelcome" and that allegations are sometimes used as a tool to get even with others.[7] Likewise, many federal employees in the 1980 survey were of the opinion that sexual harassment has been exaggerated and that people should not be so quick to take offense when someone expresses a sexual interest in them (*see* Table 2.6).

Table 2.4. Percentage of Respondents Who Consider the Indicated Behavior Can Constitute Sexual Harassment

CONDUCT DESCRIPTION	By Supervisor				By Co-Worker			
	Male		Female		Male		Female	
	1980	1987	1980	1987	1980	1987	1980	1987
Uninvited Pressure for Sexual Favors	84%	95%	91%	99%	65%	90%	81%	98%
Uninvited Deliberate Touching	83%	89%	91%	95%	69%	82%	84%	92%
Uninvited Letters and Calls	87%	76%	93%	90%	76%	67%	87%	84%
Uninvited Pressure for Dates	76%	81%	77%	87%	59%	66%	65%	76%
Uninvited Suggestive Looks	59%	68%	72%	81%	47%	60%	64%	76%
Uninvited Sexual Remarks	53%	58%	62%	72%	42%	47%	54%	64%

Source: USMSPB 1988: 13–15.

Table 2.5
Percentage of Respondents Who Agree or Strongly Agree

PERCEPTIONS OF WORK ENVIRONMENT	FEMALE		MALE	
	Victims	Nonvictims	Victims	Nonvictims
Where I work, I feel I am expected to flirt.	23%	2%	21%	2%
Where I work, I feel I am expected to make sexual comments about the opposite sex.	9%	2%	28%	5%
Uninvited and unwanted sexual attention is a problem for employees where I work.	27%	4%	22%	7%

Source: USMSPB 1981: 55.

Although the Merit Systems Protection Board studies did not inquire into the factors considered by federal employees in determining whether conduct labeled sexual harassment is "welcome" or "unwelcome," the respondents were asked about the effect of the initiator's motive. A minority of federal workers in the 1980 survey agreed that conduct should be called sexual harassment even if the person engaging in the behavior did not mean to be offensive (*see* Table 2.6).[8]

The Effect of Organizational Characteristics

The 1980 survey found that most narrator victims identified the organizational level of their harassers as coworkers or other employees (65% of females; 76% of males). Supervisors were identified as the harasser by 37 percent of the female narrator victims and 14 percent of the male narrator victims. Subordinates were identified as the harassers by some narrator victims (4% of females; 16% of males) in the 1980 survey (USMSPB 1981: 60). The 1987 survey also found that most harassers were not supervisors (*see* Table 2.7).

The notion that employees who are under the direct supervision of a female supervisor are less likely to experience sexual harassment than employees supervised by men is not supported by the Merit Systems Protection Board studies (*see* Table 2.8). Female respondents in the 1980

Table 2.6
Percentage of Respondents Who Agree or Strongly Agree

QUESTION	W	M	S	NS	V	NV
I would call something sexual harassment even if the person doing it did not mean to be offensive.	26%	28%	30%	27%	31%	26%
People shouldn't be so quick to take offense when someone expresses a sexual interest in them.	36%	48%	45%	43%	44%	43%
When people say they've been sexually harassed, they're usually trying to get the person they accuse into trouble.	7%	13%	11%	11%	9%	12%
People who receive annoying sexual attention have usually asked for it.	22%	31%	30%	27%	23%	29%
The issue of sexual harassment has been exaggerated-most incidents are simply normal sexual attraction between people.	23%	44%	43%	34%	28%	39%
Unwanted sexual attention on the job is something people should **not** have to put up with.	97%	95%	96%	95%	96%	95%

Note: W = Women; M = Men; S = Supervisor; NS = Nonsupervisor; V = Victim; NV = Non-victim.

Source: USMSPB 1981: 29.

survey reported experiencing slightly less (7%) sexual harassment when supervised by a woman than when supervised by a man. Male respondents in the 1980 survey reported experiencing more (10%) sexual harassment when supervised by a woman than when supervised by a man. The 1980 survey found evidence suggesting the male-female ratio of the immediate work group may affect the likelihood of an employee being sexually harassed (*see* Table 2.9).

Table 2.7
Percentage of Victims, by Sex, Who Claim That the Source
of Their Harassment Was in the Organizational Level Shown

POSITION OF HARASSER	1987	
	MALE	FEMALE
Immediate Supervisor	12%	12%
Higher Level Supervisor	10%	19%
Co-Worker	47%	41%
Subordinate	10%	2%
Other Employees	40%	37%
Other or Unknown	10%	10%

Source: USMSPB 1988: 20.

Table 2.8
Percentage of Respondents Who Experienced Conduct
Labeled Sexual Harassment by Sex of Immediate Supervisor(s)

Sex of Victim's Supervisor	MEN	WOMEN
Male Supervisor	13%	45%
Male and Female Supervisors	25%	44%
Female Supervisor	23%	38%

Source: USMSPB 1981: 51.

The 1980 survey found little support for a relationship between other organizational characteristics (i.e., level of privacy, supervisory status, length of service, work schedules, work hours, and the size of the work groups) and the likelihood of an employee being sexually harassed. The 1980 study also found weak relationships between geographical regions, salary and grade levels, or job classification and the likelihood of an employee being subjected to sexual harassment.

Table 2.9
Percentage of Federal Employees in Different Kinds
of Work Groups Who Experienced Sexual Harassment

TYPE WORK GROUP	1980	
	MEN	WOMEN
All men	8%	55%
Predominantly men	13%	49%
Equal numbers of men and women	19%	43%
Predominantly women	22%	37%
All women	22%	22%

Source: USMSPB 1981: 52.

Characteristics of Victims

The victims of sexual harassment include men and women of all ages, education levels, occupations, and backgrounds. The sexual and political orientations of the USMSPB respondents are unknown. Young workers are more likely than older workers to be subjected to conduct labeled sexual harassment (*see* Table 2.10). Unmarried workers are generally more likely than married workers to be subjects of sexual harassment (*see* Table 2.11). As educational levels increased, the rate of sexual harassment increased only slightly, but more so for women than for men (*see* Table 2.12). Sexual harassment also crossed racial and ethnic boundaries (*see* Table 2.13).

Conclusion

The Merit Systems Protection Board studies reflect that while sexual harassment was a problem for both men and women in the federal workforce, heightened awareness of what types of conduct can constitute sexual harassment did not result in a decrease in incident rates. Some victims are perceived as asking for it, and others are perceived as trying to get someone in trouble. Whether the alleged harasser intended to be

Table 2.10
Percentage of Federal Employees of Different Ages
Who Experienced Conduct Defined as Sexual Harassment

AGES	1980	
	MEN	WOMEN
16-19	27%	67%
20-24	20%	59%
25-34	18%	53%
35-44	14%	43%
45-54	13%	33%
55+	12%	22%

Source: USMSPB 1981: 43.

Table 2.11
Percentage of Federal Employees Who Reported
Experiencing Conduct Labeled Sexual Harassment

MARITAL STATUS	1980	
	MEN	WOMEN
Single	22%	53%
Divorced	21%	49%
Married	13%	37%
Widowed	30%	31%

Source: USMSPB 1981: 44.

Table 2.12
Percentage of Federal Employees of Different Educational
Levels Reporting Experiencing Conduct Labeled Sexual Harassment

EDUCATION LEVEL	1980	
	MEN	WOMEN
Less than high school diploma	8%	31%
High school diploma or GED	11%	35%
High school diploma plus technical training or apprenticeship	13%	39%
Some college	17%	45%
College graduate: B.A., B.S., or other bachelor's degree	14%	50%
Some graduate school	15%	53%
Graduate or professional degree	17%	48%

Source: USMSPB 1981: 45.

Table 2.13
Percentage of Federal Employees of Different Racial and
Ethnic Backgrounds Who Experienced Sexual Harassment

RACE	MEN	WOMEN
Other	27%	40%
Hispanic	18%	45%
White, not of Hispanic origin	13%	43%
Black, not of Hispanic origin	21%	43%
Asian or Pacific Islander	16%	36%
American Indian or Alaskan Native	22%	35%

Source: USMSPB 1981: 45.

offensive makes a difference to some about whether conduct should be labeled sexual harassment.

Most male (95%) and female (97%) respondents to the 1980 survey were of the opinion people should not have to put up with *unwanted* sexual attention on the job. When sexual attention is unwanted is an open question.

Chapter 3
Supreme Court Decisions and Recent Events in Congress

While many important events in the courts and Congress occurred from 1981 to 1991, of particular importance were the Supreme Court's recognition of hostile work environment sexual harassment claims in employment and public schools receiving federal financial assistance, allegations of sexual harassment being made against a Supreme Court justice, and the amendment of Title VII by the Civil Rights Act of 1991.

Meritor Savings Bank

It was not until 1986 that the first sexual harassment case was heard by the U.S. Supreme Court. In the 1986 case of *Meritor Sav. Bank, FSB v. Vinson,*[1] the Supreme Court addressed the issue of sexual harassment. A female employee met a male vice president and branch manager of a bank and was hired at the bank by this branch manager as a teller trainee in 1974. While the branch manager remained her supervisor, the employee was promoted from teller trainee to teller, and then to assistant branch manager. The promotions were based solely on merit. In September 1978, the employee notified the branch manager that she was taking indefinite sick leave. The employee was terminated for excessive use of sick leave on November 1, 1978. The employee brought suit under Title VII against both the branch manager and the bank, seeking injunctive relief, compensatory and punitive damages, and attorney's fees.

At an 11-day trial, the employee testified that shortly after her probationary period as a teller trainee, the branch manager invited her out to dinner. She accepted, and during the course of dinner, the manager suggested they go to a motel and have sexual relations. The employee testified that she consented, after first resisting, because she feared losing her job. She testified that during the next several years she consented to having intercourse with the branch manager 40 or 50 times when he demanded sexual favors from her. According to the employee, the branch manager's demands for sexual favors were usually made at the branch, during and after business hours.

In addition, the employee testified:

> [The branch manager] fondled her in front of other employees, followed her into the women's restroom when she went there alone, exposed himself to her, and even forcibly raped her on several occasions. These activities ceased after 1977, [the employee] stated, when she started going with a steady boyfriend.[2]

The employee also "testified that because she was afraid of [the branch manager] she never reported his harassment to any of his supervisors and never attempted to use the bank's complaint procedure."[3] In response to the employee's allegations,

> [The branch manager] denied [the employee's] allegations of sexual activity, testifying that he never fondled her, never made suggestive remarks to her, never engaged in sexual intercourse with her, and never asked her to do so. He contended instead that [the employee] made her accusations in response to a business-related dispute. The bank also denied [the employee's] allegations and asserted that any sexual harassment by [the branch manager] was unknown to the bank and engaged in without its consent or approval.[4]

The *Meritor* Court held that Title VII's prohibition against sex discrimination included the right to be free from a hostile working environment and remanded the case to the district court to determine whether the employee had in fact been subjected to a hostile working environment.

In *Meritor,* the Supreme Court held that "for sexual harassment to be actionable, it must be sufficiently severe or pervasive 'to alter the conditions of [the victim's] employment and create an abusive working environment.'"[5] The Court noted that "the gravamen of any sexual harassment claim is that the alleged sexual advances were 'unwelcome.'"[6] The Court distinguished between "involuntary" and "unwelcome":

> The fact that sex-related conduct was "voluntary," in the sense that the complainant was not forced to participate against her will, is not a defense to a sexual harassment suit brought under Title VII.... The correct inquiry is whether respondent by her conduct indicated that the alleged sexual advances were unwelcome, not whether her actual participation in sexual intercourse was voluntary.[7]

An alleged victim's sexually provocative speech or dress is relevant in determining whether he or she found particular sexual advances unwelcome.[8] The relevance of such evidence, however, may be outweighed by its potential for unfair prejudice in some cases.[9] The Court declined "the parties' invitation to issue a definitive rule on employer liability" but agreed "with the EEOC that Congress wanted courts to look to agency principles for guidance."[10]

One commentator announced that *Meritor* "represents an advancement of women's rights in the area of sexual harassment" (Morlacci 1987–88: 510). Terpstra and Baker (1992: 187) conducted a study of factors which affect outcomes of federal court cases (such as the existence of supporting witnesses and documents) and found the *Meritor* case "had no significant effect on the relationship between the case variables and case outcomes studied."

Hill v. Thomas

About half a decade after the Supreme Court recognized hostile work environment sexual harassment as a violation of Title VII, Clarence Thomas, now a justice of that Court, was accused of sexual harassment during his confirmation hearings. On July 1, 1991, President Bush selected Clarence Thomas as the 106th justice of the Supreme Court (Biskupic 1991c). The Senate then put into motion the process of evaluating Clarence Thomas to determine whether it would confirm him. Clarence Thomas's confirmation hearings were unique in several respects. First, Thomas discussed the unusual fact, for such a nominee, of having lived in poverty as a youngster (Reske 1991; Biskupic 1991b).[11] Second, Thomas consistently avoided taking stands on controversial issues during the initial confirmation hearings (Biskupic 1991a, 1991b, 1991c). Third, Anita Hill alleged that Thomas had sexually harassed her when she worked for him. Fourth, Thomas refused to discuss his personal life.

The confirmation hearings originally concluded on September 20, 1991, and a vote was scheduled for the week of September 23 (Biskupic 1991b). On September 27, 1991, the Senate Judiciary Committee reached a split vote, 7–7, on whether Clarence Thomas should be appointed to the Supreme Court (Biskupic 1991c). Those who voted against Clarence Thomas

> cited the nominee's refusal to give direct answers to questions during five days of testimony.
>
> Most said they were not ready to settle for evasive responses, particularly on questions of individual privacy, with a conservative court majority now in place [Biskupic 1991c: 2786].

The matter of Clarence Thomas's confirmation was then taken before the full Senate (Biskupic 1991d). A vote whether to confirm Thomas as the next Supreme Court justice was scheduled. Just a few days before the scheduled vote on Thomas's confirmation, Anita Hill's accusation that Thomas had sexually harassed her while she worked for him at the Department of Education and at the Equal Employment Opportunity Commission was made public (Reske 1991; Biskupic 1991e). Anita Hill's allegations against Clarence Thomas and his response have been summarized by one commentator as follows:

> [Clarence Thomas] denied Hill's claim of sexual impropriety and said he would not submit to questions about his private life.
> Hill directly contradicted her former boss. She said he repeatedly asked her for dates and ignored her rejections. She said she believed he wanted to have sexual intercourse with her. And she provided embarrassing details of what she said were Thomas' comments to her on the job: talk of women's breasts, the size of his penis, accounts of movies of group sex and bestiality [Biskupic 1991e: 2948].

Days of additional televised hearings were conducted to investigate Anita Hill's allegations of sexual harassment, vividly bringing the issue into the homes of millions of Americans. Joan Biskupic (1991e: 2948) asserted that "for all Americans engaged by the story, at issue are sexual harassment and how men and women treat each other on the job."[12] It has been noted that the hearings, which "produced more political steam than useful fact," suffered from several "corrupting circumstances" (Bailey 1992: 47).

Clarence Thomas suggested the charges by Anita Hill were part of a plot concocted by interest groups to destroy him (Reske 1991). It is also possible that if Anita Hill's allegations were concocted by interest groups, these interest groups were primarily interested in furthering their own interest, destroying Clarence Thomas being a subordinate interest. For example, consider the following facts: The National Women's Political Caucus (telephone 202-898-1100) received a "record $50,845 in one month and attracted more than 1,300 first-time NWPC contributors" in response to an October 25, 1991, newspaper advertisement (Siegel 1992: 22). Nine to Five (800-522-0925) "saw a 200 percent increase in volunteers during the week following the hearings" (Siegel 1992: 22). The National Organization for Women (NOW) (202-331-0066) and Women's Campaign Fund (202-234-3700) received increased donations after the Hill-Thomas hearings (Siegel 1992). NOW "signed up 13,000 members in October and November [1991], a huge jump from the average monthly rate of 100" (Siegel 1992: 22). The personal gains of public interest groups as a result of Anita Hill's allegations should not be ignored.

It has also been suggested that Anita Hill's allegations were the product of her fantasies about Clarence Thomas. One doctor, Melvin An-chell, M.D., ASPP, NAAP, has expressed the expert opinion that Anita Hill's allegations against Clarence Thomas "represents another pseudolog-ical experience in Anita Hill's life" (Anchell 1992: 44).[13] A *Newsweek* poll (1991a) of 704 respondents on October 10–11, 1991, found that most people did not believe Anita Hill (*see* Table 3.1). A *USA Today* poll of 758 respondents reached the same findings as the *Newsweek* poll (*see* Table 3.2). The *USA Today* poll (1991a) found that a lot of people changed their minds about whom to believe during the course of the confirmation hear-ings (*see* Table 3.3).

Richard Pollak (1991) has argued that "Anita Hill's case against Clarence Thomas was quite strong by the E.E.O.C.'s own ground rules." Stephanie Goldberg (1991: 90) has pointed out that "cases of harassment far worse than anything claimed by Professor Anita Hill have been thrown out of court because the incident only occurred once or because the victim failed to sufficiently protest, report the conduct, or to be traumatized by the experience." F. Lee Bailey (1992: 49) has asserted that "the evidence as it wound up—not the fault of the witnesses, but of those charged with handling it—was nowhere clear enough to support any finding of signifi-cance." Regardless of whether Hill's allegations would have stated a valid legal claim for sexual harassment had they been timely brought, her allega-tions resulted in renewed interest in and attention to sexual harass-ment.

Some people do not label the behavior as sexual harassment until they are cued to do so. Jaschik and Fretz (1991) showed a short video of a male graduate teaching assistant evaluating a term paper to 90 female undergraduates between the age of 17 and 22.[14] The undergraduates were first asked to write a few sentences describing the teaching assistant and then asked: Do you think the teaching assistant's conduct showed sexual harassment? Fewer labeled the conduct sexual harassment in their nar-rative descriptions than the number that responded yes to the direct ques-tion using the term *sexual harassment*.

Jaschik and Fretz (1991: 22) concluded that their study suggested "that women are not likely to label sexual harassment spontaneously as harass-ment, even when they confirm upon being directly asked that the behavior is indeed sexual harassment."[15] Influences in the environment in which an act takes place, such as the media and attitudes of coworkers, may have as much to do with some conduct being labeled sexual harassment as the personal opinions and views of the person alleging sexual harassment. The increased numbers of sexual harassment charges filed with the EEOC after the publicity generated by Anita Hill's allegations against Clarence Thomas may be seen as evidence of the media's cuing effect on allegations of sexual harassment.

Table 3.1

QUESTION	WOMEN	MEN
From what you've seen, heard or read, do you think Clarence Thomas sexually harassed Anita Hill?		
Yes	27%	17%
No	37%	41%
Don't Know	36%	42%

Source: Newsweek, October 21, 1991, ©1991, Newsweek, Inc. All rights reserved. Reprinted by permission.

Table 3.2

QUESTION	THOMAS	HILL	DON'T KNOW/OTHER*
Thomas has been accused of sexual harassment by Anita Hill, and he has denied the charges. Whom do you believe is telling the truth?			
TOTAL	47%	24%	29%
By Sex			
Women	45%	26%	29%
Men	49%	22%	29%

Source: Copyright 1991, *USA Today.* Reprinted with permission.

Table 3.3

QUESTION	YES	NO	DON'T KNOW
Have you found yourself believing Thomas at one point and Hill at another point since the hearings began?			
TOTAL	40%	49%	11%

Source: Copyright 1991, *USA Today.* Reprinted with permission.

Civil Rights Act of 1991

Weeks after Clarence Thomas's confirmation hearings focused widespread attention on sexual harassment, Congress passed the Civil Rights Act of 1991. The Civil Rights Act of 1991 (1991 Act) was signed by President Bush on November 21, 1991. The 1991 Act reversed a number of Supreme Court cases which made it difficult for an employee to prevail in an employment discrimination case under Title VII. Section 105(k) of the 1991 Act provides that an employment practice which has a disparate impact on a protected group constitutes discrimination unless the agency can "demonstrate that the challenged practice is job related for the position in question and consistent with business necessity."

The new Civil Rights Act made emotional distress and punitive damages, expert witness fees, and jury trials available in cases of intentional sex discrimination, including sexual harassment. Section 102 of the 1991 Act allows a party who proves intentional discrimination on the basis of sex, religion, or disability to recover compensatory and punitive damages.[16]

Punitive damages, awarded for the purpose of punishing an employer for illegal conduct, an effort to deter future illegal conduct, may cost employers significant sums of money. The 1991 Act sets limits on the amount of compensatory and punitive damages which can be awarded to an employee who proves intentional discrimination (see Table 3.4).

Prior to November 21, 1991, emotional distress damages were not available in sexual harassment cases brought under Title VII. Because research reflects that many victims of sexual harassment suffer emotionally, employers are now faced with potentially large damage awards if they are unsuccessful in defending against charges of sexual harassment.

An employee may also be able to recover the costs of expert witnesses under Section 113 of the 1991 Act. Section 102 allows a party seeking compensatory or punitive damages to demand the case be tried to a jury. Allowing an employee to recover expert witness fees and allowing jury trials may result in it being more difficult for employers to prevail on the merits of sexual harassment cases. The Civil Rights Act of 1991 clearly resulted in sexual harassment becoming more attractive to many employee-rights-oriented lawyers.

With the burden of proving discrimination made easier, increased damages, and the right to a jury trial, a new wave of employment discrimination litigation will surely occur, the stakes higher than in the past. Employers cannot afford to lose sight of the reality that higher damage awards can attract better lawyers with more resources. In a bad economy, employers are an attractive "deep pocket" in the eyes of many lawyers. Employers must reevaluate their employment practices in light of these new risk-management concerns.

Table 3.4

Number of Employees	Cap on Damages
15 - 100	$50,000
101 - 200	$100,000
201 - 500	$200,000
501 or more	$300,000

Source: Civil Rights Act of 1991, Section 102.

Sexual Harassment in Public Schools

Excessive punishment or beatings inflicted on students by public school teachers is a widespread problem in America (Roesler 1990).[17] Likewise, sexual abuse,[18] sometimes labeled sexual harassment, is a problem in America's public school system.

Title IX of the Education Amendment of 1972, 20 U.S.C. 1681–1688 (Title IX) was enacted to prohibit discrimination in educational programs receiving federal funding; 20 U.S.C. 1681(a) states in part:

> No person in the United States shall, on the basis of sex, be excluded from participation in, be denied the benefits of, or be subjected to discrimination under any education program or activity receiving Federal financial assistance.

In 1979, the Supreme Court held that a victim of sex discrimination could bring a private lawsuit against an educational program receiving federal financial assistance.[19] In 1982, the Supreme Court held that Title IX prohibits employment discrimination in educational programs receiving federal financial assistance.[20]

In a 1992 case, *Franklin v. Gwinnett County Public Schools,*[21] the Supreme Court held for the first time that monetary damages could be awarded in suits brought under Title IX. In *Franklin,* a high school student, Christine Franklin, alleged she had been sexually harassed by a coach and teacher, beginning when she was in the tenth grade in 1986. The Court summarized the student's allegations and the investigation into the allegations against the coach and teacher, Andrew Hill, as follows:

> Among other allegations, Franklin avers that Hill engaged her in sexually-oriented conversations in which he asked about her sexual experiences with her boyfriend and whether she would consider having sexual intercourse with an older man, . . . that Hill forcibly kissed her on the mouth in the school parking lot, . . . that he telephoned her at her home and asked if she would meet him socially, . . . and that, on three occasions in her junior year, Hill interrupted a class, requested that her teacher excuse [her], and took her to a private office where he subjected her to coercive intercourse. . . . The complaint further alleges that though they became aware of and investigated Hill's sexual harassment of [the student] and other female students, teachers and administrators took no action to halt it and discouraged [the student] from pressing charges against Hill. . . . On April 14, 1988, Hill resigned on the condition that all matters pending against him be dropped. . . . The school thereupon closed its investigation.[22]

Franklin filed a complaint with the Office of Civil Rights (OCR) of the U.S. Department of Education. The OCR investigation found that while Franklin had been subjected to sex discrimination in violation of Title IX, the resignation and implementation of a grievance procedure by the school district brought the school district into compliance with Title IX. The OCR then terminated its investigation. Franklin filed a lawsuit in federal court, which the court dismissed after finding damages could not be awarded under Title IX. The U.S. Court of Appeals for the Eleventh Circuit[23] affirmed the district court's decision, after which the Supreme Court agreed to hear the case. The Court held that "a damages remedy is available for an action brought to enforce Title IX."[24]

Both male and female workers have been sexually harassed at work (Dhooper 1989). Working women tend to categorize more behaviors at sexual harassment than do female students (Terpstra and Baker 1987). And both male and female students have reported being subjected to sexual harassment (Roscoe et al. 1987). Research suggests that male professors may be more likely than female professors to be harassed by students (McKinney 1990). Some male professors become involved with female students (Fitzgerald et al. 1988a; Fitzgerald et al. 1988b). Men, however, appear to be more tolerant of sexual harassment than women (Reilly et al. 1986).

Sexual Harassment in State and Local Government

Title VII's prohibition against sexual harassment applies to state and local government employers. State and local government employees have an additional remedy available for intentional sexual harassment which is not available to most private-sector employees. Title 42 U.S.C. 1983 prohibits persons acting under color of state law[25] from depriving citizens, including state government employees, of their constitutional rights.[26] A claim under Section 1983 may assert a violation of the plaintiff's constitutional right to due process and/or equal protection[27] under the provisions of the Fourteenth Amendment to the United States Constitution. In *Hubbard v. City of Middletown,*[28] the court stated:

> The Sixth Circuit has stated that "sexual harassment by government employers would violate the rights protected by the equal protection clause." *Poe v. Haydon,* 853 F.2d 418 (6th Cir. 1988) (*citing Huebschen v. Department of Health and Social Services,* 716 F.2d 1167 [7th Cir. 1983]).
> . . . .
> There is authority that sexual assault by a government agent in a position of relative authority violates the victim's fourteenth amendment right to substantive due process. *See, e.g., Stoneking v. Bradford Area School District,* 882 F.2d 720 (3d Cir. 1989).[29]

The Eleventh Amendment bars an award of monetary damages against the state. However, an award of money damages can be obtained against a supervisor or coworker individually, even for official acts. Damages available against an individual personally under Section 1983 can include compensatory damages,[30] emotional distress damages, punitive damages,[31] attorney's fees, and costs. As a general rule, claims cannot be brought under Section 1983 against private-sector employers.

Conclusion

In light of the recent media attention to sexual harassment, recent legislation substantially increasing an employer's liability upon losing a Title VII or Title IX hostile work environment sexual harassment claim and the increased number of sexual harassment charges filed with the EEOC subsequent to Anita Hill's allegations, sexual harassment must be taken more seriously than in the past. Employers must now make new risk-management decisions (the risks have changed) and gain an understanding of the myths and realities relating to sexual harassment. Employees, both male and female, must learn what offends the other sex.[32] While it is clear that Title VII prohibits sexual harassment in the workplace, what conduct constitutes "sexual harassment" prohibited by Title VII must be evaluated on a case-by-case basis in view of the totality of the circumstances.

Chapter 4
Natural Attraction as a Cause of Sexual Harassment

In 1976, federal District Court Judge Williams stated:

> The attraction of males to females and females to males is a natural sex phenomenon and it is probable that this attraction plays at least a subtle part in most personnel decisions.[1]

That same year, federal District Court Judge Stern noted that "this natural sexual attraction can be subtle."[2] Judge Stern concluded that sexual harassment and sexually motivated assault are not prohibited by Title VII's prohibition against sex discrimination because the sex of the individuals involved is "incidental" to the act in question:

> In this instance the supervisor was male and the employee was female. But no immutable principle of psychology compels this alignment of parties. The gender lines might as easily have been reversed, or even not crossed at all. While sexual desire animated the parties, or at least one of them, the gender of each is incidental to the claim of abuse.[3]

The traditional workplace is a natural environment for romantic relationships to evolve because people spend long hours on the job together, come to know each other well, and sometimes share similar values and interests which generate positive feelings. Consensual office romances exist, and no evidence suggests they will naturally disappear in the near future. Some consensual office romances involve the pursuit of a long-lasting romantic relationship or marriage. Other consensual office romances involve those not interested in pursuing an emotional relationship but desiring a sexual relationship. Others are relationships in which sexual favors are traded for job opportunities. And both parties to a relationship need not have the same goals as a prerequisite to the consensual relationship.

Even if romantic or sexual advances are naturally motivated, they may be unwelcome or offensive to the target of the advances because all people are not sexually or romantically attracted to everyone who finds them sexually or romantically attractive.[4] One-sided natural attractions can create headaches for employers because so much conduct which can be considered aggressive dating behavior by a party to a one-sided attraction can be perceived as sexual harassment by the target of the behavior if the behavior is unwelcome.

If employees manage to enter into consensual romantic or sexual relationships without engaging in conduct which has been labeled sexual harassment, the next hurdle for the employer and the parties to the relationship is dealing with the favoritism often inherent in romantic relationships and often explicitly or implicitly a condition of sexual relationships. Romantic consensual relationships often result in the parties to the relationship placing the best interest of their partner over that of strangers or others. Some argue that this type of favoritism is a natural and healthy response to becoming romantically involved with another person. Others argue that a party to a relationship should remain completely objective, showing no favoritism, when the best interests (economic, career advancement, etc.) of the other party to the relationship are at stake. The EEOC regulations state:

> Other related practices: Where employment opportunities or benefits are granted because of an individual's submission to the employer's sexual advances or requests for sexual favors, the employer may be held liable for unlawful sex discrimination against other persons who were qualified for but denied that employment opportunity or benefit.[5]

In recent years, courts have held that consensual romantic relationships are prohibited only if they result in more than a relationship. The extent to which one may show favoritism to a lover without running afoul of Title VII is unclear.

In *Candelore v. Clark County Sanitation Dist.,*[6] the court was confronted with a case in which

> Candelore alleges that one of her co-workers had an affair with one or two District supervisors and, as a result, this co-worker apparently received favorable treatment while Candelore grew increasingly frustrated in her position.[7]

The *Candelore* court affirmed the district court's grant of summary judgment to the employer, explaining:

> Much of the evidence relied on by Candelore in establishing the actual or rumored affairs involved conduct away from the workplace or outside business hours. A co-worker's romantic involvement with a supervisor

does not by itself create a hostile work environment.... Further, the isolated incidents or sexual horseplay alleged by Candelore took place over a period of years and were not so egregious as to render Candelore's work environment "hostile." ... Because Candelore has failed to identify benefits or opportunities denied as a result of discrimination, and because the isolated incidents of inappropriate behavior did not create a hostile or abusive environment, Candelore has not demonstrated the existence of any triable issues of fact on her claim of sex discrimination.[8]

According to the court, employee dating is not enough in itself to impose liability on an employer.

In *DeCintio v. Westchester County Medical*,[9] male employees alleged that a male supervisor in charge of filling a position made National Board registration a prerequisite for the position to ensure that his girlfriend would be the only qualified applicant for the position. The *DeCintio* court held that Title VII had not been violated, stating:

"Sex" when read in [the context of Title VII] logically could only refer to membership in a class delineated by gender.... The proscribed differentiation under Title VII, therefore, must be a distinction based on a person's sex, not on his or her sexual affiliations.[10]

The New Jersey Supreme Court endorsed *DeCintio* in *Erickson v. Marsh and McLennan Co. Inc.*[11]

In *Erickson*,[12] a male alleged he had been wrongfully discharged and discriminated against on the basis of his sex[13] under the provisions of the New Jersey law against discrimination when his male supervisor fired him so he could promote a woman with whom he had been romantically involved. Erickson alleged that "he was falsely accused of sexual harassment so that his superior's alleged girlfriend could be promoted to his position."[14] The court concluded that under New Jersey's law, a third-party allegation of sexual harassment requires "proof of coercion by [a supervisor] against [a coworker]." The *Erickson* court found "no reason to extend the protection of [New Jersey's law] to sex-discrimination claims based on voluntary personal relations."[15]

In *Drinkwater v. Union Carbide Corp.*,[16] a case governed by New Jersey law, a female supervisor alleged that a personal relationship between her male supervisor and a female subordinate created a hostile working environment. The supervisor had reported the incident to Patricia of the Employee Relations Department. Patricia conducted an investigation and concluded that the "plaintiff had made unfounded accusations and that [plaintiff] would be disciplined if she continued to accuse her superiors of improper conduct."[17] The *Drinkwater* court distinguished *Erickson*:

> *Erickson* held that a consensual relationship cannot form the basis of a sex discrimination claim not founded on sexual harassment, and that a consensual relationship cannot, by itself, without additional evidence of sexual hostility, give rise to a hostile environment sexual harassment claim. However, before reading too much into *Erickson* we think it is important to emphasize that it was a very different case than the one at bar. Mr. Erickson was a male *accused* of sexual harassment, not a female accusing her employer of sexual harassment. The court carefully noted that *Erickson* was not a sexual harassment case.... More importantly, there was absolutely no allegation in *Erickson* that the atmosphere in the workplace was oppressive in a way that discriminated against Mr. Erickson as a man.[18]

Unlike Erickson, the plaintiff in *Drinkwater* alleged that the affair in question created an "oppressive and intolerable environment." The *Drinkwater* court concluded that the New Jersey Supreme Court would distinguish *Erickson* and recognize third-party hostile work environment sexual harassment claims as a form of sex discrimination prohibited by New Jersey's law against discrimination. The *Drinkwater* court distinguished cases asserting discrimination based on the existence of a relationship from those grounded in the environment created by the relationship as follows:

> There are at least hints in this record that the environment was so charged with sexual innuendo as to create an atmosphere that discriminated against her as a woman. We believe that there is a critical difference between this kind of hostile environment claim and the harassment claims pled in cases like *Erickson:* in hostile environment cases, it is the environment, not the relationship, that is actionable. The relationship may contribute to the environment, but it is the workplace atmosphere that is critical.[19]

The *Drinkwater* court held that the plaintiff had failed to present enough evidence to support her claim or that the parties to the relationship "flaunted the romantic nature of their relationship, nor is there evidence that these kinds of relationships were prevalent at [Union Carbide]."[20] The court noted that had a hostile work environment been supported by evidence, a claim may have been stated:

> Such an atmosphere might have discriminated against plaintiff if sexual discourse displaced standard business procedure in a way that prevented plaintiff from working in an environment in which she could be evaluated on grounds other than her sexuality. Thus, we believe that evidence of a sufficiently oppressive environment could, in theory, give courts enough evidence to infer that the intentional discrimination prong of the *Andrews* test can be met even absent evidence of the harasser's subjective intent to discriminate.[21]

Although the *Drinkwater* court held that a consensual sexual relationship can give rise to a hostile environment claim, the court was careful to point out that "it is the environment, not the relationship, that is actionable."[22]

Employees can lose a lot as a result of entering into consensual romantic or sexual relationships in the workplace. According to attribution theory, people interpret social behavior in light of the perceived causes of the behavior. Sexuality can be emphasized by the voluntary disclosure of intimate information, such as sexual fantasies, other affairs, or dissatisfaction with a current lover (Gutek 1985). A target who dresses in a particularly seductive manner may be perceived as providing a sufficient cause for the actor's behavior (Pryor and Day 1988). Likewise, "evidence of a prior amicable relationship may serve to decrease the likelihood that socio-sexual behavior will be interpreted as sexual harassment" (Thomann and Wiener 1987: 587). As a practical matter, an employee generally loses some of the protection otherwise afforded by Title VII by entering into a consensual romantic or sexual relationship in the workplace.

Title VII does not always protect persons against adverse consequences when a relationship goes sour. For example, in *Freeman v. Continental Technical Services, Inc.,*[23] the court held that a termination based on personal animosity between an employee and her supervisor after the employee alleged she was pregnant with the married supervisor's child and planned on keeping the child did not constitute sex discrimination under Title VII. The court noted that although no "legitimate" reason existed for the employee's discharge, "Title VII does not require an employer to have good cause for its personnel decisions."[24] The court held:

> The transfer, demotion, or discharge of an employee for sexual or sex-related behavior does not constitute unlawful sex discrimination under Title VII.[25]

A review of the case law reveals that although Title VII protects employees from *unwelcome* sexual advances, it does not protect employees from the adverse consequences of *consensual* sexual behavior. Thus, while an employee may be able to use a personal relationship with a superior to get ahead in the workplace, the employee must also be ready to suffer the consequences if the relationship goes sour.

In businesses where one party to a personal relationship is related to the owner, the owner can take adverse employment actions against a nonrelated party for the purpose of preserving the traditional family unit. For example, in *Platner v. Cash & Thomas Contractors, Inc.,*[26] a female employee sued her employer, the male owner of the company, and his son's wife for sex discrimination. The owner's son and daughter-in-law worked for the company. The son's wife became extremely jealous of the female employee and suspected the employee and her husband of having an affair. The owner perceived this situation as a threat to his son's family unit and discharged the female employee to protect his son and his business interests from being affected by the tension created by this situation. The court held that the owner's personal, family-related reasons for firing the female employee constituted a legitimate, nondiscriminatory reason for discharging her.

A person entering into an office romance may be placing his or her long-term career in jeopardy, even if the person's short-term goals are furthered, if the relationship with the other party is important to reaching the long-term goal. The simple fact is that in relationships between employees of the same organization and those between employees of different firms, relationships sometimes end on a sour note with someone's feelings being hurt. These hurt feelings can result in a lot of personal animosity. In *McCollum v. Bolgers,*[27] the court held:

> Personal animosity is not the equivalent of sex discrimination and is not proscribed by Title VII. The plaintiff cannot turn a personal feud into a sex discrimination case by accusation.[28]

The personal animosity between two people at the time their relationship goes sour can result in one party taking adverse employment actions against the other party to remove the cause of personal distress, get even, or some other reason.

Many employees are subjected to conduct which can be labeled either normal dating behavior or sexual harassment. An employer is supposed to be able to know the difference and to take prompt remedial action if such conduct is unwelcome and therefore legally considered sexual harassment rather than dating behavior. Employers and employees alike must realize that they can no longer be guided by their socialization or experiences outside the workplace when pursuing an attraction to someone in the same organization for romantic or sexual purposes.

The *Drinkwater* court's reliance on the lack of prevalence of interoffice romances brings into question an employer's obligation to monitor the prevalence of consensual interoffice dating. The Merit Systems Protection Board studies suggest that organizational efforts to decrease the frequency of sexual harassment were not effective (compare USMSPB 1981 with USMSPB 1988). If sexual harassment results from natural attraction between people or natural attraction of one person to another who is not mutually attracted, sexual harassment policies, training, or other traditional organizational efforts are not likely to prevent sexual harassment (MacKinnon 1979; Tangri et al. 1982). It is unlikely that training or policies relating to sexual harassment would deter the harasser because a person who acts on a natural attraction to another without notice that the conduct is unwanted will not perceive his or her actions as harassment. One positive approach may be to enact and enforce policies requiring victims to tell any person who offends them that the conduct is unwelcome. This may reduce the duration of unwelcome one-sided attractions. Absent notice that the victim is offended, a person who is attracted to another may continue efforts to promote a personal relationship.

As a risk-management proposition, employers must begin monitoring, studying, and regulating the dating behavior of employees to avoid liability under Title VII. As a practical matter, such monitoring results in an invasion of the privacy of those employees happily pursuing a sexual or romantic relationship. However, because federal statutory laws such as Title VII control over state statutory and state tort law protecting employees' privacy rights and because privacy rights are generally personal in nature, an employer cannot assert as a defense that the monitoring necessary to determine when dating behavior becomes unwelcome or creates a hostile work environment would constitute an invasion of the privacy of its employees under state law.

Chapter 5
Power

One argument in the sexual harassment literature asserts that sexual harassment results from the exercise of "power" by one person over another in the workplace (Duldt 1982). Power is an ambiguous concept. Observed and perceived behavior result in one's attributing or inferring that another has power (e.g., sexual power, achieved power, ascribed power, situational power, organizational power, supervisory power, economic power, etc.). Perceptions relating to power are often wrong or unsupported by objective facts. Because power is attributed or inferred, it cannot be directly observed (Hinkin and Schriesheim 1990) or accurately measured.[1]

While slogans such as "Men exercise power over women" may have political appeal to many, they tell us little about the world we live in. Such slogans are broad enough to appeal to many. If the 1992 presidential primary elections were any indication of the views of the American people, the time is ripe for answers rather than rhetoric.

Courts have recognized that minorities can discriminate against their own. For example, the New Mexico Court of Appeals has held:

> Social scientists agree that members of minority groups frequently respond to discrimination and prejudice by attempting to disassociate themselves from the group, *even to the point of adopting the majority negative attitudes toward the minority.* Such behavior occurs with particular frequency among members of minority groups who have achieved some measure of economic or political success, and thereby have gained some acceptability among the dominant group.[2]

Title VII imposes liability on employers for the sexual harassment of women by women.[3] For example, in *Barlow v. Northwestern Memorial Hosp.,*[4] a female hospital secretary alleged that after she was promoted to her position, her female supervisor told her that she would have to succumb to her sexual advances to retain her position and that the employee was subsequently demoted because of her refusal to accede to her female supervisor's sexual advances.

Both Grieco (1987) and Duldt (1982) noted that some of the nurses they surveyed reported being subjected to homosexual advances. The notion that sexual harassment results from men exercising power over women fails to account for sexual harassment of women by women. Others have asserted that the degree of power over a target has little effect on the victim's perception of whether an incident constituted harassment (Fitzgerald and Ormerod 1991).

Cause of Legal Prohibition

A predominantly male Congress exercised its political power when it passed Title VII and the Civil Rights Act of 1991. A predominantly male federal judicial system exercised its political power when it adopted the EEOC's regulations defining sexual harassment as discrimination prohibited by Title VII.

Some argue the only reason the "good ole boys" gave in and enacted this legislation was the political pressure generated by feminists' efforts to bring sexual harassment to the forefront.

It appears that a person's political orientation may affect how he or she views sexual harassment. For example, poll results reported in the October 14, 1991 issue of *USA Today* suggest party affiliation may have affected the way people viewed the allegations of sexual harassment made against Clarence Thomas by Anita Hill (*see* Table 5.1).[5] Research also suggests that a feminist orientation may result in a person perceiving conduct as sexual harassment which those without a feminist perspective may not consider sexual harassment. While feminists may have taken the lead in efforts to expand definitions of sexual harassment and bring the issue to the public arena, the view of feminists is not the view of the majority of American women.

While feminism appears to be a viable political perspective,[6] a *Newsweek* poll conducted in October 1991 reflected that only 34 percent of the women surveyed identified themselves as feminists (Shapiro et al. 1991). Yet the feminist view appears to be the squeaky wheel pressuring expanded legal regulation of sexual conduct between all people in the workplace. To the extent that feminists were successful in causing conduct considered sexual harassment to become illegal under Title VII, feminists have exercised their political power in efforts to regulate the sexual relations of all people in the workplace.

Table 5.1

QUESTION	THOMAS	HILL	DON'T KNOW/OTHER*
Thomas has been accused of sexual harassment by Anita Hill, and he has denied the charges. Whom do you believe is telling the truth?			
TOTAL	47%	24%	29%
BY RACE			
BLACK	47%	20%	33%
WHITE	47%	25%	24%
BY SEX			
WOMEN	45%	26%	29%
MEN	49%	22%	29%
BY PARTY			
INDEPENDENTS	43%	23%	34%
GOP	64%	18%	18%
DEMOCRATS	38%	31%	31%

*OTHER = Neither; Both (Overall percentages are 5% for each category)

Source: Copyright 1991, *USA Today.* Reprinted with permission.

Cause of Objectionable Conduct

Sexual Sadism

Some people enjoy abusing others by engaging in conduct which could be labeled sexual harassment.[7] Some sadists act out their desires on inanimate objects, with consenting or paid partners, or by criminal acts such as rape, assault, and murder. Sadists "tend to establish dominance in interpersonal relationships and convey a lack of respect or empathy for others" (Hazelwood et al. 1992: 15). The sexual sadist may be "fascinated by violence, take pleasure in demeaning, humiliating, and frightening others, and may enjoy inflicting physical or psychological abuse" (Hazelwood et al. 1992: 15). Sadists may be hard to discharge for engaging in harassment because they often act out their sadistic desires in well-planned ways and take special steps to conceal their conduct and prevent detection.

Organizational Power

In 1976, a federal district court judge wrote: "The abuse of authority by supervisors of either sex for personal purposes is an unhappy and recurrent feature of our social experience."[8] Sexual harassment has often been said to be the result of differences in workplace power between the sexes (Gutek and Morasch 1982). Researchers have examined the notion that sexual harassment can be explained in terms of organizational power: the "organizational model" (Gruber and Bjorn 1986) or "power differential perspective" (Gutek and Morasch 1982).

The organizational model asserts that the vertical stratification of work organizations provides the opportunity for individuals to use their "power and position to extort sexual gratification from their subordinates" (Tangri et al. 1982: 37). The organizational model is not gender-specific; it recognizes that both men and women superiors may harass subordinates (Tangri et al. 1982). The power differential perspective was adopted from studies reflecting that rape is a form of the exercise of power by the rapist over the victim (Gutek and Morasch 1982). In the case of sexual harassment, the power differential perspective substitutes physical force for organizational power (Gutek and Morasch 1982).

The USMSPB's finding that both men and women reported being harassed more often by coworkers than by supervisors (*see* Table 2.7) suggests that factors other than one's position in an organization account for the cause of sexual harassment. This generalization does not appear to be without exceptions. Research reflects that those employed in the medical profession may be more likely to be harassed by a physician than those in other professions are to be harassed by a supervisor. Duldt's (1982: 337) survey of nurses found that in nursing "the typical harasser is the physician or supervisor." Grieco's (1987) survey of nurses found that patients were the most commonly reported harassers, followed by physicians, then coworkers. Gutek and Morasch (1982: 57) noted that "the finding that harassers are often not supervisors suggests that other mechanisms besides *organizational power* difference might contribute to the occurrence of sexual harassment." While the power differential perspective acknowledges the hierarchical nature of work environments, it neglects other important elements which affect an organization's environment (Gutek and Morasch 1982).[9] The fact that sexual harassment occurs in public places and schools also suggests that factors other than specific workplace power differentials play a part in sexual harassment in work organizations (Glass 1988).

If sexual harassment results from the exercise of power by one person in the workplace over another, it may be that the best approach is to address the distribution of "power" within the workplace. If the view that sexual harassment results from the exercise of power by one person over another is correct, personnel policies, grievance procedures, and employee education programs relating to sexual harassment would not be expected to be effective in reducing the occurrence of hostile work environment sexual harassment because these measures do not address the distribution of organizational power in the organization (Livingston 1982). The organizational model appears better suited to address quid pro quo sexual harassment than hostile work environment sexual harassment.

Many have suggested that employee education programs should be enacted as a method of preventing sexual harassment (James 1981; Duldt 1982; Grieco 1984). It would seem, however, that educational programs would not prevent sexual harassment if sexual harassment results from the exercise of organizational power by one person over another because educational programs do not address the distribution of intraorganizational power (Livingston 1982). Although a redistribution of power may result from employees learning how to file complaints outside the organization for which they work, this does little to aid the organization in its efforts to prevent sexual harassment and may be seen as counterproductive to many employers.

Sociocultural Power

Another model or theory asserts that sexual harassment results from differences in social "status" and "power" between classes of people, such as men and women—the "socioculture model" (MacKinnon 1979; Tangri et al. 1982; Gruber and Bjorn 1986). Tangri et al. (1982: 40) argued that one version of the sociocultural model is based on the assumption that "sexual harassment is one manifestation of a larger patriarchal system in which men rule and social beliefs legitimize their rule." The sociocultural model asserts that male dominance is maintained by cultural patterns of male-female interaction, that men are socialized to engage in "aggressive and domineering sexual behaviors and females for passivity and acquiescence," and that these behaviors or roles are rewarded by society (Tangri et al. 1982: 40). Because women are socialized to evaluate their self-worth in light of what others think of them, especially men, "they are predisposed to try to interpret male attention as flattery, making them less likely to define unwanted attention as harassment" (Tangri et al. 1982: 40).

The sociocultural model claims that "the function of sexual harassment is to manage ongoing male-female interactions according to accepted sex status norms, and to maintain male dominance occupationally and therefore economically, by intimidating, discouraging, or precipitating removal of women from work" (Tangri et al. 1982: 40). The version of the sociocultural model outlined by Tangri fails to account for the fact that some women sexually harass other women[10] and some men sexually harass other men.[11] And this version of the sociocultural model fails to account for the fact that women sexually harass men.[12]

Economic Power

Some have suggested that sexual harassment results from the economic dependence of employees on their jobs. If this is true, we would expect sexual harassment rates to increase as the proportion of women in the workplace who are economically dependent on their jobs increases. The economic condition of women as a class has deteriorated since Title VII's enactment.

The wages paid many American workers, both men and women, have decreased since Title VII's enactment. Increased numbers of workers result in increased competition for jobs and the willingness of workers to sell their labor power at a cheaper rate simply to exist. "Between 1973 and 1989, the median wages of hourly workers (adjusted for inflation) fell by 17 percent among women younger than 25, 19 percent among men ages 25 and older, and a stunning 29 percent among men younger than 25" (The State of America's Children 1991: 24). The value of the federal minimum wage has also decreased. Increasing numbers of children are living in one-parent families. The Children's Defense Fund has offered the following explanation of why more children are living in one-parent families:

> As earnings among young men have fallen further and further below what it takes to support families, their marriage rates also have plummeted. This pattern reflects, in part, their growing inability to assume the financial responsibilities of marriage and their diminishing attractiveness as marriage partners. Although social changes also underlie declining marriage rates, statistics suggest that falling earnings are a major contributing factor. As the marriage rate falls, the number of mothers and children in one-parent families increases. [The State of America's Children 1991: 25].

In 1989, 52 percent of all poor families were headed by women. Children living in one-parent families are more likely to be poor than are children growing up in two-parent families (The State of America's Children 1991). The Children's Defense Fund has concluded:

> Children living only with their mothers are far more likely to be poor. Fifty-one percent of such children were poor in 1989, compared with only 22 percent in male-headed, one-parent families and 10 percent in two-parent families. The immediate causes of this disparity are obvious. First, women generally earn less than men. In 1989 women's median weekly earnings were 69 percent of men's for year-round, full-time employment. Second, there is no second wage earner in a one-parent family to help

offset losses when earnings fall and wages fail to keep pace with inflation, leaving both male- and female-headed, one-parent families more likely than married-couple families to be poor. [The State of America's Children 1991: 25].

In 1991, the Children's Defense Fund reported that "a total of 12.6 million children now live below the poverty line, an increase of more than 2.5 million from only a decade ago" (The State of America's Children 1991: 23).

Poverty rates for married-couple families with children have also increased during the past decade (The State of America's Children 1991). Poverty may be "the strongest predictor of violent crime by teenagers" (The State of America's Children 1991: 97). Today, most women work because they must, either because they are a single parent supporting their children or because one income is insufficient to satisfy the financial needs or desires of their family (The State of America's Children 1991). Title VII has resulted in more women being required to work in order to exist.[13]

If sexual harassment results from women being economically dependent upon their jobs, traditional training programs, policies, and other employer efforts are not likely to reduce harassment because these efforts will not change the fact that most people must work for wages and are extremely dependent upon their earning capacity to pay their rent, buy food, and pay other bills.

The reality, according to Marxists, is that in a capitalist society most men and women are "slaves" of the owners of the means of production. Marx noted a common consensus that "wages are the sum of money paid by the capitalist for a particular labour time or for a particular output of labour" (Marx 1849: 204).[14] Employees sell their labor, and capitalists buy their labor; labor is a commodity bought and sold like sugar (Marx 1849). Marx argued that because employees must sell their *life activity* to another to secure the necessary *means of subsistence,* an employee's life activity is only a means to enable him to exist: "He [or she] works in order to live" (Marx 1849: 204).

While the free laborer does not belong to the owner of the factory, a certain amount of time during a certain number of days belongs to the person who purchases the free laborer's labor power (Marx 1849). While an employee may generally quit a job whenever he or she likes and the employer can discharge an employee, providing the employer does not violate the law in doing so,

the worker, whose sole source of livelihood is the sale of his labour power, cannot leave the *whole class of purchasers, that is, the capitalist class,* without renouncing his existence. He belongs not to this or that capitalist but to the *capitalist class,* and, moreover, it is his business to

dispose of himself, that is, to find a purchaser within this capitalist class
[Marx 1849: 205].

In 1848, Marx (1848: 479) predicted that "the less the skill and exertion of
strength implied in manual labour, in other words, the more modern industry becomes developed, the more is the labour of men superseded by
that of women. Differences of age and sex have no longer any distinctive
social validity for the working class. All are instruments of labour, more
or less expensive to use, according to their age and sex."

Mary-Alice Waters (1971: 23) argued that neither men nor women
workers are "paid for the full value of what they produce. . . . The entire
economic system is organized to exploit and oppress. . . . It is a system based
on production for the purpose of increasing the individual wealth of a few;
. . . a system which *must* produce racism, sexism, and extreme prejudices
of every kind in order to prevent those who produce all the wealth from
uniting to demand control of what they produce. . . . The individual
worker has absolutely no function in society except to sell her or his labor
power at whatever rate is attainable."

If one's economic dependence on a job is the cause of sexual harassment, there is nothing an employer can do short of retaining every
employee regardless of productivity. If capitalism results in sexual harassment, we must then ask whether we are better off with a capitalist system
resulting in sexual harassment or another form of economy that may result
in less sexual harassment. A change from a capitalist economy to another
form does not appear to be a popular idea.

Sexual Power

Is the "reasonable woman" the woman who uses her sexuality to get
ahead in the business world? Consensual sexual relationships (office
romances) do exist in the workplace (Anderson and Fisher 1991) and have
been used by both men and women to get ahead in the business world.
Stringer et al. (1990) have referred to the use of sex to get ahead in the
business world as "sexual power."

While some people simply enjoy sexual jokes and flirting, others are
willing to exchange sexual favors for privileges at work (Gutek 1985; Backhouse and Cohen 1981). Some people are romantically attracted to someone they work with. A consensual romantic relationship between employees of the same firm can create an uncomfortable work environment for
other employees. The perception that an employee can use sexual favors
for job advancement appears to be widespread. The 1980 Merit Systems
Protection Board study found that many federal employees perceived that
the use of sexual favors for job advancement occurred where they worked

Table 5.2.
Percentage of Respondents Who Agree or Strongly Agree

STATEMENT	FEMALE		MALE	
	VICTIM	NON-VICTIM	VICTIM	NON-VICTIM
Where I work, employees use their sexual favors for advancement on the job.	30%	23%	27%	22%

Source: USMSPB 1981: 55.

Table 5.3.
Percentage of Respondents Who Agree or Strongly Agree

STATEMENT	W	M	S	NS	V	NV
Morale at work suffers when some employees seem to get ahead by using their sexuality.	93%	90%	92%	91%	94%	90%
There's nothing wrong when women use their sexuality to get ahead on the job.	4%	4%	4%	4%	4%	4%
There's nothing wrong when men use their sexuality to get ahead on the job.	3%	4%	4%	4%	4%	4%
I think it's all right for people to have sexual affairs with people they work with.	17%	26%	21%	23%	23%	23%

Legend: W=Women; M=Men; S=Supervisor; NS=Nonsupervisor; V=Victim; NV=Nonvictim

Source: USMSPB 1981: 29.

(*see* Table 5.2). Most of the respondents to the 1980 study agreed that morale suffers when employees seem able to use their sexuality to get ahead (*see* Table 5.3).

Office romances exist, and no evidence suggests they will disappear in the near future. Differences do exist in the way people react to office romances and the way those engaged in office romances are perceived by others. The perception of office romances by others (for example, an

EEOC investigator, judge, or jury) should be considered prior to litigation. Women are often seen as entering into office romances to move up the organizational ladder or for other gain, while men are often perceived as entering into ego-related affairs. And women are more often seen as seeking a lasting relationship than the "fling" men are seen as seeking when entering into an office romance (Anderson and Fisher 1991). Both a romantic consensual personal relationship and a consensual exchange of sexual favors for job advantages can result in favoritism being shown a party to the relationship. The favoritism, rather than the relationship, may result in many romantic personal relationships being perceived as the use of sex to get ahead. As a general rule, favoritism based on consensual romantic or sexual relationships does not in and of itself constitute sex discrimination[15] or sexual harassment[16] under Title VII.

Many employment decisions affect the lives of more than one employee. For example, if ten people apply for a promotion and one is promoted, all ten applicants' employment status is either advanced or it is not. When nine employees perceive an affair as the reason they were not promoted, they may become angry and feel cheated of an opportunity to compete based on merit. Some relationships begin as romantic relationships and become relationships in which sex is traded for job advancement. In other cases, relationships involve an explicit agreement to exchange sexual favors for job advancement.

While an employer is generally not prohibited from accepting offers of sexual favors and promoting the career of a subordinate who offers sexual favors, an employer is prohibited from offering a subordinate the *opportunity* to engage in sexual favors to get ahead. It is only where an employer engages in a long-term practice of advancing the careers of those who are willing to offer sex for job benefits that Title VII generally imposes legal obstacles or civil liability.

Power of Allegations of Sexual Harassment

Fear of civil liability under Title VII is not a concern only for men. Both men and women often feel they are unfairly accused of sexual harassment (*see* Table 5.4). Men are often perceived as the villains and women as the innocent victims in conversations about sexual harassment. Civil liability under Title VII must be a real concern for employers regardless of the sexual composition of the work force. An employer with a 100 percent female work force can still be held liable under Title VII for conduct defined as sexual harassment because women do sexually harass women (*see* Table 2.3).

Both men and women felt some charges were unfair because their

Table 5.4. Number and Percentage of Accused Harassers Who Responded to Whether They Thought the Charge Was Fair

QUESTION	WOMEN		MEN	
	NUMBER	%	NUMBER	%
Total accused harassers	1,100	---	10,500	---
Thought charge unfair	900	83%	8,100	82%
Did not know if charge was fair	190	17%	980	10%
Thought charge was fair	0	0%	780	8%

Source: USMSPB 1981: D-21.

Table 5.5. Percentage of Accused Harassers Who Gave Reasons for Why They Thought the Charge Was Unfair

RESPONSE	WOMEN	MEN
There was nothing wrong with what I did	16%	29%
Accuser misunderstood my motives	38%	48%
Accuser wanted to create trouble	21%	45%
Management found the charge to be false	41%	35%
Total Respondents	900	8,000

Source: USMSPB 1981: D-24.

accusers misunderstood their motives or wanted to create trouble (*see* Table 5.5). A large number of the charges against both men and women were found false by management (*see* Table 5.5). While most respondents thought that if a person did not intend his conduct to be offensive, the conduct should not be labeled sexual harassment (*see* Table 2.6), it appears that the motives of both men and women are often misunderstood. False allegations of harassment can be viewed as a tool available to exercise power over another.

Conclusion

Although the abuse of one's position, economic status, or other superior position to elicit sexual favors is often referred to as the "use of power" in the sexual harassment literature, most cases are better understood in the context of the "lack of power" if power is one's ability to cause the victim to submit to conduct labeled sexual harassment.

An abundance of social science research reflects that men and women have historically been socialized differently, men being socialized to be "masculine" and women socialized to be "feminine." Thus, while biological sex is determined at birth, "gender" is what one becomes as a result of the socialization process (masculine or feminine). And both men and women have historically been expected to play appropriate "gender roles." Much of the behavior, attitudes, and expectations held by men and women about themselves and others is shaped by the socialization process rather than biological sex. Changes in the socialization process, then, can affect the behavior, attitudes, and expectations of both men and women about themselves and others.

The characterization of many of men's dominant and women's passive attributes are social (learned), not biological (natural), in origin. Mary-Alice Waters (1971: 25) argued that equating "male" with "violence, conquest, destruction, and glory-seeking" is improper because "in reality [these are] characteristics not of men *per se* but of class society, of a competitive system based on each one for herself or himself, a system where the stronger *do* take advantage of the weaker. To place women in power instead of men, without fundamentally changing that *system,* would alter nothing."

Chapter 6

The Process of Evaluating Sexual Harassment Claims

Defining sexual harassment involves the process of grouping a set of behaviors into a category and labeling them sexual harassment. The sexual harassment literature reflects that everything from rape to suggestive looks has been labeled sexual harassment by one researcher or another. The Merit Systems Protection Board surveys included sexual remarks, suggestive looks, pressure for sexual favors, letters and calls, and rape or attempted rape when reporting that 42 percent of female respondents alleged they had been sexually harassed.[1]

As a prerequisite to an employer responding to sexual harassment in the workplace, the employer must be able to identify what it is that constitutes harassment. For an employee to know when he or she has been sexually harassed, the employee must first be able to define sexual harassment. For coworkers or supervisors to refrain from engaging in sexual harassment, they must be able to identify the line separating sexual harassment from other behavior. The definition of sexual harassment is very important to all concerned: employer or employee, male or female.

Personal Level

Conduct is evaluated and labeled at numerous stages. First, an employee must decide, sometimes with the "cuing" of others, whether specific conduct constitutes sexual harassment. At this stage, the personal views of the possible victim are very important.[2] Research suggests that a person's background and age affects what that person perceives as sexual harassment (Reilly et al. 1982), that men and women have different perceptions about what constitutes sexual harassment (Powell 1986; Kenig and Ryan 1986), and that women do not agree about what constitutes sexual harassment among themselves (Schneider 1982). Sexual orientation (Schneider 1982), sex-role attitudes (Malovich and Stake 1990), and self-esteem (Malovich and Stake 1990) have also been found to affect the attitudes of victims toward conduct labeled sexual harassment.

Many factors other than an incident in the work force can affect what one labels sexual harassment. Thus, it is reasonable to conclude that some unsuccessful sexual harassment cases result from differing views about what constitutes sexual harassment in a given situation. Charges may be false or may not be substantiated (Conte 1990).[3] As the fact finder changes, the personal views of the person who believes he or she has been sexually harassed and those who cue the employee become less important. For example, if the employee files an internal grievance with the employer, the employer's policies and the views of the fact finder designated by the employer will determine whether the conduct constitutes sexual harassment. The views expressed in an employer's personnel policies may not be the same as those which resulted in the internal charge in the first place.

Organizational Level

Many personnel policies prohibiting sexual harassment fail to provide sufficient guidelines regarding what constitutes sexual harassment to those who must apply the personnel policies. Thus, the interpretations given the language used in personnel policies by those who must apply them are very important in determining what types of conduct are prohibited. An example of a personnel policy under which supervisors and others must apply the broad language used in EEOC policy statements was found in Bernalillo County, New Mexico. The *Bernalillo County Personnel Rules and Regulations,* adopted June 18, 1991, set forth the following sexual harassment policy:

Section 1100, Prohibition of Sexual Harassment

Employees of Bernalillo County are prohibited from sexually harassing any other County employee(s). Sexual harassment is any unwanted sexual attention or such attention when submission to such conduct is made, either explicitly or implicitly, a term of an individual's employment; submission to or rejection of such conduct by an individual used as the basis for employment decisions affecting such individual; or such conduct having the purpose of affecting or unreasonably interfering with an individual's work performance or creating an intimidating, hostile, or offensive working environment.

Section 1101, Policy Regarding Sexual Harassment

Bernalillo County is committed to enforcing a policy prohibiting sexual harassment that:

A. Provides for a work environment free from all forms of sexual harassment.

B. Applies to the actions of all County employees, elected and appointed officials, volunteers, and contractors.

C. Provides for training of all County employees, elected and appointed officials, volunteers, and contractors regarding sexual harassment.

D. Ensures that appropriate corrective measures, up to and including discharge and appropriate legal action, will be taken if this policy is violated.

E. Establishes a complaint procedure that is fair and confidential and protects against retaliation for filing of, or testifying as a witness to, a complaint.

F. Ensures that all complaints are investigated promptly, thoroughly, and fairly.

G. Ensures that all elected officials, managers, and supervisors are fully trained in their responsibilities under this policy.

Section 1102, Sexual Harassment Complaint Procedures

A. Employees of Bernalillo County are encouraged to resolve complaints of sexual harassment with the lowest level supervisor who is independent of the complaint and has supervisory authority over the alleged harasser. The supervisor shall document the complaint on a County approved form and provide a copy to the complaining employee and the County's Equal Employment Opportunity ("EEO") office, which shall keep all such forms on file.

B. The immediate supervisor who is independent of the complaint and has supervisory authority over the alleged harasser shall meet with the alleged harasser immediately and in no event more than three (3) working days from the filing of the complaint. The purpose of the meeting will be to investigate the matter and, if necessary, take prompt corrective action. The investigation shall be complete, confidential, and well documented. The principles of progressive discipline, up to and including termination from County employment, shall be followed by the supervisor for a person who is determined to have violated the sexual harassment policy. The discipline will vary depending on the basis of the complaint.

C. Nothing in these procedures shall prohibit employees from filing a complaint directly with the County EEO Office, the Federal Equal Employment Office, or the New Mexico Human Rights Division, if any employees feel that they cannot obtain appropriate relief within the steps above. Employees are encouraged to seek consultation through the County EEO Office before filing a formal sexual harassment complaint to determine whether an action constitutes unlawful behavior under the Civil Rights Act. If there appears to be a violation constituting sexual harassment/discrimination, the EEO office shall advise the employee of his rights and make a recommendation to the County Manager if any administrative action is warranted.

D. If the complaint filed requires an investigation by the County EEO office, the investigation shall be complete, confidential, and well documented. The results of the investigation will be forwarded to the County Manager in writing for his action.

Under the above policy, the "lowest level supervisor who is independent of the complaint and who has supervisory authority over the alleged harasser," must meet with the alleged harasser, "investigate the matter and, if necessary, take prompt corrective action."

The meanings applied by low-level supervisors to the terms used in Bernalillo County's sexual harassment policy initially determines whether sexual harassment occurred and whether corrective action is necessary.

The lack of guidance in personnel policies regarding what conduct constitutes "sexual harassment" and the lack of guidance for determining whether conduct has created an "intimidating," "hostile," or "offensive" working environment can result in a lack of uniformity in the application of the policy.

The lack of uniformity regarding who is the "lowest level supervisor who is independent of the complaint and who has supervisory authority over the alleged harasser," may, however, give an employee some leeway in determining which supervisor to file a complaint with.

Under the Bernalillo County policy, a lower-level supervisor who receives a sexual harassment complaint must document the complaint and provide a copy of it to the county's EEO office. An employee can also file a complaint directly with the county EEO office.

The person who determines whether an EEO complaint requires an investigation and how the investigation will be conducted, and analyzes the evidence to reach the results of the investigation must also interpret the policy language.

And finally, the views of the Bernalillo county manager regarding the policy language are important where an EEO investigation has been conducted because the county manager must decide what action to take based on the investigation.

While policies using the language used in broad, theoretical EEOC policy statements may be sufficient for purposes of limiting legal liability under Title VII, they do little if anything in providing practical guidance to employees and managers who must interpret and apply the policy in the workplace.

Such policies often seem to reflect a commitment to reducing civil liability by enacting a policy as recommended by the EEOC rather than a commitment to combating sexual harassment in a particular workplace. Subjective interpretations of those charged with interpreting and enforcing sexual harassment policies are very important and should not be disregarded.

Administrative Level

Within a short time after the last instance of sexual harassment, an employee must decide whether to file sexual harassment charges with a state or federal administrative agency.

As a prerequisite to filing a lawsuit under Title VII, an employee must exhaust the EEOC administrative remedies.[4] These administrative remedies are different for federal employees than for employees of state and local governments and private-sector employees. In *E.E.O.C. v. Commercial Office Products Co.,*[5] the Supreme Court held that a complaint alleging discrimination must generally be filed with the EEOC within 180 days.

However, if the complaint is initially timely filed with a state agency charged with prohibiting discrimination, the time constraint is extended to 300 days. Since the EEOC must defer jurisdiction of the complaint to the state agency for a period of 60 days, the complaint must be filed with the EEOC within 240 days for the EEOC to have jurisdiction within the 300-day time frame.

Most states have state administrative agencies charged with combating sexual harassment and other forms of employment discrimination in the workplace. State laws control the time within which charges must be filed with the state agency and the right to proceed to state court once state administrative remedies are exhausted.[6] When charges of discrimination are filed with the EEOC by nonfederal employees, the charge is generally sent to the state administrative agency for investigation. The state has exclusive jurisdiction over the charge for a period of 60 days (a "deferral" period). If an employee files with the state agency prior to filing with the EEOC, the EEOC obtains jurisdiction over the charge once the charge has been filed with the state agency for a period of 60 days, regardless of the date a charge of discrimination is filed with the EEOC. The reason for the 60-day deferral period is to provide states with an opportunity to rectify employment discrimination within their boundaries in the first instance.

The EEOC charge is very important because it establishes the scope of the allegations against an employer and the parties against whom the charge is brought. Generally, an employee may include in a Title VII suit only those violations alleged in the EEOC charge or related allegations which could reasonably be expected to arise out of the violations alleged in the charge.[7] An employee need not always file additional charges of discrimination if the employee is subjected to additional discrimination or retaliation after the initial charge is filed with the EEOC involving the same party.[8]

A person not made a party to the EEOC charge can generally be named as a defendant in a subsequent Title VII suit only if there is an identity of interest between the unnamed person and those charged sufficient to create a presumption that the EEOC investigation and conciliation efforts would include the unnamed person or the unnamed person is identified in the body of the charge.[9] In some jurisdictions, employees of the EEOC prepare charges of discrimination for targets of discrimination to sign. And in some cases the employee of the EEOC fails to name all appropriate parties or to include all appropriate allegations, resulting in the employee being deprived of his or her right later to pursue a lawsuit under Title VII.

If a charge is filed with a state or federal agency, the agency must evaluate the conduct and determine whether that conduct constitutes sexual harassment as a matter of law, as interpreted by agency regulations and standards.

The definition of sexual harassment applied by a state administrative agency may be different from the definition of sexual harassment applied by the federal EEOC or the courts in Title VII cases in the same jurisdiction (Terpstra and Baker 1992).

Research suggests that equal employment opportunity investigators often fail to do an effective investigation (USGAO 1988; O'Connell 1991). Terpstra and Baker (1988) examined 81 case reports of sexual harassment filed with the Illinois Department of Human Rights between July 1, 1981, and June 30, 1983, in an effort to determine whether the types of conduct alleged and supporting evidence affected the disposition of the charges. This study found that "the type of harassment behavior, the presence or absence of witnesses, and notice to management ... were significantly related to charge outcomes" (Terpstra and Baker 1988: 191). Only 31 percent of these charges resulted in favorable outcomes for the complaining party (Terpstra and Baker 1988: 192).

The perspective of those preparing an administrative complaint, those investigating the complaint, and those rendering an administrative decision can affect the outcome of the administrative agency's decision.

If the agency fails to find in favor of the employee, the employee must determine whether to file a lawsuit. Courts may discount allegations of sexual harassment in a lawsuit which were not made in the EEOC proceedings.[10]

In cases involving federal employees, an EEO counselor must be notified within 30 days of the discriminatory event unless equitable considerations excuse noncompliance.[11] Failure to file a proper complaint within 30 days after receipt of an EEOC decision can result in dismissal of a Title VII claim.[12] The failure properly to name the defendant, the head of the federal agency in question, can also result in dismissal of a Title VII claim.[13]

Trial Court Level

If an employee decides to file a lawsuit in court under Title VII's provisions, either a judge or a jury will determine whether the evidence presented is sufficient to prove sexual harassment under the circumstances. Prior to the enactment of the Civil Rights Act of 1991, the presiding judge generally determined what a reasonable person, or a reasonable person of the same sex as the victim, would perceive as sexual harassment. The Civil Rights Act of 1991 provides for jury trials in cases of intentional discrimination. What can constitute sexual harassment in the eyes of a reasonable person or a reasonable person of the same sex as the plaintiff will now more likely be determined by a jury.

The chances of a man obtaining an all-male jury or a woman obtaining an all-female jury are not very good. And the Supreme Court has held that a party cannot disqualify a juror based on her membership in a class,[14] such as the juror's sex. If men are unable to understand a woman's point of view in the workplace, or vice versa, it is unclear how that inability to understand will suddenly disappear in the jury box.

Research Level

In recent years, some courts have held that whether conduct is sufficiently severe or pervasive to alter the conditions of employment must be determined from the perspective of a reasonable person of the same sex as the victim. Empirical research relating to what a "reasonable woman" or "reasonable man"[15] considers harassment is now much more important in sexual harassment cases. In *Ellison v. Brady,* the Ninth Circuit stated:

> A complete understanding of the victim's view requires, among other things, an analysis of the different perspectives of men and women. Conduct that many men consider unobjectionable may offend many women.
> . . . .
> We realize that there is a broad range of viewpoints among women as a group, but we believe that many women share common concerns which men do not necessarily share.[16]

Social scientists often define the term *sexual harassment* based on their view of the world. Other studies attempt to define sexual harassment based on the respondent's point of view. It is important to understand the limitations of social sciences research. Social scientists recognized sexual harassment as a legitimate topic of scientific inquiry soon after the media and courts did so (Brewer and Berk 1982). There is no commonly accepted definition of sexual harassment by social science researchers (Somers

1982). Linda Rubin and Sherry Borgers (1990: 397) have noted that "a clear definition of sexual harassment has yet to be commonly accepted in the psychology research." Amy Somers (1982: 31) reviewed the social sciences literature and found a consensus that "sexual harassment includes a range of behaviors, from physical assault to verbal innuendos and threats. Most of the definitions include some concept of coercion or the misuse of differential power."

The lack of a common social sciences definition is important because incident rates in research vary, depending on which definition is used (Somers 1982). Because legal definitions of sexual harassment are seldom the operational definitions used by researchers, most studies are of limited use in harassment litigation. Cross-study comparisons of the frequency and nature of sexual harassment are difficult because of the varieties of populations sampled, sampling techniques, and operational definitions of sexual harassment (Somers 1982).

David Terpstra and Douglas Baker (1987: 601) have noted that "research investigating the types of behaviors actually considered to be sexual harassment seems a necessary step toward reducing the individual and organizational costs associated with the problem. In addition, the results of such research can assist in the formulation of organizational policies and the development of training and awareness programs." Even though a survey may accurately reflect the nature and extent of a problem in the organization, it may not accurately reflect the nature and extent of the problem generally or in another organization. The best way for an employer to determine the types of behaviors its employees consider sexual harassment is to survey its employees.

Effect of Identification on Incident Rates

Incident rates can be obtained at each level of the process. At the personal level, survey studies of employees reflect the highest incident rates. Fewer complaints are filed under organizational policies prohibiting sexual harassment than the number of employees who report being subjected to sexual harassment in surveys of employees. The October 21, 1991 issue of *Newsweek* reported that in 1981 there were 3,661 sexual harassment complaints filed with the EEOC.[17] *Newsweek* reported that in 1990 the number of sexual harassment complaints filed with the EEOC had risen to 5,694.[18] While 5,694 complaints signal a problem, it is far from the 40 percent or more of the women in the work force reporting sexual harassment in survey studies of female employees.

Chapter 7

The Process of Litigating a Sexual Harassment Case

A Title VII lawsuit has a life of its own which begins when a *complaint* is filed (a complaint is a document which sets forth the legal and factual bases for the lawsuit). The complaint is assigned a case number and served on the employer. The employer must then answer the complaint and defend against the lawsuit. The complaint must state more than conclusionary allegations, or it can be dismissed for "failure to state a claim."

This discussion is limited in assuming that the lawsuit will be filed in federal court and that there are no local rules inconsistent with the Federal Rules of Civil Procedure for U.S. district courts. The Federal Rules of Civil Procedure apply to civil proceedings in all federal courts. However, each district generally has an additional set of rules of its own. The violation of one of these rules by a plaintiff in a Title VII case can result in the case being thrown out without its merits being considered.

The first legal challenge made to a plaintiff's complaint is often that the complaint "fails to state a claim upon which relief can be granted." The employer generally argues that if the facts set forth in the plaintiff's complaint are taken as true, the plaintiff cannot recover under existing law. This type of challenge is to the *facial* validity of the complaint itself. "When a federal court reviews the sufficiency of a complaint, before the reception of any evidence either by affidavit or admissions, its task is necessarily a limited one. The issue is not whether a plaintiff will ultimately prevail but whether the claimant is entitled to offer evidence to support the claims."[1]

In reviewing the sufficiency of a complaint in the context of a motion to dismiss, this court must "treat all of the well-pleaded allegations of the complaint as true."[2] Not only must the facts alleged in the complaint be taken as true, but the facts set forth in the complaint must also "be construed favorably to the pleader."[3] Taking all the well-pleaded allegations as true and construing the complaint in the light most favorable to the plaintiff, "a complaint should not be dismissed for failure to state a claim

59

unless it appears beyond doubt that the plaintiff can prove no set of facts in support of his [or her] claim which would entitle him [or her] to relief."[4]

At any time after the complaint is filed and served on the defendant, "discovery" may begin. Under the Federal Rules of Civil Procedure (FRCP), a party may move for discovery regarding any matter, not "privileged," relevant to the subject matter involved in the pending action. Rule 26 (b) (1) provides in part:

> The frequency or extent of use of the discovery methods set forth in subdivision (a) shall be limited by the court if it determines that:
> (i) the discovery sought is unreasonably cumulative or duplicative, or is obtainable from some other source that is more convenient, less burdensome, or less expensive;
> (ii) the party seeking discovery has had ample opportunity by discovery in the action to obtain the information sought; or
> (iii) the discovery is unduly burdensome or expensive, taking into account the needs of the case, the amount in controversy, limitations on the parties' resources, and the importance of the issues at stake in the litigation.

The scope of discovery is especially broad in employment discrimination cases.[5] Discovery is not limited to issues raised by the pleadings because discovery is designed to help define and clarify the issues the court has been called upon to resolve.[6] Thus, "relevancy" for the purpose of Rule 26 cannot be equated with admissibility at trial.[7] Since direct evidence of discrimination is rarely obtainable in employment discrimination cases, employees must often rely on circumstantial evidence, statistical data, and evidence of an employer's overall employment practices.[8] The party opposing discovery has the burden of showing that the discovery request should not be granted.[9]

Pursuant to Rule 33, a former employee can request that the employer, and other appropriate persons under certain circumstances, answer written "interrogatories." Interrogatories are questions which the employer, through an authorized person, answers in a narrative form, in writing and under oath. A former employee can request, pursuant to Rule 34, that an employer produce specified documents. As a general rule, all nonprivileged documents in the possession of an employer can be requested.

The courts have held that discovery of *comparative* information is often necessary to afford a former employee a fair opportunity to develop his or her case and may be relevant to establish the pretextual nature of an employer's conduct.[10] A former employee generally has a right to information that would show that other groups or employees were not treated in the same way as the former employee in a similar situation.[11] For example, in *Weahkee v. Norton,*[12] the court held that an employee was entitled to discover personnel files of other employees who had been promoted over him where qualifications and job performance of those employees in comparison with his qualifications and performance were at the heart of the controversy, since it could not be determined from the record whether the requested documents might have changed the result. The *Weahkee* court noted that the "denial of discovery is ordinarily prejudicial in the absence of circumstances showing it is harmless. Here, since we cannot determine from the record whether the requested documents might have changed the result in this trial, we cannot say the error was harmless."[13]

One of the common items requested very early by employees' attorneys in employment discrimination cases is a complete copy of the employee's personnel file and the personnel files of other employees, including that of the harasser. The personnel file of the harasser may lead to evidence of the sexual harassment training given the harasser, employer notice of prior complaints, or other evidence tending to prove that the harasser is a bad actor.

In many types of sexual harassment cases in which a plaintiff is terminated, comparative evidence showing that an employer departed from established procedures or made less of a paper trail than normal may serve as evidence of the pretextual nature of an employer's proffered reasons for termination. In cases involving the failure to promote or hire a plaintiff, evidence that an employer denied an applicant or employee the chance to demonstrate his or her qualifications, evidence that an item was in an employee's personnel file for a long time before it was used in an adverse manner against the employee, and a comparison of the qualifications of the plaintiff with the person who obtained the job or promotion may be relied upon to show the pretextual nature of an employer's failure to hire or promote an employee.

Many plaintiffs' lawyers also request information relating to sexual harassment or related complaints by other employees against the harasser in question and against the employer very early in the case.

Evidence of preceding or succeeding discrimination may be relevant to show motive and intent regarding a practice.[14] In *Spulak v. K Mart Corp.,*[15] the court held that "as a general rule, the testimony of other employees about their treatment by the [employer] is relevant to the issue of the employer's discriminatory intent." The *Spulak* court held this rule applicable to former employees of an employer as well as current employees.[16]

Records reflecting similar complaints may provide a former employee with information from which he or she can obtain testimony against the employer that the former employee was otherwise unaware of. Evidence of sexual harassment of other employees can be "relevant in establishing a generally hostile work environment."[17] Evidence of the absence of sexual harassment in the workplace or by a particular person can be relied upon by a court in concluding that a plaintiff failed to prove a hostile work environment claim.[18]

(This discussion is based on the FRCP and case law decided under those rules. These rules generally guide employment discrimination cases brought in the federal courts against employers. It should be pointed out, however, that an employment discrimination case may be brought in state court. State court cases are governed by the rules of judicial procedure in that state rather than the federal rules discussed here.)

When an employee files a lawsuit, the employer has a right to conduct an investigation to defend the lawsuit. An employer may discover information unknown to the employer at the time of the acts which gave rise to the lawsuit. For example, an employer may defend a sexual harassment case in some jurisdictions based on an employee's misrepresentations on an employment application if the misrepresentation would have prevented the employer from hiring the employee.

Once sufficient discovery has been conducted, the plaintiff or the defendant may ask the court to enter "summary judgment." As a general rule, a party moving for summary judgment submits a motion which states that based upon the evidence obtained during discovery, the moving party is entitled to a ruling in its favor without the benefit of a trial. Rule 56 (c) provides that summary judgment may be granted "if the pleadings, depositions, answers to interrogatories, and admissions on file, together with the affidavits, if any, show that there is no genuine issue as to any material fact and that the moving party is entitled to a judgment as a matter of law.... The mere existence of *some* alleged factual dispute between the parties will not defeat an otherwise properly supported motion for summary judgment; the requirement is that there be no *genuine* issue of *material* fact."[19] However, all doubts as to the existence of a genuine issue of material fact should be resolved against the moving party,[20] and summary judgment should not be granted unless it is clear that a trial is unnecessary.[21]

Although it is clear that "one of the principal purposes of the summary judgment rule is to isolate and dispose of factually unsupported claims or defenses, and ... it should be interpreted in a way that allows it to accomplish this purpose,"[22] it is equally clear that "at the summary judgment stage the judge's function is not himself to weigh the evidence and determine the truth of the matter but to determine whether there is a genuine issue for trial.... The inquiry performed is the threshold inquiry of determining whether there is the need for a trial—whether, in other words, there are any genuine factual issues that properly can be resolved only by a finder of fact because they may reasonably be resolved in favor of either party."[23] To survive a defendant's motion for summary judgment, a plaintiff "need only present evidence from which a jury might return a verdict in his favor. If he does so, there is a genuine issue of fact that requires a trial."[24]

If the court decides summary judgment is improper, that portion of the case not dismissed will be tried. A party who loses after a trial can appeal the decision to a U.S. court of appeals. A party who loses in the court of appeals can then ask the Supreme Court to hear the case and reverse the decision of the court of appeals.

Many reported sexual harassment cases are decided on motions to dismiss or motions for summary judgment. The facts set forth in those reported cases are relied upon in this book. These representations of fact are not intended to reflect what happened or would have happened had there been a trial on the merits. Remember, I am reviewing facts found by the judiciary.

Chapter 8

Theories of Liability Under Title VII

Harassment on the basis of sex is a violation of Sec. 703 of Title VII. Unwelcome sexual advances, requests for sexual favors, and other verbal or physical conduct of a sexual nature constitute sexual harassment when (1) submission to such conduct is made either explicitly or implicitly a term or condition of an individual's employment, (2) submission to or rejection of such conduct by an individual is used as the basis for employment decisions affecting such individual, or (3) such conduct has the purpose or effect of unreasonably interfering with an individual's work performance or creating an intimidating, hostile, or offensive working environment.

In determining whether alleged conduct constitutes sexual harassment, the Commission will look at the record as a whole and at the totality of the circumstances, such as the nature of the sexual advances and the context in which the alleged incidents occurred. The determination of the legality of a particular action will be made from the facts, on a case by case basis [29 C.F.R. 1604.11 (a), (b); footnote omitted].

There are several recognized theories of liability in sexual harassment cases. The most common types of cases are those for "quid pro quo" sexual harassment, hostile work environment sexual harassment, constructive discharge, and retaliation.

Quid Pro Quo Sexual Harassment

Quid pro quo sexual harassment occurs when matters such as promotions and pay increases are granted or denied based upon whether an employee submits to a superior's requests for sexual favors. In *Bowen v. Valley Camp of Utah, Inc.,*[1] the court held that a plaintiff must prove the following elements to prevail on a quid pro quo sexual harassment claim:

(1) the employee is a member of a protected group; (2) the employee was subject to unwelcome sexual harassment; (3) the harassment complained

of affected a "term, condition, or privilege" of employment (*quid pro quo* or created a hostile environment), and (4) the employer is subject to liability based on agency principles.[2]

It has been said that employers are "automatically liable for supervisory misconduct in quid pro quo cases involving tangible job detriments" (Lindemann and Kadue 1992: 220).

In *Hicks v. Gates Rubber Co.,*[3] a woman who had been hired as a security guard and subsequently discharged sued her employer for sexual harassment. The employee alleged that she had been sexually harassed by coworkers and supervisors. One male supervisor was accused of reaching over and rubbing the employee's thigh, stating, "I think you're going to make it."[4] The employer asserted that the employee had misconstrued an innocent and harmless gesture of encouragement as sexual harassment. The district court found that no sexual advance was intended. Another male supervisor was accused of telling the employee "he would put his foot up [her] ass so far that [she] would have to go to [the] clinic to take it out."[5] It was alleged that the following day this supervisor touched the employee on her buttocks and said, "I'm going to get you yet."[6] The employee testified that some time later, this supervisor drove up to where she was taking a break, grabbed her breasts, and when she fell over, got on top of her.

The district court held that there was no evidence that submission to this supervisor's sexual advances was related to favorable supervisory treatment by the supervisor or a requirement of continued employment and that the record was unclear whether these incidents were brought to the attention of the supervisor or the company's guard division.

Both the district court and court of appeals held that because the evidence did not support a conclusion that the employee's continued employment was conditioned upon her submission to her supervisor's advances, the employee failed to state a claim for quid pro quo sexual harassment. The court of appeals noted:

> The gravamen of a *quid pro quo* sexual harassment claim is that tangible job benefits are conditioned on an employee's submission to conduct of a sexual nature and that adverse job consequences result from the employee's refusal to submit to the conduct.[7]

The court of appeals remanded the case to the district court to determine whether the employee had been subjected to hostile work environment sexual harassment, an issue the district court had not addressed.

The lapse of time between the unwelcome sexual advance and the adverse employment action, comparative evidence showing that those who did submit were treated more favorably, and evidence relating to whether the alleged harasser took part or influenced the adverse personnel decision are often important factors in determining whether the adverse employment action occurred as a result of the rejection of a sexual advance (Lindemann and Kadue 1992). An "employer may introduce evidence of poor work performance, excessive tardiness or absenteeism, insubordination, a violation of company policy, or a lack of work" as a justification for an adverse employment action alleged to constitute quid pro quo sexual harassment (Lindemann and Kadue 1992: 153–54). Sexual harassment claims have been rejected where no evidence existed that the alleged harassers participated in or were consulted about the adverse employment action.[8]

Hostile Work Environment

Hostile work environment cases are the most common type of sexual harassment cases. Hostile work environment occurs when an employee is subjected to working conditions in which harassment is sufficiently severe or pervasive to alter the conditions of employment and create an abusive work environment. In *Meritor Sav. Bank, FSB v. Vinson,*[9] the Court held that to be actionable under Title VII, the harassment must be "sufficiently severe or pervasive 'to alter the conditions of [the victim's] employment and create an abusive working environment.'"[10] Whether harassment is sufficiently severe or pervasive to be actionable is generally determined based on the totality of the circumstances.[11] To show that the discrimination was based on sex, the plaintiff must show that if he or she had been of the opposite sex, the employee would not have been the object of sexual harassment. In *Haehn v. City of Hoisington,*[12] the court stated:

> In other words, the sexual harassment "must be sufficiently severe or persuasive 'to alter the conditions of [the victim's] employment and create an abusive working environment.'" ... Whether the sexual conduct meets this threshold is determined from the totality of the circumstances.... To be actionable, the alleged sexual conduct must be sustained, repeated or persistent. ... In some instances, the severity of the offensive conduct may reduce the need for sustained exposure.[13]

Isolated incidents will generally not support a hostile environment sexual harassment claim. The plaintiff bears the burden of proving a hostile work environment claim by a preponderance of the evidence.[14] A sexual harassment claim may arise when an employee is subjected to advances made by a same-sex supervisor.[15] Title VII does not protect against employment discrimination because of homosexuality,[16] or transsexuality.[17] The fact that an employee is later terminated for legitimate reasons does not prohibit an employee from challenging the hostile environment while employed.[18]

An employer's liability for hostile work environment sexual harassment is not automatic (Lindemann and Kadue 1992). Title VII, on its face, prohibits an "employer" from engaging in prohibited conduct; 42 U.S.C. 2000e (b) defines the term *employer:*

> The term "employer" means a person engaged in an industry affecting commerce who has fifteen or more employees for each working day in each of twenty or more calendar weeks in the current or preceding calendar year, and any agent of such a person.

Individuals can also be considered an employer under Title VII. "Courts have generally held that to be an employer for purposes of Title VII, an individual must be an officer, director or supervisor of a Title VII employer, or otherwise involved in managerial decisions."[19] Individual liability can be imposed under Title VII where the individual meets the definition of employer and actively engages in discriminatory conduct.[20] Courts have held that failure to prevent sexual harassment once it becomes known is not enough in itself to impose individual liability upon one who is found to be an employer for purposes of Title VII.[21]

In *Meritor Sav. Bank, FSB v. Vinson,*[22] the Court declined "the parties' invitation to issue a definitive rule on employer liability" but agreed with the EEOC that "Congress wanted courts to look to agency principles for guidance in this area."

> With respect to conduct between fellow employees, an employer is responsible for acts of sexual harassment in the workplace where the employer (or its agents or supervisory employees) knows or should have known of the conduct, unless it can show that it took immediate and appropriate corrective action [C.F.R. 1604.11 (d)].

An employer can be charged with knowing of sexual harassment that occurs on regular basis. Employers have been relieved of liability where prompt action has been taken in response to a claim of sexual harassment. Although a coworker cannot be held liable for sexual harassment under Title VII, a coworker may be held liable under state tort law.[23]

> Applying general Title VII principles, an employer, employment agency, joint apprenticeship committee or labor organization (hereinafter collectively referred to as "employer") is responsible for its acts and those of its agents and supervisory employees with respect to sexual harassment regardless of whether the specific acts complained of were authorized or even forbidden by the employer and regardless of whether the employer knew or should have known of their occurrence. The Commission will

examine the circumstances of the particular employment relationship and the job [f]unctions performed by the individual in determining whether an individual acts in either a supervisory or agency capacity [29 C.F.R. 1604.11 (c)].

In determining whether an employer is liable for hostile environment sexual harassment by a supervisor, the courts have concluded that an employer may be held liable under the following theories:

> (A) harassment within the harasser's scope of employment, (B) harassment within the harasser's apparent authority, and (C) employer negligence in failing to prevent or remedy the harassment [Lindemann and Kadue 1992: 226].

Any one of these three bases of liability is sufficient to hold an employer liable for a supervisor's hostile work environment sexual harassment.[24] An employer can be held liable for hostile environment harassment by supervisors even though the employer had no knowledge of the harassment.[25]

In *Hirschfeld v. New Mexico Corrections Dept.,*[26] a female typist at the Central New Mexico Correctional Facility, a medium-security prison, was temporarily reassigned after an inmate was discovered watching her from an empty room across from her office and an anonymous letter had been received by prison officials detailing a plan to rape her.[27] Shortly after the typist was returned to the post she had previously held, she became the target of sexual harassment by a male captain who hugged her and kissed her or attempted to kiss her on two occasions. The target reported both incidents to superiors. After the second incident, the captain was placed on administrative leave.

The target filed a formal complaint, and at a formal interview the captain admitted to hugging and kissing the target and another female employee at the prison. The captain was demoted to lieutenant.[28] After filing the formal complaint, the target was the subject of rumors and received anonymous obscene telephone calls at her home. The target filed suit for sexual harassment.

The district court held that the captain's conduct, "in combination with the incident of sexual harassment by an inmate, constituted sexual harassment which gave rise to an intimidating and offensive work environment."[29] *Hirschfeld* was appealed to the Tenth Circuit Court of Appeals, which identified and discussed the three alternative bases for holding an employer liable for hostile environment sexual harassment.

Acting Within the Scope of Employment

Where the harassing supervisor is not acting within the parameters of his or her job description and the employer does not explicitly require or consciously allow its supervisors to harass subordinates sexually, the harasser does not act within the scope of his or her employment when sexually harassing a subordinate.[30] If the harasser is not acting within the scope of his or her employment when engaging in harassment, an employer cannot be held liable for the harasser's conduct under this theory of liability.[31]

Employer Negligence or Recklessness

"Employer negligence or recklessness in failing to respond to hostile work environment sexual harassment by employees may result in liability.... Employer negligence in this context is defined as 'failing to remedy or prevent a hostile or offensive work environment of which management-level employees knew, or in the exercise of reasonable care should have known.'"[32] In *Hirschfeld,* the warden interviewed the harasser the same day he was informed of the plaintiff's complaint and placed the alleged harasser on administrative leave. Once the investigation was completed, the alleged harasser was demoted, a decision which was upheld by the secretary of corrections.

Because the alleged victim did not believe the grievance procedure would be effective, she did not file a formal grievance as requested by the warden for his investigation. The evidence did not support the victim's conclusion that the grievance procedure would have been ineffective.[33] After this incident, the victim had no subsequent problems with the alleged harasser. The *Hirschfeld* court agreed with the district court's conclusion that the remedial action was prompt, adequate, and effective. The court found important to its decision the fact that once the prompt remedial action was taken,[34] no subsequent incidents of the victim being sexually harassed by the same harasser occurred. The *Hirschfeld* court concluded that the Department of Corrections was not liable for the harasser's conduct under the theory of employer negligence or recklessness.

Authority or Agency Relationship Aiding Harasser

The *Hirschfeld* court held that an employer may be liable for the acts of an employee "acting outside the scope of delegated authority if 'the servant purported to act or to speak on behalf of the principal and there was reliance upon apparent authority, or he was aided in accomplishing the tort by the existence of the agency relation.'"[35] The fact that an employee would not have been at the worksite except for his job is insufficient in itself to establish liability under this theory.[36] The court held that since the alleged harasser was not the plaintiff's supervisor and the alleged harasser did not use his authority over the guards he supervised for the purpose of facilitating his harassment of the plaintiff, the Department of Corrections could not be held liable under this theory.

Constructive Discharge

Sometimes the working conditions created when an employee complains of sexual harassment or rejects sexual advances results in the working conditions becoming so intolerable that a reasonable person would quit: a "constructive discharge." An employee who asserts that a hostile work environment resulted in her quitting her job may be deemed constructively discharged.[37] "The test for a constructive discharge claim brought under Title VII is 'whether a reasonable person would view the working conditions as intolerable.'"[38] The employee alleging constructive discharge "bears the burden of proving she was constructively discharged by a preponderance of credible evidence; mere uncontroverted evidence, if not credible, is insufficient."[39] The employee must prove that he or she resigned because of the sexual harassment. Where a plaintiff is affirmatively terminated, no constructive-discharge action under Title VII can be brought.[40]

Retaliation

Sometimes complaints of sexual harassment result in retaliation. However, "not every action taken by management, perceived as adverse by the employee, can be explained by a claim of an environment hostile to women or of retaliation for asserting claims of sexual harassment."[41] To make a prima facie case of retaliatory firing, an employee must generally show

> 1. that he or she engaged in protected opposition to Title VII discrimination;
>
> 2. adverse action by the employer subsequent to or contemporaneous with such employee activity; and
>
> 3. a causal connection between the protected activity and the adverse employment action.[42]

In some jurisdictions, internal complaints can constitute "protected" activity.[43] In *Kotcher v. Rosa & Sullivan Appliance,*[44] the court held:

> In this case, Kotcher had not filed a formal agency complaint before she was fired, but she did make an internal complaint to company management, protesting the sexually harassing actions of their supervisors. Surely

this opposition to the unlawful practice of sexual harassment is protected activity within the policies of Title VII.[45]

"A causal connection may be proven by circumstantial evidence that justifies an inference of retaliatory motive."[46] "A showing by Plaintiff that she was discharged following protected activity of which the employer was aware establishes a prima facie case of retaliatory dismissal."[47]

Chapter 9
From Whose Eyes
Do We Look?

It is clear that the definition of sexual harassment will vary depending upon whether the totality of the circumstances is viewed through the eyes of the victim, the harasser, or an objectively reasonable bystander, a "reasonable" man or woman. The reality is that there is no standard by which to measure the reasonable person.

When the *Meritor* case was decided, it was assumed that courts viewed hostile work environment claims from the perspective of a reasonable person.[1] In some jurisdictions, sexual harassment claims are still analyzed by the courts from the perspective of a reasonable person. Subsequent to the *Meritor* decision, however, a number of courts have held that allegations of harassment must be viewed from the perspective of a reasonable person of the same sex as the employee who alleges he or she was subjected to a hostile environment.

For example, in *Yates v. Avco Corp.,*[2] the Sixth Circuit Court of Appeals recognized that allegations of harassment of a female subordinate by a male supervisor should be viewed through the eyes of "a reasonable woman" when determining whether an employee was subjected to such difficult or unpleasant working conditions that a reasonable person in the employee's situation would have felt compelled to resign (a constructive discharge).

A comparison of the cases decided under these different standards indicates that an employer's liability does change, depending upon which perspective the court utilizes.

The Reasonable Person Standard

In *Babcock,*[3] a postal worker, Babcock, had a consensual, intimate, personal relationship with her married supervisor, Musso, for over a year. Babcock filed a sexual harassment complaint with her supervisor alleging sexual harassment by another employee and was transferred because the alleged harasser was confined to a wheelchair. Babcock filed a second harassment complaint against Musso. Babcock alleged that when their affair ended the first time, Musso told her to keep quiet about the affair or she would lose her job.

The affair resumed and finally ended in July 1988. Babcock alleged that when she refused to resume the affair with Musso, he threatened to destroy her career. Babcock was subsequently issued a letter of warning for insubordination, which she alleged had been fabricated by Musso. An investigation found no support for Musso's allegations but found that Babcock had had affairs with other employees. Babcock requested that either Musso or she be transferred. Babcock was offered a job she had previously applied for, which could have resulted in the separation of Babcock and Musso, but she was never transferred because Musso took sick leave and was terminated a short time later.

Musso appealed to the Merit Systems Protection Board and accepted a demotion and transfer in lieu of termination. While the appeal was pending, Babcock asked that she be promoted to Musso's position. Musso's position was filled by a woman more qualified than Babcock. Babcock alleged that the failure to promote her to Musso's former position was retaliation for her filing the complaint against Musso. Babcock filed a third complaint, alleging retaliation.

Babcock began taking sick leave and in response to her supervisor's concerns about the amount of sick leave being used, requested a transfer to a job that met her requirements. Her supervisor was unable to find a job that met all her criteria after making efforts to do so. Babcock told her supervisor she was having a drink at night to help her fall asleep, and the supervisor referred her to counseling. After Babcock had taken 180 hours of sick leave in a 3-month period, her supervisor required her to obtain medical documentation for any further sick leave.

Babcock filed a fourth complaint, alleging she was being retaliated against for taking sick leave to attend therapy sessions for the harassment she had been subjected to. Babcock's attendance improved once medical documentation was required, and this requirement was subsequently lifted. Once the medical documentation requirement was lifted, Babcock used 172 hours of sick leave in 2.5 months, working elsewhere as a teacher part of the time. Babcock alleged that she was sexually harassed at another facility when male managers[4] said, "Don't say anything around Miss Babcock, because she'll file an EEOC at the drop of a hat." An investigation concluded that Babcock's allegation about the statement by male managers was false. Disciplinary action was taken against Babcock, but later rescinded.

The court had the following to say about Babcock's other allegations:

Babcock also testified that while Musso was in the office, Anthony Paciullo, a supervisor and friend of Musso's, kept a picture of a half-naked woman pinned to a bulletin board and would kiss the picture. However, Adrienne Wells, a Data Collection Technician and Babcock's friend, testified that she never saw the picture nor the practice. In the absence of any contemporaneous record of complaint, and given the extent of the documentation of Babcock's other complaints, this incident is disregarded and discounted.

Babcock further testified that Corcoran called her a scorned woman. Corcoran denied the allegation. Although Corcoran admitted telling Babcock that she should not be working around men, Corcoran said that this statement was an immediate and unconsidered reaction to reading Babcock's deposition. Corcoran did, as Babcock claims, assign her the duty of measuring furniture because the ETU was moving into a new facility and all the furniture and equipment had to be measured. However, such a task was considered normal for lower-level managers, such as Babcock.

The only social contact between Corcoran and Babcock consisted of Corcoran and his wife taking Babcock and her son out for ice cream. Corcoran gave Babcock red lace underwear as a gag gift at the Christmas party in 1986, but such joke gifts were common at the office's Christmas parties.[5]

Babcock submitted her letter of resignation. Babcock was not aware of the fact that at the time of her resignation, disciplinary action against her (termination) was being considered because of her irregular attendance.

The *Babcock* court held that the plaintiff failed to show quid pro quo sexual harassment: "Absent facts showing an actual, rather than threatened, employment decision resulting in a denial of a tangible employment benefit, Babcock cannot prove sexual harassment based on a *quid pro quo* theory."[6] The *Babcock* court analyzed the hostile work environment claim under a *reasonable person* standard:

Actionable sexual harassment must consist of more than just isolated incidents or casual comments that express harassment or hostility.... Whether such conduct reaches the level of actionable sexual harassment is determined by a totality of the circumstances under a reasonable person standard....

Babcock did establish a severe or pervasive practice of sexual harassment with respect to Musso's actions. However, because Musso's [Letter of Warning] to Babcock was expunged from Babcock's file, this brief incident had no lasting effect. Where, as here, the claimed incident [sic] are few in number and occurred over a short period of time, they fail to rise to a level that would create a hostile working environment....

The other incidents that Babcock claims were sexually harassing are equally insufficient to establish a hostile working environment. Occasional or isolated utterances of offensive epithets, although repugnant, are not so pervasive as to affect the conditions of employment to a degree which violates Title VII....

The other two alleged incidents that occurred in 1988 — the throwing of the pencils by Haishun and Traveli's note recommending that Babcock wear a hairpiece — were isolated events that cannot be deemed severe or pervasive nor sexually derived. The episodes while Babcock was working at the Monticello were not established, nor did Babcock name the employee who she claimed physically harassed her.

While the gift of red lace underwear as a gag gift at an office Christmas party does not seem amusing in retrospect, it does not rise to the level of harassment, nor was it so perceived by Babcock at the time.

The picture of a half-naked woman pinned to the wall of Paciullo's office may have been offensive to Babcock, but it was not observed by others and it was not the subject of any complaint, contemporaneous or otherwise.

The incidents of harassing conduct alleged by Babcock simply are not sufficient to establish a hostile working environment. At most, the above incidents were a few isolated incidents that Babcock may not rely on to prevail here, . . . and the Postal Service responded promptly to all of Babcock's complaints. Taken together, the absence of a hostile environment was demonstrated.[7]

The court held that even if sexual harassment had occurred, the Postal Service could not be held liable for hostile environment sexual harassment because it took prompt and reasonable corrective action.[8]

The *Babcock* court held that "a plaintiff must prove that her employer deliberately acted or refrained from acting, rendering her working conditions so intolerable as to force her resignation"[9] to prevail on a constructive discharge claim. The court rejected the plaintiff's constructive discharge claim:

Babcock claims constructive discharge on the grounds that, after she filed her complaint against Musso, her supervisors were arranging to relocate her to another facility and into a lower level position. However, in response to her request to be reassigned, Corcoran decided to transfer Babcock to an OIC position in another facility. Placing her in such a position not only would have separated Babcock from Musso, but also would have provided Babcock with the opportunity to enhance her employment credentials. Smith said that Babcock had requested such an assignment prior to the Musso incident because OIC assignments are a training device. Babcock, though, was never transferred because Musso left the ETU on sick leave. Being considered for a transfer in 1988 which she herself requested cannot amount to a retaliatory or constructive discharge of Babcock by the Postal Service in 1989.

Babcock further claims that she was penalized for using sick leave. However, the record incontrovertibly shows that Babcock did in fact use an excessive amount of sick leave. Indeed, the record shows that she used some of her sick leave to work in another job as a teacher. Moreover, according to Smith, Babcock's placement on sick leave restriction was simply an administrative measure and was not considered an adverse action.

DeEttore also told Babcock that restricted sick leave was not a disciplinary device.

In sum, Babcock has not proved that her working conditions at the Postal Service were so intolerable that a reasonable person would have resigned in the same situation. Moreover, the evidence established that the Postal Service did not act deliberately in making Babcock's working conditions so intolerable that she should have felt compelled to resign.[10]

In *Saxton v. AT&T*,[11] the female plaintiff met Jerome Richardson, a supervisor in another department, had several lunches with him, and transferred to his department. A few months later, the plaintiff agreed to have drinks with Richardson at a bar after work one night and after a couple of hours at the bar, agreed to go to a jazz club with Richardson. Richardson rubbed his hand on the plaintiff's upper leg and kissed her, but when the plaintiff opposed the conduct, he quit.

A few weeks later, the plaintiff had lunch with Richardson again, and the two drove to a park where Richardson "lurched" at her from behind a bush. Richardson became quiet when the plaintiff opposed the conduct and never displayed sexually inappropriate conduct after the park incident. The plaintiff alleged that after the park incident, Richardson harassed her by not speaking to her, acting in a condescending manner, and teasing her about her personal relationship with a coworker.

The plaintiff reported sexual harassment to management. An investigation found inconclusive evidence of sexual harassment but found that Richardson exercised "poor management judgment" in pursuing the personal relationship with the plaintiff and a "communication problem" between the plaintiff and Richardson. The investigator concluded that the plaintiff and Richardson should obtain additional sexual harassment training, which Richardson did not do. The plaintiff accepted an offer to work at home until Richardson was transferred. The plaintiff was offered a job but felt she would do better in another job and requested time off. The investigator told plaintiff the option to work at home was void and continuously requested that she return to work. The plaintiff was terminated when she refused to return.

The *Saxton* court held that Richardson's condescending remarks, impatient attitude, and teasing about her relationship with another employee were insufficient to constitute a hostile work environment under Title VII. The court found significant the fact that plaintiff and Richardson had been friends and held that whether a work environment was so intolerable as to justify the plaintiff's resignation "must be determined by a reasonable person standard." The court rejected plaintiff's constructive discharge claim:

After the AT&T investigation of Saxton's charges and the subsequent corrective action, Saxton unreasonably refused to continue her employment, resulting in a voluntary resignation. The record reveals that after Richardson was transferred Saxton was offered additional work in the project management tools group. Although Saxton admitted there was work available for her in this area, she refused to work in the group because she believed she should have been offered a position in requirement development or as a project coordinator. Why Saxton believed she was entitled to a higher position is not clear. What is clear, however, is that Saxton's working conditions were not "so difficult or unpleasant that a reasonable person in the employee's shoes would have felt compelled to resign." *Bourque v. Powell Electrical Manufacturing Co.,* 617 F. 2d 61, 65, [22 FEP Cases 1191] (5th Cir. 1980) (quoting *Alicea Rosado v. Garcia Santiago,* 562 F. 2d 114, 119 [1st Cir. 1977]. Saxton could have pursued a number of other courses while remaining on the job. Instead, she ignored repeated attempts by her manager, admonishing her to report to work. "An employee must seek legal redress while remaining in his or her job unless confronted with an 'aggravated situation' beyond 'ordinary' discrimination." *Brooms,* 881 F. 2d at 423 (quoting *Bailey,* 583 F. Supp. at 929). Saxton has not only failed to establish a genuine issue as to any ordinary discrimination, but she falls way short of showing that it would be reasonable to conclude that she was confronted with an aggravated situation beyond ordinary discrimination. In short, as a matter of law, her refusal to report to work was tantamount to a voluntary resignation and not a constructive discharge as required by Title VII.[12]

A constructive discharge generally requires a resignation very close in time to the last act of sexual harassment.[13]

The *Saxton* court held that even if the allegations did constitute sexual harassment, the employer was not liable because it took appropriate corrective action:

Holmes, pursuant to AT&T procedure, promptly began a thorough investigation. He interviewed the principals as well as the witnesses whom Saxton proffered to corroborate her version of the facts. These witnesses not only failed to corroborate Saxton's version of the facts, but Trespalacious went so far as to accuse Saxton of spreading false rumors about her and Richardson. Holmes found, and we agree, that there was inconclusive evidence of sexual harassment. He also found, and we also agree, that Richardson acted improperly and that the separation of Richardson and Saxton was in the best interest of all concerned. Holmes, after learning that Saxton was not interested in a transfer, immediately began the process of transferring Richardson. In a month's time Richardson was transferred to another department, one-half mile from Saxton. During this entire process Saxton was allowed to work at home. Nevertheless, Saxton contends that the corrective action did not have the "desired effect." She points to two or three occurrences of seeing Richardson in her department after his transfer was effective, for about two seconds per instance. We agree with AT&T's assessment that what Saxton perceives to be the "desired effect" is not the proper inquiry. The question is whether the course of action taken by AT&T was "reasonably likely to prevent the misconduct from recurring." *Guess,* 913 F. 2d at 465. The misconduct in this case was Richardson's condescending comments, teasing, and impatience. After Richardson was transferred, this conduct ceased. Saxton has not alleged that any of the complained of conduct has recurred. Therefore, as a matter of law, AT&T's actions were reasonable.[14]

As illustrated by *Saxton,* even letters, calls, and requests for dates that can be considered sexual harassment cannot be used as a basis for employer liability if the employer takes prompt remedial action which results in the complained of conduct being stopped.

The Reasonable Woman Standard

In *Ellison v. Brady,*[15] a female IRS agent, Kerry, was asked to lunch by a male coworker, Sterling, in June 1986. Kerry and Sterling's workstations were about 20 feet away from each other. Kerry accepted the invitation to lunch. Thereafter, Sterling allegedly "started to pester [Kerry] with unnecessary questions and hang around her desk."[16] On October 9, 1986, Sterling asked Kerry to have a drink with him after work. She declined but suggested they have lunch the following week.

Kerry tried to avoid Sterling during lunchtime because she did not want to have lunch alone with him. A week after Sterling had asked Kerry to have a drink with him, he showed up at work in a three-piece suit and asked Kerry to have lunch with him, which she declined to do. On October 22, 1986, Sterling handed Kerry a note: "I cried over you last night and I'm totally drained today. I have never been in such constant term oil [sic]. Thank you for talking with me. I could not stand to feel your hatred for another day."[17]

Kerry became "shocked and frightened and left the room."[18] Sterling followed Kerry into the hall and "demanded that she talk to him, but she left the building."[19] Kerry later showed the note to her supervisor. Although the supervisor noted the conduct constituted sexual harassment, Kerry asked the supervisor not to do anything about it because "she wanted to try to handle it herself." Kerry "asked a male co-worker to talk to [Sterling], to tell him that she was not interested in him and to leave her alone."[20]

Kerry went out of town for training before she worked with Sterling again. Sterling sent Kerry a typed three-page single-spaced letter which stated in part:

> I know that you are worth knowing with or without sex. . . . Leaving aside the hassles and disasters of recent weeks. I have enjoyed you so much over these past few months. Watching you. Experiencing you from O so far away. Admiring your style and elan. . . . Don't you think it odd that

two people who have never even talked together, alone, are striking off such intense sparks. . . . I will [write] another letter in the near future.[21]

In the middle of the letter, Sterling wrote: "I am obligated to you so much that if you want me to leave you alone I will. . . . If you want me to forget you entirely, I can not [*sic*] do that."[22] Kerry explained her reaction to this letter as follows: "I just thought he was crazy. I thought he was nuts. I didn't know what he would do next. I was frightened."[23]

Kerry immediately called her supervisor, told her supervisor she was upset, and requested that either Sterling or she be transferred because she "would not be comfortable working in the same office with him."[24] The same day, Kerry's supervisor held a counseling session with Sterling and told him to leave Kerry alone, and reminded Sterling many times over the following few weeks that he was not to contact Kerry in any way. Sterling was transferred to another office before Kerry returned from training.

A grievance was filed, and the settlement resulted four months later in Sterling being returned to the office where Kerry worked and a promise by Sterling that he would not bother Kerry. On January 28, 1987, Kerry was notified by a letter from her supervisor that Sterling would be returning and was assured that additional action would be taken if the problem recurred. When she read the letter, Kerry became "frantic," filed a formal complaint alleging sexual harassment on January 30, 1987, and obtained permission to transfer temporarily to another office when Sterling returned to the office.

Although the person who investigated Kerry's formal complaint agreed that the complained of conduct constituted sexual harassment, the Treasury Department rejected Kerry's complaint "because it believed that the complaint did not describe a pattern or practice of sexual harassment covered by the EEOC regulations."[25] The EEOC affirmed the decision of the Treasury Department on the grounds that adequate action was taken by the agency to prevent the repetition of Sterling's conduct.

In September 1987, Kerry filed a lawsuit in the U.S. District Court for the Northern District of California. The district court granted the government's motion for summary judgment, finding that Kerry had "failed to state a prima facie case of sexual harassment due to a hostile working environment."[26]

On appeal, the Ninth Circuit Court of Appeals reversed the district court's decision after concluding as a matter of law that a *reasonable woman* would perceive Sterling's conduct as sufficiently severe and pervasive to alter the conditions of Kerry's employment and create an abusive working environment. The fear that letters, calls, and requests for dates may lead to sexual assault or rape appears to be a legally recognized fear of the reasonable woman.

In *Ellison v. Brady*,[27] the Ninth Circuit held that "well-intentioned compliments by co-workers or supervisors can form the basis of a sexual harassment cause of action if a reasonable victim of the same sex as the plaintiff would consider the comments sufficiently severe or pervasive to alter a condition of employment and create an abusive working environment. That is because Title VII is not a fault-based tort scheme." The *Ellison* court also held that when evaluating the severity and pervasiveness of sexual harassment, the court must focus on the perspective of a reasonable person of the same sex as the victim.

The Ninth Circuit has adopted the perspective of the reasonable person of the same sex as the victim primarily because "a sex-blind reasonable person standard tends to be male-biased and tends to systematically ignore the experiences of women."[28] According to the Ninth Circuit, the same sex standard allows the standard of behavior acceptable under Title VII to change as the views of reasonable men and women change.[29]

While feminists have been credited with defining sexual harassment and causing it to become and remain a public issue, it is far from clear that the views of the feminist are those of the "reasonable woman." There are many female feminists in America, but they do not appear to be the majority. An October 1991 *Newsweek* poll "revealed that while 45 percent of women believe that the women's movement has done well in improving women's lives and an additional 23 percent believe that it hasn't gone far enough, only 34 percent identify themselves as feminists" (Shapiro et al. 1991: 44). Research suggests that feminists are more likely to perceive as more offensive conduct labeled sexual harassment than nonfeminists (Brooks and Perot 1991). Not surprisingly, research also reflects that complaints of sexual harassment by a feminist may be taken less seriously because his or her feminist ideology, rather than the conduct complained of, is perceived as the cause of the complaint (Summers 1991). If the view of the reasonable woman is the view of the majority of women, there appears to be no justification for the reasonable woman standard being that of the feminist. Under the reasonable woman standard, an employer may be required to believe the views of a nonfeminist over those of a feminist about what constitutes sexual harassment. But then, the prostitute, nymphomaniac, or exhibitionist will probably not be found a reasonable woman either.

Conclusion

The extent to which calls, letters, and requests for dates can form the basis of liability under Title VII will depend in part on whether the courts in a particular jurisdiction apply the reasonable person or reasonable person–same sex standard. The law varies by what the courts in a given jurisdiction have said. Employees and employers must make decisions about whether to litigate a sexual harassment case under Title VII in light of the law as interpreted in the jurisdiction in which the conduct occurred.

The process of labeling conduct sexual harassment also results in labeling people. For example, under the reasonable man standard, men who hold views inconsistent with those of the reasonable man are, at least implicitly, unreasonable men. If most men cannot see what women see and the reasonable man is a member of the majority, all men who have adopted the feminists' view of sexual harassment may well be unreasonable men in some jurisdictions.

Is it fair to label the man who can see what women see unreasonable? The Ninth Circuit's *Ellison* decision would seem to require such a result. Likewise, under the reasonable woman standard, women who hold views inconsistent with those of the reasonable woman are, at least implicitly, unreasonable women. By assuming that men cannot see what women see, men are given an excuse for sexually harassing behavior because the law recognizes that men do not understand which behavior offends women.

Chapter 10

Sexual Teasing, Jokes, Gifts, Remarks, or Questions

There is a vast difference between what has been labeled sexual harassment by researchers and victims and what constitutes sexual harassment prohibited by law. For example, research suggests that the most common types of sexual harassment are unwelcome sexual teasing, jokes, remarks, or questions (USMSPB 1988; Dhooper et al. 1989). Some have argued that sexually explicit language offends women more than men (Lublin 1991). Poll results appearing in the October 21, 1991 issue of *Newsweek* showed that 35 percent of women reported experiencing sexual remarks.

Many employees have unsuccessfully challenged sexist or sexually degrading comments by coworkers and supervisors as sexual harassment. The courts are reluctant to find this type of conduct sexual harassment prohibited by Title VII, even though research suggests that many people believe this conduct can constitute sexual harassment. For example, 53 percent of males and 62 percent of females in the 1980 USMSPB survey thought that uninvited sexual remarks by a supervisor could constitute sexual harassment. By the time the 1987 USMSPB survey was conducted, these figures had risen to 58 percent of males and 72 percent of females. The percentage who considered uninvited sexual remarks by coworkers sexual harassment was less: 1980, 42 percent of males, 54 percent of females; 1987, 47 percent of males, 64 percent of females. Experiencing uninvited sexual remarks was reported by 10 percent of males and 33 percent of females in the 1980 USMSPB survey. The number of respondents who reported experiencing uninvited sexual remarks rose slightly in the 1987 USMSPB survey (12% of males, 35% of females).

Long before the enactment of Title VII, workers had tolerated harassment by their superiors in many industries. Some courts have held that Title VII was not intended to alter work environments in which rough language, sexual jokes, sexual conversations, and girlie magazines were present prior to the plaintiff's entering the work environment.[1] Barbara Lindemann and David Kadue (1992: 184) noted that courts have found no hostile environment at a chemical plant where sexually oriented dialogue was "customary plant language" and "no better or no worse than it had been before [the complainant] arrived," at a security trading house where coarse references to male and female genitalia and to sexual activity were "the language of this marketplace," at a patrol station where nearly everyone used profanity, in a "back shop" environment "replete with sexual innuendo, joke telling and general vulgarity," and in a convention center work environment "permeated by profanity" [footnotes omitted].

Under this view, Title VII prohibits treating women differently than men in the existing environment. Women entering the workplace take the environment as they find it but are protected from being treated differently than men in that environment by Title VII.

Other courts have held that Title VII requires an employer to take affirmative action to change the workplace norms to accommodate women (Lindemann and Kadue 1992).[2] This view requires employers to take affirmative action to accommodate women in the workplace (i.e., to change the workplace). These changes can include changing the language used by employees, removing pictures that have been hanging on the wall for years, and absorbing the cost of a personnel system to address sexual harassment training, policies, and remedies.

An employer is also required to monitor interoffice dating to ensure that requests for sexual favors or dates are not a condition of employment and are not creating a hostile work environment. The reasonable accommodation approach, as applied by many courts, requires an employer to monitor activity many would call private, beyond an employer's control, and legitimate business concerns. To some extent, including requests for dates and other unwelcome verbal conduct in conduct giving rise to a hostile environment under Title VII results in an invasion of an employee's right to privacy. As Title VII becomes more inclusive, an employer will be required to monitor more and more conduct previously considered private and beyond the legitimate interests of an employer.

To establish a prima facie case of hostile environment harassment against an employer under Title VII, an employee must generally show that

1. plaintiff belongs to a protected group;

2. plaintiff was subjected to unwelcomed sexual harassment;

3. the harassment was based on plaintiff's sex;

4. the harassment was so pervasive that it altered the conditions of plaintiff's employment and created a hostile work environment; and

5. the employer is liable based upon applicable agency principles —

employer knew or should have known of the harassment and failed to take proper remedial action.[3]

It has been stated that while "acts underlying a hostile environment claim do not have to be clearly sexual in nature," they "must be sufficiently severe or pervasive to alter the condition of the victim's employment and create an abusive work environment. . . . Whether the sexual conduct complained of is sufficiently pervasive to create a hostile work environment must be determined from the totality of the circumstances."[4]

Member of Protected Group

To establish a prima facie case of hostile environment, an employee must first prove that he or she was a member of a protected class. This requirement has led to little litigation because whether an employee is male or female is most often easily ascertainable and rarely disputed. Title VII, as a theoretical matter, prohibits hostile environment harassment against all employees, both male and female. Because all people are either male or female, all people are in a protected class.

Subjected to Unwelcome Sexual Conduct

In *Meritor Sav. Bank, FSB v. Vinson,*[5] the Supreme Court said, "The gravamen of any sexual harassment claim is that the alleged sexual advances were 'unwelcome.'"[6] "Unwelcomeness means that an employee did not solicit or invite the alleged behavior."[7] Determining whether sexual teasing, jokes, gifts, remarks, or questions are unwelcome is a complicated task. Men and women perceive "friendliness" and "sexiness" as different when observing women's social interactions (Saal et al. 1989). The extent to which one smiles or is friendly can affect perceptions about friendliness or sexual interest (Deutsch et al. 1987; Abbey 1987).

A person's knowledge about the sexual conduct of another must also be considered in determining whether conduct is unwelcome. For example, in *Burns v. McGregor Electronic Ind.,*[8] the court held that evidence of an employee's posing for nude photos published in magazines outside the workplace may be relevant in explaining the comments and actions of those accused of sexual harassment. When allegations of sexual harassment are made by an employee, the employer is often unaware of many circumstances which must be taken into account in determining whether conduct is unwelcome.

Organizational communication experts have recognized the importance of nonverbal information on a person's perception of a speaker. For example, in their textbook *Perspectives on Organizational Communication,* Tom Daniels and Barry Spiker had the following to say about nonverbal behavior:

> Nonverbal information also is important in organizational communication, but the concept of nonverbal communication is troublesome because many nonverbal behaviors may be ambiguous and unreliable signs of emotional states or even random activities that occur without awareness or intent on the part of a source. Although an observer is likely to interpret such behaviors, they lead to no shared meaning. Popular notions that nonverbal behaviors are consistent indicators of specific messages and conditions that can be interpreted reliably if one knows the rules are misleading. One should exercise caution when attaching interpretations to nonverbal behavior.
>
> Three important forms of nonverbal information are paralanguage, body movement (kinesics), and space (proxemics). Paralanguage cues such as volume, rate, rhythm, inflection, tone, and pitch help us to interpret verbal behavior. These cues also influence our perceptions of a speaker [Daniels and Spiker 1987: 40].

Because people interpret verbal communication in light of their perceptions of nonverbal behavior, nonverbal behavior must be taken into account when attempting to determine whether verbal communication is perceived as unwelcome.

Sexuality can be emphasized by a person choosing to wear tight or revealing clothing (Gutek 1985). It has been argued that clothing is one cue upon which people base their impressions and judgments about others (Kaiser 1990). Items we attach to or wear on our bodies, the body itself, and any visible modifications to the body constitute appearance. The social psychology of clothing is the study of "the various means people use to modify the appearance of the body, as well as the social and psychological forces that lead to, and result from, processes of managing personal appearance" (Kaiser 1990: 4). The attention, decisions, and actions of a person relating to his or her appearance are all included in the concept known as *appearance management* (Kaiser 1990).[9]

Appearance *perception,* on the other hand, refers to "the process of observing and making evaluations or drawing inferences based on how people look" (Kaiser 1990: 7). A person's physical appearance can have an effect on the way his or her actions are perceived by others. For example, research suggests that "unattractive individuals are typically perceived as more aggressive, antisocial, and dishonest than those considered attractive" (Wertlieb 1991: 333). Thus, conduct engaged in by unattractive individuals may be perceived as less welcome than the same conduct engaged in by an attractive person. A target who dresses in a particularly seductive manner may be perceived as providing a sufficient cause for the actor's behavior (Pryor and Day 1988). Likewise, "evidence of a prior amicable relationship may serve to decrease the likelihood that socio-sexual behavior will be interpreted as sexual harassment" (Thomann and Wiener 1987: 587).

Because "traditional ideas about what a woman should look like are not legitimate criteria for evaluating women in the workplace," an undue preoccupation with what female employees look like, when the same scrutiny is not given to males, may give rise to a hostile environment claim.[10] A few isolated comments about what a woman looks like has generally been held insufficient to establish a hostile environment harassment claim under Title VII.[11] A woman's appearance, however, may be relevant to an analysis of whether conduct is unwelcome. The symbolic-interactionist perspective asserts that people act toward others in a manner consistent with their perception of the meanings of the appearances of others (Kaiser 1990).

In *E.E.O.C. v. Newtown Inn Associates,*[12] female cocktail waitresses filed sexual harassment complaints because their employer, the Ramada Inn, required them to "project an air of sexual availability to customers and to dance, both with customers and alone, in a sexually provocative and degrading fashion."[13] Not surprisingly, the consequence was that "employees were subjected to unwelcome sexual proposals and both verbal and physical abuse of a sexual nature."

In 1980, a federal court in Michigan stated: "A sexually provocative dress code imposed as a condition of employment which subjects persons to sexual harassment could well violate the true spirit and the literal language of Title VII."[14] An employee who perceives another as making efforts to appear sexually attractive may believe the sexually attractive person is seeking sexual attention or advances. In light of the continuing wave of sexual harassment litigation, dress codes must be reevaluated.

Unwelcome Conduct Must Be Based on Sex

Some courts have held that "because of sex" and "sexual in nature" are separate concepts for purposes of Title VII:

> Sexual harassment or unequal treatment of employees on the basis of sex, does not have to take the form of sexual advances or contain sexual overtones.... Unequal treatment or harassment based on the sex of the employee is the touchstone of the action.[15]

Other courts have required the harassment to be sexual in nature. In *Trotta v. Mobil Oil Corp.,*[16] the court noted:

> Many courts have required that the alleged harassment take the form of
> sexual advances, requests for sexual favors, or other verbal or physical
> conduct of a sexual nature. . . . Some courts, however, have held that the
> alleged conduct need not be sexual.[17]

The nature of the "because of sex" requirement appears to vary among
jurisdictions.

Sexual comments alone are generally not enough to constitute sexual
harassment prohibited by Title VII.[18] Courts have held that where a supervisor or coworker engages in the same conduct with both sexes, there is no
harassment because of gender or sex.[19] In many cases, both men and
women have engaged in conduct considered sexually offensive by the person who files a Title VII suit.

In *Ebert v. Lamar Truck Plaza,*[20] the court noted that "Congress did
not intend for Title VII to obliterate the use of foul language in the American work-place."[21] In *Ebert,* former female employees of a newly opened
truck restaurant in Colorado unsuccessfully brought a sexual harassment
suit against their employer. An assistant manager and shift supervisor were
accused of using offensive gestures and language, and touching various
female employees on the breasts and buttocks.

The evidence showed that "rough language" was used by both males
and females, supervisors and coworkers. Vulgar language was used by,
and directed at, male and female employees. Some of the employees who
brought the suit were also found to have used vulgar language. A female
waitress testified that the language used by one of the plaintiff-employees
was as offensive to her as that of male kitchen employees. At trial, several
witnesses testified that the type of language at issue was "typical of that
used in the restaurant business."

All incidents of offensive conduct were not reported to the restaurant
manager. When incidents were reported to the manager, prompt remedial
action was taken. The *Ebert* court relied partly on the following statement
in *Rabidue v. Osceola Refining Co.,*[22] in concluding that the employees'
claims were insufficient under Title VII:

> It cannot be seriously disputed that in some work environments, humor
> and language is rough hewn and vulgar. . . . Title VII was not meant to—
> or can—change this. It must never be forgotten that Title VII is the
> federal court mainstay in the struggle for equal employment opportunity
> for the female workers of America. But it is quite different to claim that
> Title VII was designed to bring about a magical transformation in the
> social mores of American workers.

The *Ebert* court held that the employees had not shown that the conduct
in question occurred because of their sex or that the conduct sufficiently
affected their working environment.

In *Bowen v. Department of Human Services*,[23] a female employee's female supervisor allegedly used vulgar and offensive language in the presence of both men and women. Males and females used language Thelma Bowen found offensive. Ms. Bowen resigned, and her supervisor refused to allow her to withdraw her resignation. Ms. Bowen filed a charge of discrimination alleging a hostile environment with the Maine Human Rights Commission, which found reasonable grounds to believe she had been subjected to sexual harassment.

Ms. Bowen filed suit against her supervisor and employer without waiting for the commission to take further action. The lower court granted the supervisor's and employer's motion for summary judgment. On appeal, Ms. Bowen argued that genuine issues of material fact existed regarding whether she had been subjected to a hostile environment. The Maine Supreme Judicial Court rejected Ms. Bowen's claim:

> The constant use of vulgar language in the workplace is without question offensive and unprofessional conduct. Nonetheless, the record does not support Bowen's assertion that the vulgar language was used in her presence or directed at her because she was a woman. It was directed at, and used by members of both sexes. A reasonable male could also find the behavior offensive.[24]

In response to Ms. Bowen's complaints that her supervisor called her an offensive nickname, told her she should wear a bathing suit at a stress relief session occurring primarily around a swimming pool, and referred to her predecessor in a vulgar fashion, the court stated:

> There is nothing in the record that suggests that when Bartley gave Bowen the offensive nickname it was because Bowen was a woman; rather it would appear that it was because she was a new employee. Bartley did not call her that again after Bowen asked her not to. When Bartley criticized Bowen for not wearing a bathing suit to the stress relief session it was not because she was a woman, but rather because her attire was not compatible with the occasion. There is nothing in the record that supports Bowen's contention that when Bartley referred to Bowen's predecessor in a vulgar fashion it was because she was [a] woman. This conduct was not sexual in nature and Bowen failed to generate any factual issue that would support an inference that it would not have occurred but for her gender.[25]

The *Bowen* Court noted that the female supervisor "allowed people working under her to relieve stress by using coarse language."[26]

In *Porras v. Montefiore Medical Center*,[27] a voluntary nonprofit acute-care hospital with a contract to provide medical and mental health services to prisoners was sued for sexual harassment by Porras, a 47-year-old female unit chief for Mental Health Services at the Correctional Institute for Men on Rikers Island. After Porras supported an investigation into brutality, she began to receive intense harassment from a female, Gale Siegal, deputy director of Mental Health Services for the corporation. Porras's performance evaluation dropped, and complaints were made by subordinates about her work performance.

Porras was assessed by a psychiatrist as "suffering from tremendous emotional distress resulting from the harassment of Siegal and others creating a hostile and dangerous work environment."[28] Siegal subsequently left her employment.

At the first meeting between Porras and a new male director, Scimeca, the director allegedly threw a computer printout at Porras and thereafter "singled Porras out for an unrelenting barrage of yelling, screaming and hostility."[29] Porras's emotional state became much worse, resulting in her seeing her psychiatrist more often. As a result of allegations made by the same two persons who had made complaints about Porras to Siegal, Scimeca began monitoring Porras's work more closely. In May 1988, a prisoner attempted suicide, and Porras didn't report the incident for several days. Scimeca told Porras she should begin to look for other work, and a heated exchange ensued. Porras was given the option of resigning or being terminated. When Porras refused to resign, she was terminated. The day after her termination, Porras was discovered secretly tape-recording another meeting regarding her termination. A termination notice and recommendation not to rehire was issued and affirmed after a termination hearing, "allegedly because of Porras' overall poor record."[30]

Porras subsequently filed suit alleging in part disparate treatment and a hostile environment. The employer and Scimeca obtained summary judgment in their favor. The *Porras* court stated:

> Porras also fails to establish a claim for sexual harassment, that is harassment not sexual in form but in circumstances from which a gender-based motive can be inferred. Although Porras claims that Scimeca and presumably Siegal yelled at and intimidated her because of her sex, there is no evidence to support her claim that the harassment in this form was gender-induced. Although various affidavits both support and negate Scimeca's alleged practice of yelling or "shrieking" at women, even assuming Scimeca's yelling at the female Unit Chiefs constituted gender-induced harassment, there is no evidence presented that could support a claim that this harassment rose to a level sufficient to be considered pervasive or severe so as to create a hostile working environment.[31]

Thus it appears clear that Title VII does not require employers to prohibit the use of abusive language in the workplace as long as both men and women are subjected to the abusive language.

Sufficiently Severe or Pervasive to Alter the Conditions of Employment

In *Meritor*,[32] the Supreme Court held that to be actionable under Title VII, the sexual harassment must be "sufficiently severe or pervasive 'to alter the conditions of [the victim's] employment and create an abusive working environment.'"

In *Lehtinen v. Bill Communications*,[33] the court stated: "Sporadic offhand remarks or casual comments are insufficient to give rise to a Title VII violation."[34] In *Rabidue v. Osceola Refining Company*,[35] the Sixth Circuit Court of Appeals determined that sexual harassment rising to the level of creating a hostile work environment requires conduct which would interfere with the reasonable individual's work performance and affect seriously the psychological well-being of a reasonable person under like circumstances. Isolated sexually suggestive or offensive comments are generally insufficient to establish a hostile environment claim.[36]

In rejecting the hostile environment claim, the *Porras*[37] court concluded that "unfair, overbearing, or annoying treatment of an employee, standing alone, cannot constitute a Title VII sex discrimination claim."[38] The court held that although some evidence supported the employee's claim that the supervisor habitually yelled at women, these allegations, taken as true and assuming such conduct constituted gender-based discrimination, were insufficient to support a claim that the harassment rose to a level sufficient to be considered so pervasive or severe as to alter the conditions of employment and create a hostile working environment.[39]

The *Bowen*[40] court held that sexually suggestive or offensive jokes made by male and female employees around a pool during a stress relief session, taken as true, were insufficient to create a genuine issue of material fact whether the conduct was so severe and pervasive that it altered the conditions of employment and created a hostile environment.

In *Downum v. City of Wichita, Kan.*,[41] a terminated fire fighter and dispatcher alleged that a fellow recruit said he refused to take orders from a "damn bitch" and that on another occasion the plaintiff was invited to join the men in the shower since she was "doing a man's job."[42] The court held that no claim for sexual harassment was stated because "the conduct complained of constitutes an annoying, but fairly insignificant part of the total job environment."[43] The court concluded that this conduct was "not so significant that an average female recruit would have found her overall work experience to be substantially and adversely affected."[44]

Table 10.1. Percentage of Federal Workers Who Agreed or Disagreed with Statement: Nearly All Instances of Unwanted Sexual Attention Can Be Stopped If the Person Receiving the Attention Simply Tells the Other Person to Stop

FEDERAL WORKERS	AGREE	DISAGREE
Women	62%	35%
Men	74%	22%
Supervisors	73%	24%
Nonsupervisors	68%	28%
Victims	60%	37%
Nonvictims	73%	23%

Source: USMSPB 1981: D-23.

Individual Remedial Action

Most respondents to the 1980 USMSPB survey thought that an employee could end unwanted sexual attention by simply asking the person engaging in the offensive conduct to stop (*see* Table 10.1). The 1980 USMSPB survey found that asking that person to cease the conduct did make things better most of the time for victims of "less severe" harassment, i.e., pressure for dates, sexually suggestive looks or gestures, and sexual teasing, jokes, remarks or questions (*see* Table 10.2). Thus, it appears that victims of this type of conduct may be well advised simply to tell the harasser to stop.

Organizational Remedial Action

In *Kotcher v. Rosa & Sullivan Appliance,*[45] Pamela Kotcher alleged that her superior Herbert Trageser sexually harassed her, in part by the use of vulgar comments and gestures. "This treatment included, but was not limited to, comments to the effect that if Trageser had the same bodily 'equipment' as Kotcher, his sales would be more substantial. In addition, Trageser often pretended to masturbate and ejaculate at Kotcher behind

**Table 10.2. Percentage of Narrators Who Indicated
That Taking These Informal Actions "Made Things Better"**

ACTION	LESS SEVERE	
	WOMEN	MEN
Transferred, disciplined or gave a poor performance rating to the person	59%	33%
Asked or told the person(s) to stop	60%	68%
Reported the behavior to the supervisor or other officials	52%	17%
Avoided the person(s)	54%	58%
Made a joke of the behavior	43%	57%
Threatened to tell or told other workers	36%	21%
Ignored the behavior or did nothing	36%	45%
Went along with the behavior	18%	13%

Source: USMSPB 1981: 68.

her back to express his anger with her. This treatment took place on a regular basis, often in front of others at the store."[46]

The trial court concluded that these acts were unwelcome and of such a degrading nature that "no ordinary person would welcome them."[47] Although the court found these allegations sufficient to state a hostile environment claim, it refused to hold the employer liable because (1) Kotcher failed to report the harassment promptly through the employer's established grievance procedure, (2) the employer commenced an investigation within 24 hours after Kotcher reported the incident, and (3) the employer quickly transferred and demoted the harasser.[48]

Kotcher was instructed to take time off while the investigation was conducted. It is unclear whether Kotcher was terminated or refused to return to work.[49] Five months after his transfer, Trageser was returned to the position he held before Kotcher's complaint. The *Kotcher* court held that the reinstatement of the alleged harasser created a "cloud of suspicion" that the employer's remedial action was a sham and remanded the case to the district court for further consideration. In response to Kotcher's argument that the employer had prior actual notice of Trageser's propensity to engage in harassment because another female employee had alleged he harassed her and he had been given a written warning, the *Kotcher* court stated:

> Although the district court did not specifically address this question, it implicitly held that the prior incident was not sufficiently egregious to require severe remedial actions by the employer. Of course, not every response to a complaint should take the form of discharge, and we conclude that the district court could reasonably have found that the employer had responded appropriately because the written warning was sufficient to make Trageser aware that the harassment would not be tolerated on its premises.[50]

In response to Kotcher's allegation that the employer knew or should have known of the harassment because other employees and supervisors in the store knew of Trageser's conduct, the court stated:

> At some point, even under the *Vinson* dichotomy between quid pro quo claims and hostile work environment claims, the actions of a supervisor at a sufficiently high level in the hierarchy would necessarily be imputed to the company. But we do not think that this case presents such a situation, and the district court could reasonably have found that the company, whose main office was in Rochester, did not have constructive notice of Trageser's behavior in Oswego.[51]

The location of employees and supervisors in relation to the firm's main office appears to be relevant in determining whether an employer knew or should have known of sexual harassment at a firm's satellite office.

Conclusion

Contrary to much feminist literature, there is no evidence that as a class, women supervisors are less likely than male supervisors to use sexually explicit or offensive language in the workplace when they are free to do so. Many sexual harassment cases filed by female employees support the argument that placing females in a supervisory position over other women will not reduce the verbal sexual harassment female employees are confronted with in the workplace. For example, in *E.E.O.C. v. Hacienda Hotel*,[52] a female executive housekeeper called female subordinates names such as "dog," "whore," and "slut." Sometimes females supervisors fail to make efforts to assist their female subordinates who complain about sexual harassment or then conspire with men to harass women.

While it is possible for an employee to prevail on a hostile environment claim under Title VII based on unwelcome sexual teasing, jokes, remarks, or questions, an employee is less likely to prevail on such a claim where the conduct is directed toward both men and women or where the victim has engaged in similar conduct. In cases where abusive or offensive language is directed toward both male and female employees, a state-law claim for intentional infliction of emotional distress may be easier to prove than a claim under Title VII. Employees who wish to be free from such conduct should consider telling the offender to stop the conduct because it is offensive.

Chapter 11

Letters, Calls, and Pressure for Dates or Sexual Favors

Pressure

Some consider letters, calls, and requests for dates in appropriate circumstances normal courting behavior. However, a person may be attracted to person who does not find him or her attractive: a one-sided attraction. In the workplace, these one-sided attractions or infatuations can manifest themselves in unwelcome calls, letters, and requests for dates directed to a coworker or subordinate. These requests for dates may then be labeled sexual harassment.

Most male and female respondents in both the 1980 (87% of males, 93% of females) and 1987 (76% of males, 90% of females) USMSPB surveys thought that uninvited letters and calls by a supervisor could constitute sexual harassment. Likewise, the majority of respondents in both the 1980 (76% of males, 87% of females) and 1987 (67% of males, 84% of females) USMSPB surveys thought that uninvited letters and calls by a coworker could constitute sexual harassment. Although most male and female respondents were of the opinion that uninvited letters and calls could constitute sexual harassment, the number of both men and women holding this opinion decreased between 1980 and 1987. The reported incident rate, however, increased between 1980 (9% of females, 3% of males) and 1987 (12% of females, 4% of males). Poll results appearing in the October 21, 1991 issue of *Newsweek* showed 12 percent of women experiencing such letters and calls.

Most men and women thought that uninvited pressure for dates by a supervisor could constitute sexual harassment in the 1980 USMSPB survey (76% of males, 77% of females) and in the 1987 USMSPB survey (81% of males, 87% of females). As for uninvited pressure for dates by coworkers, 59 percent of males and 65 percent of females in the 1980 survey, 66 percent of males and 76 percent of females in the 1987 USMSPB survey, thought this conduct could constitute sexual harassment. The number of male and female respondents who reported experiencing uninvited pressure for dates decreased between the 1980 (7% of males, 26% of females) and the 1987 (4% of males, 15% of females) USMSPB surveys. Poll results appearing in the October 21, 1991 issue of *Newsweek* found that 15 percent of the women reported experiencing pressure for dates.

The 1980 USMSPB survey showed that 65 percent of the male respondents and 81 percent of the female respondents thought that uninvited pressure for sexual favors by a coworker could constitute sexual harassment. In 1980, 84 percent of male respondents and 91 percent of female respondents indicated that uninvited pressure for sexual favors by a supervisor could constitute sexual harassment. Only 9 percent of the female and 2 percent of the male federal employees responding to the 1980 USMSPB study reported experiencing uninvited pressure for sexual favors. The 1987 USMSPB survey reflected an increase (90% of males, 98% of females) in the number of respondents who thought that uninvited pressure for sexual favors by a coworker could constitute sexual harassment.

The same patterns[1] emerged in relation to uninvited pressure for sexual favors by supervisors. The 1987 USMSPB survey reflected an increase (95% of males, 99% of females) in the number of respondents who believed uninvited pressure for sexual favors by a supervisor could constitute sexual harassment. Both men and women considered uninvited pressure for sexual favors sexual harassment. The 1987 USMSPB survey reflected no change in the number of female employees (9%) reporting uninvited pressure for sexual favors. The number of male employees experiencing uninvited pressure for sexual favors rose between the 1980 (2%) and 1987 (3%) USMSPB surveys.[2] Poll results appearing in the October 21, 1991 issue of *Newsweek* showed 9 percent of the women experiencing pressure for sexual favors.

Unwelcome Sexual Conduct

While it is clear that uninvited pressure for sexual favors is perceived as offensive by many people, there are times when a reasonable person may question whether such conduct is unwelcome. In *Thoreson v. Penthouse International,*[3] Marjorie Thoreson filed suit against Penthouse International, the publisher of *Penthouse* magazine, and its founder, Robert Guccione. Ms. Thoreson, at age 20, agreed to appear as "Pet of the Month" in the September 1973 issue of *Penthouse,* was photographed in London by the founder, and became intimate with him. Ms. Thoreson signed a management agreement with *Penthouse* in which she gave *Penthouse* exclusive control over her career in the entertainment industry in exchange for a promise that *Penthouse* would use its best efforts to assist her.

Ms. Thoreson then appeared on the cover of the December issue of *Viva,* a magazine published by Guccione. Guccione agreed to make Ms. Thoreson "Pet of the Year" in 1975 and asked her to live with him, which she did. In 1976, Ms. Thoreson was led to believe she could get a part in a movie being produced by Penthouse, *Caligula,* and agreed to have surgery to enlarge her breasts. After the breast surgery, Ms. Thoreson learned the part for which she had agreed to the surgery had been given to someone else[4] but was promised another part. Guccione decided to incorporate two new scenes in *Caligula.* The court described the plaintiff's part in these scenes:

> Guccione returned to the set in January, 1977, with plaintiff and other Penthouse pets to shoot the scenes. One scene graphically captured plaintiff performing oral sex on a man. The second showed plaintiff and Penthouse pet Lori Wagner having sex with each other. Plaintiff claims to have performed in the scenes reluctantly and only after having been persuaded that it would further her career.[5]

In 1977, plaintiff began working in a starring role in the movie *Messalina, Messalina.* Thereafter, Ms. Thoreson alleged, Guccione asked her to perform sexual favors for him:

> He told plaintiff to seduce the advisor and to encourage him to move to this country. Plaintiff refused. Defendant insisted that plaintiff do so because it was important to him and to the Penthouse empire. Plaintiff capitulated. Her sexual affair with the financial advisor, carried on during his periodic trips to New York, and guided by Guccione, lasted eighteen months.
> In the summer of 1980, defendant encountered difficulty in raising money to open a gambling casino in Atlantic City. Defendant asked plaintiff to sleep with a furniture manufacturer from Milan, who, defendant believed, could assist him with this venture. Plaintiff refused. Defendant told her that she had to do it because she owed him. She did.[6]

In 1980 *Caligula* was released. A dispute about promoting *Caligula* resulted in Ms. Thoreson being fired:

> Caligula was released in 1980. Promotions were done by plaintiff and Guccione. Defendant told plaintiff that he wanted her to promote Caligula in Japan. Plaintiff refused because her experience on the United States promotional tour had been degrading and humiliating. Defendant refused to discuss plaintiff's reluctance to go. Plaintiff did not go, as a consequence of which she was fired. She never did another film.[7]

Thoreson filed a claim under New York's human rights laws alleging sexual harassment. The New York Supreme Court, New York County, concluded that Thoreson had been sexually harassed:

> The credible evidence reveals that defendant Guccione utilized his employment relationship with plaintiff to coerce her to participate in sexual activity with the furniture manufacturer and with his financial advisor in order to advance his business. He compelled plaintiff to continue the relationship with his advisor, which he helped to choreograph, for a period of eighteen months.
>
> Plaintiff's testimony concerning these matters was controverted only by defendant Guccione's blanket denial that the events took place. I do not believe him.[8]

The court entered a judgment in Thoreson's favor for $60,000 in emotional distress (compensatory damages) and $4 million in punitive damages. The New York Supreme Court, Appellate Division, vacated the $4 million punitive damages award after finding punitive damages were not available under New York's human rights law.[9]

In *Burns v. McGregor Electronic Ind.,*[10] Lisa Ann Burns alleged that a manager-trainee, Marla Ludvik, made sexual comments as Burns left the bathroom,[11] made almost daily comments to other workers about Burns,[12] and tried to get Burns to date male employees. Burns complained to both male and female supervisors, but no corrective action was taken. The owner allegedly showed Burns advertisements for pornographic films in *Penthouse,* talked to her about sex, asked her to watch pornographic movies with him, made lewd gestures, and asked her for dates at least once a week. Burns alleged that the owner's behavior made her "angry, upset, and 'real nervous,' and that sometimes she would cry at work or at home."[13]

Burns stated that her work slowed down and she voluntarily left her employment the first time on August 10, 1981. Burns returned to work on September 15, 1981, allegedly as a result of her needing work. Burns was placed in a higher-paying quality control job by the new plant manager, Virginia Kelley. The owner allegedly continued to ask Burns for dates and also asked her to engage in oral sex. During this second period of employment, Marla Ludvik circulated a petition seeking the termination of Burns because nude photos of Burns taken by Burns's father appeared in *Easyrider* and *In the Wind*. After Ludvik showed the owner the photographs, the owner asked Burns to pose nude for him. In addition to these events and plant gossip, Burns testified that June Volske, a supervisor, tried to get her to sit on the owner's lap and that a male supervisor called her vulgar names, creating a hostile environment and resulting in her quitting again on June 20, 1983. On September 26, 1983, Burns again returned to work at McGregor and was repeatedly asked out by the owner, asked to pose nude and to watch pornographic movies. Burns quit again on July 19, 1984, after being called vulgar names and being the object of misconduct by Eugene Ottaway.

The district court held that Burns had not shown she was constructively discharged from her third period of employment. The district court held that "in view of [Burns's] willingness to display her nude body to the public in Easy Riders publications, crude magazines at best, her testimony that she was offended by sexually directed comments and Penthouse or Playboy pictures is not credible."[14] The district court further held that Burns failed to prove the sexual harassment to which she was subjected was sufficiently severe or pervasive to alter the conditions of Burns's employment and create an abusive work environment. Burns appealed. The court of appeals reversed the case for reconsideration in light of the totality of the circumstances including the first two periods of employment.

Many an average man and woman would suspect that requesting sexual favors from a person who portrays his or her nude body in magazines or movies for money would be less offensive than requesting sexual favors from someone who has never engaged in such conduct. Because requests for sexual favors from those who publicly exploit their sexuality for financial gain can give rise to civil liability, it is clear that requests for sexual favors from those who do not engage in such activity will most often be viewed as unwelcome.

It is interesting that the use of provocative women is often a feature of advertising directed at women. "The use of attractive persons, sexual fantasies, and nude and scantily clad models is prominent in advertising. . . . Sex appeal in ads does seem to have a high attention-getting value for both men and women. . . . Ads featuring provocative pictures of women are read more often by women than by men. . . . A similar phenomenon occurs with ads using pictures of attractive men; the messages are more often read by men than by women" (Schultz and Schultz 1986: 534–35).

Some of those ads directed at women could give rise to civil liability in some jurisdictions. In *Robinson v. Jacksonville Shipyards, Inc.,*[15] the court held that a sexual harassment claim may be based on the presence of nude and seminude photos in the workplace and remarks demeaning to women made by coworkers and supervisors.[16] Requests for sexual favors appear to be considered unwelcome "as a matter of law" in some jurisdictions.

Chapter 12

Deliberate Touching, Assault, Actual or Attempted Rape

It appears clear that unwelcome deliberate touching, assault, and actual or attempted rape are considered offensive conduct by most people under most circumstances. The long-standing public policy against this type of conduct is reflected in criminal laws prohibiting rape and sexual assault long before the 1960s and 1970s when this conduct was included in the definition of sexual harassment.

Deliberate Touching

Most men and women were of the opinion that uninvited deliberate touching by a supervisor could constitute sexual harassment in the 1980 USMSPB survey (83% of males, 91% of females). Likewise, most men and women thought that uninvited deliberate touching by a coworker could constitute sexual harassment in the 1980 USMSPB survey (69% of males, 84% of females). Most men and women thought uninvited deliberate touching by a supervisor could constitute sexual harassment in the 1987 USMSPB survey (89% of males, 95% of females); likewise, uninvited deliberate touching by a coworker could constitute sexual harassment in the 1987 USMSPB survey (82% of males, 92% of females).

While the number of female respondents reporting uninvited deliberate touching rose between 1980 and 1987 (15% to 26%), the number of males who reported experiencing this form of sexual harassment more than doubled between 1980 and 1987 (3% to 8%). Poll results in the October 21, 1991 *Newsweek* showed 26% of the women experiencing deliberate touching.

In *Gallagher v. Wilton Enterprises, Inc.,*[1] the court summarized the facts in the light most favorable to the plaintiff:

> Plaintiff was hired by defendant as a sales representative for its Boston territory on November 12, 1984. Defendant sold cakeware and cake

decorating accessories to retail stores and outlets; it also, through its sales representatives, ran cake decorating classes at some of its customer's stores. Because of her success as a sales person, plaintiff's territory was enlarged twice, first, to include Springfield, Massachusetts, Hartford, Connecticut, and Bangor and Portland, Maine. In 1986 her supervisor, Michael Olsen, the villain of the piece, expanded her territory to encompass all of New England because she "was doing a really good job." Plaintiff received a number of awards from the defendant for her sales performances: the "100 Percent Plus Club" for fiscal 1987; "High 5 Member" status in 1987 (achieving 105% or more of her sales quota); and a plaque for achievement of 100% of her sales quota for the first quarter of 1987. Plaintiff met or exceeded her sales quotas for every full quarter she was employed by defendant. Plaintiff received accolades from defendant's executive officers for her sales performances. Despite plaintiff's outstanding sales record she was fired without notice or warning on January 27, 1988, by her supervisor Michael Olsen.

Plaintiff testified that she was fired because of refusal to allow Olsen to kiss, squeeze and hug her, as was his wont with other female sales representatives, and because she rebuffed his sexual advances. In answer to a question as to how Olsen conducted himself toward her, plaintiff testified: "Every time I met him, left him, he was always reaching out and squeezing me, hugging me, touching me. He always was kissing me. I'd always turn my face, so he would end up on my cheek." This behavior by Olsen started when he first became supervisor in 1985 and continued through the day he discharged her.

Plaintiff testified that in November of 1987 Olsen told her that "our personal relationship had better improve." She further testified that at another time, "he [Olsen] looked me straight in the face and he said that our relationship had better improve." Plaintiff interpreted the statements about improving "our relationship" as sexual advances.

On the day that she was fired, plaintiff picked up Olsen at the Providence, Rhode Island Airport and drove him to the Holiday Inn, where they both stayed. Olsen told her to meet him in the lounge after she had checked in. She did so, and, after she sat down, Olsen said: "Our relationship better improve." Plaintiff ignored the remark. Olsen then told her that she was fired as of the coming Friday. Plaintiff was shocked and just looked at Olsen, who said, "You know what it is, it's our relationship."[2]

The *Gallagher* court upheld the judgment of $165,750 against the employer for back pay, front pay, and emotional distress.

Unwelcome Sexual Conduct

In *Lehtinen v. Bill Communications,*[3] an editor of a trade magazine, *Plastics Technology,* alleged that the publisher and editor in chief of the magazine "routinely harassed her and made offensive remarks about women in her presence" and that the publisher "publicly insulted and 'touched [her] in an offensive manner' at a company social function."[4] The plaintiff alleged that when she mentioned taking legal action against the publisher as a result of the incident at the social function, the president of the firm "indicated she would be fired if she took such action."[5] Shortly thereafter, the plaintiff filed a charge of discrimination and was terminated the same day. The court denied the employer's motion to dismiss for failure to state a hostile environment claim under Title VII.

Unwelcome Conduct Must be Based on Sex

In *Campbell v. Board of Regents of State of Kan.*,[6] the plaintiff alleged that the following facts constituted sexual harassment:

> Dr. Deyoe crowded plaintiff in her office and made knee to knee contact with her that made her feel uncomfortable; he used obscenities in talking to her about others; he threatened plaintiff at least a half dozen times to slap her on the butt; on December 22, 1987, Dr. Deyoe slapped plaintiff on the butt after she had just delivered a message to him, and plaintiff made it clear that this conduct was unwelcome; in January 1988, Dr. Deyoe told plaintiff that he would hit her again but obviously she did not like it; Dr. Deyoe had previously threatened a former secretary, Kim Hoffman, that he would hit her on the butt and also threatened to inseminate her.[7]

In response to defendant's argument that the conduct had little to do with the fact that plaintiff was female, the court stated:

> Wherever else such conduct might be acceptable, a slap on the buttocks in the office setting has yet to replace the hand shake, and the court is confident that such conduct, when directed from a man towards a woman, occurs precisely and only because of the parties' respective gender.[8]

It appears that some conduct is perceived as gender-motivated as a matter of law in cases involving physical contact.

Sufficiently Severe or Pervasive to Alter Conditions of Employment

n *Hirschfeld v. New Mexico Corrections Dept.*,[9] a female typist at Central New Mexico Correctional Facility, a medium-security prison, temporarily reassigned after an inmate was discovered watching her in an empty room across from her office and an anonymous letter had been received by prison officials detailing a plan to rape her.[10] Shortly after typist was returned to the post she had previously held, she became the target of sexual harassment by a male captain who hugged her and kissed her or attempted to kiss her on two occasions. The target reported both incidents to superiors.

After the second incident, the captain was placed on administrative leave. The target filed a formal complaint, and at a formal interview, the captain admitted hugging and kissing the target and another female employee at the prison. The captain was demoted to lieutenant.[11] After filing the formal complaint, the target was the subject of rumors and received anonymous obscene telephone calls at her home. The target filed suit for sexual harassment.

The district court held that the captain's conduct, "in combination with the incident of sexual harassment by an inmate, constituted sexual harassment which gave rise to an intimidating and offensive work environment."[12]

Prompt Remedial Action

In *Chrysler Motors v. Allied Ind. Workers,*[13] the undisputed facts relating to an allegation of sexual harassment were as follows:

> During a telephone conversation, Gallenbeck put down the telephone receiver and approached the co-worker from behind and grabbed her breasts as she inspected a door panel nearby. He then returned to the telephone and stated, "Yup, they're real."[14]

The union filed a grievance on behalf of the harasser, who had been discharged for the conduct, asserting that he had not been discharged for "good cause." The arbitrator held termination too severe a remedy:

> Although Chrysler presented evidence that Gallenbeck had committed four other incidents in which he intentionally grabbed and/or pinched female co-workers, the arbitrator found that Chrysler acquired this information after the discharge and therefore the arbitrator refused to consider it. The arbitrator also found that the evidence upon which Gallenbeck's discharge was based did not indicate that he could not be rehabilitated. The arbitrator concluded that severe discipline short of discharge would be adequate to deter him from further misconduct and to demonstrate to all employees Chrysler's opposition to sexual harassment. The arbitrator determined that Gallenbeck was not discharged for "good cause" and reduced the penalty to a 30-day suspension and directed Chrysler to reinstate Gallenbeck with back pay.[15]

The district court refused Chrysler's request to set aside the arbitrator's award as contrary to the public policy against sexual harassment. The Seventh Circuit Court of Appeals held that although the public policy against sexual harassment is well recognized, the district court properly enforced the arbitration award.

Actual or Attempted Rape or Assault

While rape accounts for only a small fraction of allegations of sexual harassment, those rape cases which have made their way to the courts have been used to gain legal protection from much less severe conduct included in the package of conduct labeled sexual harassment. For example, in *Meritor,* the case in which the Supreme Court recognized that Title VII prohibited some types of hostile work environments, the employee alleged she had been forcibly raped on several occasions. The legal principles announced in *Meritor* have been used to hold employers liable for conduct much less egregious than the conduct alleged in *Meritor.*

Actual or attempted rape or assault was reported by 0.3 percent of male and 1 percent of female federal employees surveyed by the Merit Systems Protection Board in 1980. Actual or attempted rape or assault was reported by less than 1 percent (female 0.8%, male 0.3%) of federal employees surveyed in 1987 (USMSPB 1981; USMSPB 1988). Poll results appearing in the October 21, 1991 *Newsweek* showed 0.8 percent of the women experiencing actual or attempted rape or assault.

In *Capitol City Foods v. Superior Court,*[16] the court held that where an employee voluntarily and without coercion goes into the bedroom of an off-duty supervisor and is thereafter raped, the employer is not liable for the rape. The *Capitol City* court discussed the facts before it:

> Mary T. began working at defendant's Burger King franchise in January of 1989. Vernon Johnson was the night shift supervisor. On January 29, Mary and a co-worker asked Johnson to go with them for a drink. Johnson could not go then, but suggested another time. Mary and Johnson made arrangements to go out on the 31st. They both believed the co-worker would accompany them. Neither Johnson nor Mary was scheduled to work that day, but unbeknownst to Johnson, Dan Singh had changed the schedule and scheduled Mary to work that day at 5 P.M. At that time Mary was still in training and had a flexible schedule as she learned the job along side more experienced workers. On January 31, as arranged, Johnson picked up Mary, who was in her Burger King uniform, at a grocery store at 4 P.M.; the co-worker did not show up. They drove around for 45 minutes, during which time Johnson made two phone calls. He called the Burger King and told Dan Singh that he should not have changed the schedule without Johnson's approval and that if Mary wanted to work she would come in late. He also called his parents' house. Johnson took Mary to his parents' house, where they had sexual intercourse. Johnson then dropped Mary off at an auto repair store, and he went to Burger King. The next day Mary told the manager what had happened, and quit shortly thereafter.
> . . . .
> The first cause of action alleged there was unlawful discrimination on the basis of sex (sexual harassment) against Mary, which included requiring

her "to work in an intimidating, hostile and offensive environment." The primary factual allegation to support this cause of action read: "On January 31, 1989, defendant Johnson, abusing his position of authority as shift manager and supervisor of plaintiff Mary [T.], instructed plaintiff Mary [T.], who was dressed in her Burger King uniform and about to enter the premises at 2335 Florin Road, Sacramento, California, to report to her regularly assigned shift, to get into his car and accompany her [sic] to his residence. Defendant Johnson advised her he had made arrangements so that she would not have to punch in on the time clock at work at that time. Defendant Johnson thereupon transported plaintiff Mary [T.] to his residence at 3445 Gates Way, Sacramento, California 95832 and raped her." The complaint further alleged Mary was required to then work in the presence of Johnson although he was a known sexual harasser.[17]

The court held the employer could not be held liable for date rape after an employee's working hours in the privacy of a supervisor's home.

In *EEOC v. Wilson Metal Casket Co.,*[18] Mr. and Mrs. Ellis worked for the same employer, a firm owned by Mr. Wilson. The court found:

> When Mr. Ellis left Wilson for surgery, Mr. Wilson transferred Barbara Ellis to a small facility away from the main casket plant. Mr. Wilson required Mrs. Ellis to perform oral sex on him several times. He also subjected her to touches on her breasts and buttocks, sexual comments, kisses, and requests to meet him after working hours.
>
> When her husband returned to work, Mrs. Ellis was transferred back to the main plant. Although the demands for oral sex ceased, the other forms of harassment continued.[19]

Mr. Ellis's request that Mr. Wilson cease the affair apparently upset Mr. Wilson's wife, and both Mr. and Mrs. Ellis were terminated.

The court held that Mrs. Ellis had been subjected to a hostile work environment prohibited by Title VII:

> Here, the proof was that Mr. Wilson required Barbara Ellis to perform oral sex on him from time to time, that he frequently fondled her breasts and buttocks, requested that she meet him after working hours, and made other comments of a sexual nature. Although Barbara Ellis capitulated to some of these demands for sexual services, Mr. Wilson's advances were nonetheless unwelcome and thus violated Title VII. *See Vinson*, 477 U.S. at 68.
>
> Furthermore, Mr. Wilson's harassment of Barbara Ellis occurred with some frequency at least during the nine months in 1982 when William Ellis was out of work with back surgery. Barbara Ellis testified that Mr. Wilson's sexual harassment disturbed her psychological well-being and interfered with her work performance. The undersigned finds that Barbara Ellis' reaction to Mr. Wilson's sexual advances was that of a reasonable person's reaction to such a working environment. Accordingly

the undersigned finds that Barbara Ellis has proved that she was subjected to sex discrimination within the meaning of Title VII.[20]

The following facts were sufficient to make a prima facie case of retaliatory discharge:

> Barbara and William Ellis claim that they were discharged in retaliation for William Ellis' act of protesting Mr. Wilson's sexual harassment. On the evening of September 18, 1984, William Ellis became upset because he believed that Mr. Wilson was sexually harassing Barbara Ellis. William Ellis came to this conclusion because of comments made to him by Barbara Ellis, and because he thought that he had seen Mr. Wilson sexually harass other female employees. That evening, William Ellis telephoned Mr. Wilson at his home and requested that Mr. Wilson cease making sexual contact with Barbara Ellis. Both Mr. Wilson and Mrs. Wilson were disturbed by the phone call. William Ellis and Barbara Ellis were terminated the next afternoon on account of the phone call.
> . . . .
> William Ellis had a good faith and reasonable belief that Barbara Ellis was sexually harassed by Mr. Wilson. Although Barbara Ellis had not told her husband the entire story of Mr. Wilson's harassment, William Ellis had enough information to reasonably believe that harassment was taking place. There is no contention that the Ellis' did not subsequently suffer adverse employment action, and it is clear that a causal link existed between William Ellis' phone call and the subsequent discharges.[21]

The court rejected the employer's argument that Mr. Ellis's method of protesting the sexual harassment was unreasonable:

> William Ellis' phone call may have embarrassed Mr. Wilson and even strained Mr. Wilson's marriage, but this was more on account of the nature of William Ellis' complaint rather than the method of complaint. Furthermore, William Ellis' method of protest did nothing to disrupt the productivity of the workplace at Wilson Metal Casket Company.
> Defendant has not rebutted plaintiff's *prima facie* case of discrimination. William Ellis has proved by a preponderance of the evidence that he was discharged for protesting what he reasonably believed to be Mr. Wilson's illegal activities. Barbara Ellis was discharged for aiding William Ellis' opposition activities and is thus also protected by 42 U.S.C. §2000e (3) (a).[22]

Fear of Crime and the Reasonable Woman Standard

The Ninth Circuit has held that fear of violent crime justifies inclusion of less severe conduct within the scope of conduct prohibited by Title VII. The *Ellison v. Brady*[23] court concluded:

Table 12.1. Question: How Fearful Are You
of Being the Victim of a Violent Crime in the 1990s?

RESPONSE	SEX OF RESPONDENT	
	MALE	FEMALE
Very fearful	8%	16%
Somewhat fearful	38%	49%
Not fearful at all	54%	33%
Don't Know/No Answer	less than 1%	2%

Source: Sourcebook of Criminal Justice Statistics — 1990, 181.

Because women are disproportionately victims of rape and sexual assault, women have a stronger incentive to be concerned with sexual behavior. Women who are victims of mild forms of sexual harassment may understandably worry whether a harasser's conduct is merely a prelude to violent sexual assault. Men, who are rarely victims of sexual assault, may view sexual conduct in a vacuum without a full appreciation of the social setting or the underlying threat of violence that a woman may perceive.[24]

The *Ellison* court relied in part on literature reflecting that men and women have varying views about what constitutes sexual harassment and statistics which reflected that in 1988 "an estimated 73 of every 100,000 females in the country were reported rape victims"[25] to conclude that the conduct in question could be offensive to a reasonable woman. Fear of rape appears to justify a finding that less severe conduct constitutes sexual harassment in the Ninth Circuit if a reasonable woman could share the fear.

It appears that women may fear crime more than men do. Data obtained from 1,001 telephone interviews in the summer of 1989 found a little more than half the respondents "very fearful" or "somewhat fearful" of being "the victim of a violent crime in the 1990s" (*see* Table 12.1). A 1986 survey conducted by the U.S. Census Bureau of 13,711 inmates convicted of violent offenses and residing in state prisons, found that men were more often targets of all violent offenses, including assault (*see* Table 12.2). Women, however, have been convicted of rape and assault (*see* Tables 12.2 and 12.3). It appears that women's fear that some types of conduct, such as the display of sexual materials, will lead to rape is declining (*see* Figure 12.1).

Table 12.2. Violent Offenders in State Prisons

CURRENT OFFENSES	SEX OF VICTIM(S)		
	MALE	FEMALE	BOTH
All violent offenses	53.0%	39.0%	8.1%
Homicide	70.4%	26.4%	3.2%
Rape/Sexual Assault	11.0%	87.0%	2.0%
Robbery	55.6%	29.4%	14.9%
Assault	68.2%	24.6%	7.2%
Other	39.4%	52.3%	8.4%

Source: Sourcebook of Criminal Justice Statistics — 1990, 621.

Table 12.3. Arrests by Offense Charged, Sex, and Age Group, United States, 1989 and 1990

ARRESTS (ACTS)	MEN			WOMEN		
	1989	1990	% CHG	1989	1990	% CHG
Forcible rape	25,210	27,264	8.1	316	290	-8.2
Aggravated assault	257,333	289,208	12.4	38,844	43,583	12.2
Other assaults	548,791	610,312	11.2	103,199	117,563	13.9
Prostitution and commercialized vice	23,218	27,503	18.5	54,138	53,385	-1.4
Sex offenses (except forcible rape and prostitution)	66,354	69,994	5.5	5,611	5,831	3.9
Offenses against family and children	38,900	45,746	17.6	8,305	10,244	23.3

Source: Sourcebook of Criminal Justice Statistics — 1991, 443.

Figure 12.1

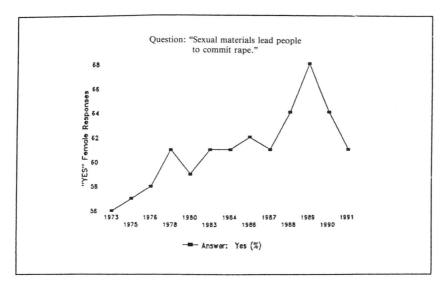

Source: Sourcebook of Criminal Justice Statistics—1991, 250–51.

Title VII Is Decreasing the Seriousness of Rape and Increasing the Defenses of Rapists

Including rape and physical sexual assault in the package of behaviors labeled sexual harassment may have been seen as advantageous to feminists when attempting to gain recognition of sexual harassment as a social issue. Such conduct was already considered a problem worthy of legal sanctions and was perceived by lawmakers and most citizens, men and women, as highly inappropriate conduct.[26]

However, including such egregious conduct as rape in the package of behaviors labeled sexual harassment tended to mitigate the seriousness of rape in the eyes of many. As sexual harassment law evolved, employers became civilly liable for the criminal conduct of their employees, even where the crime was unauthorized and appalling. Because it is the employer who is sued under Title VII rather than the rapist, corporate defense lawyers were called upon to defend rapists' actions. This required defense counsel to defend or attempt to mitigate the unauthorized conduct of a rapist.

Was it in the best interest of women to create a situation where highly skilled corporate defense attorneys come to defend the conduct of rapists?

I think not. Another question worth asking is: What deterrent effect does Title VII have on rape when the judgment must be paid by the employer rather than the rapist? Does Title VII encourage rape by those who realize it is the employer who will be held liable for a judgment under Title VII?

Title VII Allows Perpetrators to Escape Personal Civil Liability

Some believe that being charged as a criminal damages the public image of a person more than allegations of violations of civil laws. Some conduct defined as sexual harassment clearly constitutes conduct which also violates criminal laws[27] prohibiting sexual assault or rape.[28] Publicizing Title VII's civil remedy and educating employees about Title VII's prohibitions can be seen as in the best interest of employees who engage in sexual assault and rape at work because it increases the likelihood that victims of sexual assault and rape will seek civil rather than criminal redress.[29] A judgment under Title VII would most likely be paid by the employer rather than the person engaging in the illegal conduct.

These circumstances may encourage one who wishes to engage in sexual assault or rape to do so at work. Including sexual assault and rape within the meaning of sexual harassment prohibited by Title VII may have given victims of sexual harassment some hope of more meaningful relief (money) than that obtained in seeking criminal prosecution (often no tangible economic compensation). While Title VII may further the interests of victims of sexual assault and rape by providing them a way to collect damages from an employer, it is unclear that this new cost of doing business will help prevent employee rape.

Chapter 13

Duty to Take General Preventive Measures: Policy Statements and Training Programs

> Prevention is the best tool for the elimination of sexual harassment. An employer should take all steps necessary to prevent sexual harassment from occurring, such as affirmatively raising the subject, expressing strong disapproval, developing appropriate sanctions, informing employees of their right to raise and how to raise the issue of harassment under Title VII, and developing methods to sensitize all concerned [29 C.F.R. 1604.11 (f)].

That an employer takes steps to prevent sexual harassment does not necessarily prevent a finding of liability, although it is one factor to be considered.[1] Policy statements that sexual harassment will not be tolerated and training programs designed to increase the awareness of employees about what kinds of conduct can constitute harassment may be enough to relieve an employer from liability under Title VII. These efforts by themselves, however, seem to do little to reduce the prevalence of conduct labeled sexual harassment.

After the 1980 Merit Systems Protection Board study uncovered what was perceived as widespread sexual harassment in the federal workplace, federal agencies made additional efforts to prevent or deter sexual harassment. The executive summary of the results of the 1987 study conducted by the Merit Systems Protection Board reported:

> Among the 22 largest Federal departments and agencies surveyed, all had issued policy statements or other internal guidance during the 7-year period from FY 1980 through FY 1986 concerning prohibitions against sexual harassment.... Most employees ... said they are aware of their agency's policies regarding sexual harassment and the internal complaint procedures available to victims.
>
> ....
>
> Every agency maintained it provided training on the issue of sexual

harassment, although most efforts were directed at managers and personnel and equal employment opportunity officials rather than nonsupervisory employees.

. . . .

Most agencies maintained that they have taken a number of different
actions in an effort to reduce sexual harassment and that, in most cases,
those actions have been effective.

. . . .

Compared to 7 years ago, Federal workers are now more inclined to
define certain types of behavior as sexual harassment.

. . . .

In 1987, 42 percent of all women and 14 percent of all men reported
they experienced some form of uninvited and unwanted sexual attention.
Despite the apparent increase in the level of sensitivity about what
behavior may be considered sexual harassment, there has been no significant change since the Board's last survey in 1980 in the percentage of
Federal employees who say they have received such uninvited and unwanted attention [USMSPB 1988: 2–4].

Programs designed to increase employees' awareness of conduct
labeled sexual harassment did not reduce the incidence of such conduct.
The frequency of allegations of sexual harassment did not change significantly between the 1980 and 1987 USMSPB surveys. The Merit Systems
Protection Board's findings suggest that increased awareness of what constitutes sexual harassment and how to respond to sexual harassment
through established procedures does not result in a decrease in the frequency of sexual harassment in the workplace. The Merit Systems Protection Board findings suggest that employee training programs focused on
increasing the awareness of employees about these issues are rather ineffective if the goal is reducing the frequency of sexual harassment.

Policy Statements

Hope Comisky (1992: 199) has explained that an effective policy is required:

An employer must have an "effective" policy against sexual harassment
in place. "Effective" means one about which all employees have knowledge. "Effective" means that employees are educated on a periodic basis
about sexual harassment. "Effective" means that managers also are
educated about sexual harassment on a periodic basis and trained in how
to deal with such complaints. "Effective" also means that more than one
person is designated to receive sexual harassment complaints. If the immediate supervisor, for example, is the harasser, an employee has someone else to complain to about the offensive behavior.

Well-drafted policies may be relied upon by an employer asserting a lack-of-knowledge defense. The extent to which policy statements deter or prevent sexual harassment is unclear. Use of good policies, however, may result in the employer being given an opportunity to deal with the problem prior to hearing from a government agency.

The *Kay v. Peter Motor Co., Inc.*[2] court was confronted with the following facts:

> Appellant Peter Motor Company, Inc. is a closely held corporation, owned in part by Peter Lillemoe, which primarily sells new and used automobiles. In October 1988, respondent Bobbie Kay began work for Peter Motors as a salesperson. The record reveals that Lillemoe and Kay developed a friendly relationship and that Kay would often share her personal problems with Lillemoe and he would give her advice.
>
> However, the record also reveals a number of incidents which demonstrate another side to their relationship which forms the basis of her complaint. At a sales meeting in March 1990, Lillemoe asked respondent when she last experienced an orgasm. Also in March, Lillemoe displayed a wind-up toy penis to Kay while at work. Sometime in the spring, Lillemoe also participated in collecting money in an attempt to encourage another female employee to shake her breasts. Lillemoe asked respondent for some change for this fund, although he did not fully explain why he was asking for the money.
>
> On May 5, 1990, Lillemoe directed a number of sexually derogatory remarks to Kay. Among other statements, Lillemoe asked, in the presence of other salespersons, when respondent had last been "gang banged." Later in the day, Lillemoe informed Kay that he had been at a party where he had watched a woman suck on her own nipples. Still later in the day, Lillemoe announced over the intercom, while customers and employees were present, "Let's have a gang bang." Respondent testified that she told Lillemoe about the presence of customers and he answered "so let them join in." Thereafter Lillemoe held a quarter pitching contest with male salespersons to determine who would get to "have Bobbie" first. Testimony also revealed that Lillemoe referred to Kay as a "fat pig in heat" to another employee and asked "how would you like to jump in the sack with that?" Lillemoe stated that these comments were merely friendly comments which should not be taken out of context.
>
> Respondent's employment terminated on May 16, 1990, after Lillemoe stated that she had mishandled a deal and it would be better if they parted company. Kay never filed a complaint with Peter Motors alleging sexual harassment by Peter Lillemoe while she was employed by the company.[3]

The employer defended in part on the ground that plaintiff had not given the employer notice of the harassment prior to the charge being filed. The *Kay* court reviewed the decisions relating to mandatory reporting requirements:

No reported case has required a complaint where the employer's grievance procedures do not outline a mandatory complaint procedure. *See Bersie,* 417 N.W. 2d at 294 (Lansing, J., dissenting) (employer not entitled to complaint on harassment perpetrated by supervisors, "particularly if the employer has not established an express policy against sexual harassment or any procedure for resolving harassment claims") (citing *Meritor Savings Bank, FSB v. Vinson,* 477 U.S. 57, 72–3, 106 S. Ct. 2399, 2408, 91 L. Ed. 2d 49 [1986]). *Compare Heaser v. Lerch, Bates & Assocs., Inc.,* 467 N.W. 2d 833, 835 (Minn. App. 1991) (where manager commits sexual harassment, such knowledge is imputed to employer and absent specific, detailed company policy, victim not required to make further complaints) *with Weaver v. Minnesota Valley Lab., Inc.,* 470 N.W. 2d 131, 135 (Minn. App. 1991) (where company has written reporting policy, victim had duty to complain to identified individual in order to preserve sexual harassment claim against company). [fn. 1] In this case the employer had no express grievance reporting procedure and no policy for reporting wrongful harassment. Moreover, the employer has shown no training program or policy announcements which demonstrate a sincere desire to receive harassment complaints and respond to them.[4]

In note 1, the court stated:

We also note that there is no reason to require an employee to complain to their supervisor when the supervisor is the harasser because the employee would not likely have a "reasonable expectation of assistance." *True-Stone Corp. v. Gutzkow,* 400 N.W. 2d 836, 838 (Minn. App. 1987); *see also Dura Supreme v. Kienholz,* 381 N.W. 2d 92, 95 (Minn. App. 1986) (no expectation of assistance where supervisor viewed harassment as "joke"); *Porrazzo v. Nabisco, Inc.,* 360 N.W. 2d 662, 664 (Minn. App. 1985) (employer deemed to have knowledge of continuing harassment where supervisor was source of many problems).[5]

The *Kay* court concluded that since no specific sexual harassment policy required the plaintiff to report the incident, she was not required to file an internal complaint with her employer prior to bringing suit under Minnesota's law prohibiting sexual harassment. The court affirmed a judgment against the employer in the amount of $56,593. Policy statements should require employees to report sexual harassment within a short, specified period of time. The report should be made to a party not engaged in the conduct complained of. Enforcement of mandatory reporting requirements, however, may be seen as retaliation prohibited by Title VII.

Policy statements designed to enhance an employer's chances of dealing with sexual harassment should define the conduct the employer wants to know about. Identifying the specific conduct prohibited may enhance an employer's lack-of-knowledge argument where the conduct is specifically identified in the policy and not brought to the employer's attention. Specific prohibitions also make the policy less likely to be challenged as failing to put harassers on notice of prohibited conduct. If the conduct the employer wishes to address is "requests for sexual favors," the policy should explicitly identify requests for sexual favors as a type of conduct which is prohibited and requires reporting. A waiver of the reporting requirement should exist where the complainant explicitly tells the harasser the conduct is unwelcome, in which case reporting is required within a specified period after the recurrence of conduct prohibited by the policy.

Policy statements may most appropriately be analyzed under an unconstitutionally-void-for-vagueness standard. Courts have held that standards "usually employed to scrutinize legislation ... are just as applicable to judicially fashioned law."[6] One principle well founded in constitutional law is that a statute which prohibits conduct in terms the average man would not understand is unconstitutionally void for vagueness. An abundance of literature supports the argument that men do not understand what sexual harassment is. Some of this literature stands for the proposition that men will never understand what sexual harassment is. If it is true that reasonably intelligent men cannot understand what is prohibited by Title VII's prohibition against sexual harassment, it may also be true that Title VII is unconstitutionally void for vagueness.

In *New Mexico v. City of Albuquerque,*[7] a female employee filed a formal written complaint with the city of Albuquerque accusing Cleo F. Hughes of sexual harassment. Hughes was placed on administrative leave while the allegations were investigated. Hughes was given notice of the allegations against him, represented by counsel during the investigation, and allowed to testify personally and identify favorable witnesses. The investigators found evidence to support the allegations against Hughes, and he was given notice of a pretermination hearing. At the hearing, Hughes was allowed to defend against the allegations. After the hearing, Hughes was terminated.

Hughes appealed his termination to the city personnel board, which upheld the termination after another hearing. Hughes appealed the decision to uphold his termination to the state district court. The district court affirmed the decision of the city personnel board, and Hughes appealed the decision to the New Mexico Court of Appeals.

Hughes argued that the findings of the city personnel board did not establish that the board believed the allegations of sexual harassment[8] and that the findings of the board were insufficient to justify his termination. The New Mexico Court of Appeals agreed that the city personnel board's findings and conclusions were insufficient to support Hughes's termination, stating in part:

> The conclusions state only that the alleged victims *construed* Hughes' actions as sexual harassment. The City argues that this conclusion "falls

within the definition of sexual harassment set out by the Board[.]" We disagree. The City relies on Administrative Instruction No. 44, which defines sexual harassment as "unwelcomed sexual advance, request for sexual favors, and other verbal or physical conduct of a sexual nature." Although the perception of the victim is a factor in determining whether conduct satisfies the definition, that perception must be reasonable. *See Ellison v. Brady*, 924 F. 2d 872 [54 FEP Cases 1346] (9th Cir. 1991) (applying "reasonable woman" standard to claim of sexual harassment under Civil Rights Act of 1964); *cf. Green v. City of Albuquerque*, ___ N.M. ___, 819 P. 2d 1342 (Ct. App. 1991) (No. 12,701) (employee is not entitled to benefits under Workers' Compensation Act for disability caused by *perceived* harassment). The board's conclusion does not justify Hughes' termination because it does not include the necessary language that the complainant's perception was reasonable. The reasonableness of the perception does not follow from the unchallenged findings as a matter of law; and because of our uncertainty as to which allegations the board believed, we are reluctant to presume that the board concluded that the complainant's perception of harassment was reasonable.[9]

The city of Albuquerque also argued that Hughes's termination should be sustained because Hughes failed to comply with prior instructions to refrain from engaging in behavior which could be *interpreted* as sexual harassment. The New Mexico Court of Appeals rejected the city's position, stating in part:

The propriety of such a ruling would depend, however, upon whether the board found that Hughes had been given simply a general warning to refrain from behavior that could be construed as sexual harassment or whether he was warned against engaging in certain specified conduct that could be so construed. Failure to comply with a specific directive might be proper grounds for discipline, even termination. On the other hand, a general directive not to engage in conduct that could be construed as sexual harassment might not provide adequate notice to refrain from particular conduct. *Cf. Chavez v. Employment Sec. Comm'n*, 98 N.M. 462, 649 P. 2d 1375 (1982) (for purposes of Unemployment Compensation Law, discharge was not for misconduct because alleged misconduct was not preceded by adequate warnings). To illustrate this point, we consider the possibilities in the case before us. Shortly before the incident involving complainant, Hughes had been accused of similar conduct. To avoid the future occurrence or appearance of sexual harassment, the City might have instructed Hughes not to engage in certain particular conduct that could be perceived as sexual harassment, such as inviting a female subordinate into his home during working hours or taking a female subordinate on a business trip when her presence serves no evident business purpose. The board might then have sustained Hughes' termination if it found that Hughes had violated such a directive and that the directive was reasonable. If, however, the board found that he was simply told in general terms to refrain from any conduct that might be construed as sexual harassment, the board could not sustain Hughes' termination unless it also found that he engaged in conduct that was reasonably construed as sexual harassment. Hence, we cannot affirm the board on the ground that Hughes violated a directive because on this record we cannot tell whether the board found that Hughes violated only a general directive or violated a specific directive prohibiting particular conduct.[10]

The New Mexico Court of Appeals reversed and remanded the case to the district court with instructions to remand the case to the city personnel board for entry of more specific findings and conclusions. It appears tha the language used in Title VII may not be sufficiently clear to constitute a specific warning of prohibited conduct. While Title VII may be void for vagueness, employers' personnel policies should not suffer from the same deficiency. *Sexual harassment* might be a term to avoid in identifying the types of conduct prohibited by a personnel policy, were it not for the EEOC's regulations.

Employers struggle to understand what is prohibited as sexual harassment by Title VII, often without success. Employers should try not to put their employees in the same frustrating situation. Employees are more likely to know what is expected of them when an employer says "Requests for sexual favors from any other employee will not be tolerated in this firm" than when an employer says "Sexual harassment will not be tolerated in this firm."

Training Programs

Training programs should address behavior which has been labeled a social problem. The problem behavior targets both men and women, and both men and women perpetrators exist. Additionally, not all unwelcome behavior of a sexual nature is heterosexual in nature. Stereotyping this social problem in training presentations as a problem of men harassing women may be counterproductive.[11] Training programs should include examples of both men and women perpetrators and victims.

The fear of AIDS, the Disabilities Act of 1990's prohibitions relating to the termination of persons with AIDS, and homophobia may need to be addressed in workplaces where those issues could affect whether behavior is perceived as less welcome, more offensive, or more sexual in nature.

Training programs should begin from the baseline that men and women perceive the world differently. The goal of the trainer is to assist diverse people to understand each other and work together productively and efficiently. The means of reaching this goal is training people about the options available to them for taking responsibility for their own work environment and safety. An effective program must be designed to teach people how to interact with each other in a manner which does not violate any laws in spite of their personal views of the world (i.e., how to be more assertive about expressing their opinions and how to accept differing views and criticism).

If the goal is stopping the behavior in the fastest and most cost-effective manner, programs should include a component designed to teach employees about the options and methods available to them to respond informally and immediately to conduct they find offensive. The training program should stress that the firm supports informal resolution for most forms of sexual harassment, as evidenced by the waiver of the mandatory reporting requirement for victims who affirmatively tell the offender the conduct is unwelcome at the time of the incident.

Many victims do nothing when they are sexually harassed. Avoiding the harasser or ignoring the behavior are common responses (Tangri et al. 1982). Livingston (1982) found that victims were more likely to respond assertively when the harassment was serious or created emotional distress. Sexual harassment can affect victims' emotional or physical condition, decrease their ability to work with others, and decrease their satisfaction with their work even though no formal action is taken against the harasser by the victim (Tangri et al. 1982). Victims need to learn to be more assertive about their views.

As a general tort law principle, all citizens have a duty to take reasonable measures to protect themselves. The *comparative negligence* doctrine requires that damages be awarded consistent with each party's fault for the conduct resulting in injury. The Merit Systems Protection Board found that informal responses to sexual harassment are often much more effective than other responses:

> When victims of sexual harassment did take positive action in response to unwanted sexual attention, it was largely informal action and, in many cases, was judged to be effective. The most effective and frequently taken informal action was simply telling the harasser to stop. Forty-four percent of the female victims and 25 percent of the male victims said they took this action and, in over 60 percent of the cases, both groups said it "made things better" [USMSPB 1988: 3].

The 1980 USMSPB survey found that asking the person engaging in the offensive conduct to cease the conduct often made things better for victims of "severe" harassment—letters, phone calls, display of materials of a sexual nature, pressure for sexual favors, and deliberate touching (*see* Table 13.1). Victims of these types of conduct may be well advised to tell the person engaging in the offensive conduct the conduct is unwelcome and offensive and request that it be stopped.

The 1980 USMSPB study found that telling the offender to stop or

Table 13.1. Percentage of Narrators Who Indicated
That Taking These Informal Actions "Made Things Better"

ACTION	SEVERE	
	WOMEN	MEN
Transferred, disciplined or gave a poor performance rating to the person	79%	87%
Asked or told the person(s) to stop	53%	69%
Reported the behavior to the supervisor or other officials	54%	46%
Avoided the person(s)	42%	51%
Made a joke of the behavior	32%	45%
Threatened to tell or told other workers	35%	29%
Ignored the behavior or did nothing	24%	41%
Went along with the behavior	3%	32%

Source: USMSPB 1981: 68.

reporting the behavior to officials often made things better for victims of the "most severe" harassment, actual or attempted rape or assault (*see* Table 13.2).

Although telling such a person to stop appears to make things better in many cases, many victims do not timely identify the conduct which offends them. And victims of sexual harassment have no legal obligation to confront a harasser informally before filing a sexual harassment charge with the EEOC, even though that may be the most effective response.

Training programs should be designed to teach employees prompt informal responses informing others what they find offensive. Management's support for those who engage in informal responses should be overwhelming. Employees should get the message that they are expected to join in the fight to end sexual harassment and that they must be part of the solution. Employer support for the mandatory reporting requirements where informal resolutions are not tried or not effective should be stressed. Employees should be told of the employer's commitment to ending prohibited conduct and that this can be accomplished only if it is aware of the conduct.

**Table 13.2. Percentage of Narrators Who Indicated
That Taking These Informal Actions "Made Things Better"**

ACTION	MOST SEVERE	
	WOMEN	MEN
Transferred, disciplined or gave a poor performance rating to the person	72%	9%
Asked or told the person(s) to stop	40%	13%
Reported the behavior to the supervisor or other officials	57%	11%
Avoided the person(s)	20%	32%
Made a joke of the behavior	52%	7%
Threatened to tell or told other workers	30%	19%
Ignored the behavior or did nothing	12%	27%
Went along with the behavior	14%	46%

Source: USMSPB 1981: 68.

Employee training programs should address sex roles. A is a woman who brings a cake to work for her boss's birthday because she thinks that is expected of her since she is the only female employee in the office. While the cake may be appreciated the first year, the only expectations may be A's. After five years of bringing the cake, A may not feel like bringing in the cake anymore but believes the cake is expected. By now, the boss may expect a cake. But that expectation can be based on the history of bringing cakes rather than on the sex of the baker. And what about the legal secretary who on her own began making coffee every morning until she grew tired of this task, confronted the boss about being required to do this "women's work," and took a deep breath when the boss responded, "I've been meaning to get that coffeepot out of here ever since I quit drinking that stuff last year"?

Women may be more concerned than men about the cleanliness of their work environment. Josephine Townsend (1992: 53) made the following comments about the differences between male and female police officers:

> Women officers are more concerned with their environment than their male counterparts. It's more important to a woman that the patrol car she is driving looks good and that the squad room doesn't look like a cyclone struck it. Appearance might be important to male officers as well, but usually not to such great detail. Many supervisors have experienced female officers complaining that the guys don't pick up after themselves at the station or their car.

After noting men's propensity to replace items when they are needed and women's propensity to replace things before they need them, Townsend (1992: 53) noted:

> Certainly it is important to replace supplies as they are needed — but who needs reminding of this, and why, is just as important. Women tend to be judgmental in this regard, assuming that her male counterparts are taking advantage of her. The fact is, women are raised as caretakers and many times assume the role. There is nothing wrong with that, but what may be wrong is that she also assumes that this caretaker role is what is expected of her.
>
> Most men wouldn't care if they replaced the stock or not. The fact that the female officer did so was nice, but, "it would have been replaced eventually."

A training program should try to address realistic differences between the sexes in the work environment and distinguish this sex-role spillover from affirmative harassment because of sex. While men and women may have different views about baking cakes, cleaning, or replacing supplies, these events need to be placed in perspective in an effort to prevent each difference in perspective from being perceived as sexual harassment.

Employer-sponsored programs should focus on the personal liability of employees rather than the liability of employers under Title VII. Specific types of conduct should be discussed (kissing, touching, requests for a date, etc.) and broad terms like *sexual harassment* avoided. Coworkers cannot be held liable under Title VII, although they are most often the harassers.

Thus, training programs directed at nonsupervisory employees which focus on Title VII's prohibition may have little if any deterrent effect. It seems that a better approach to training nonsupervisory employees for deterring sexual harassment would be to focus on the employee's personal liability in job security and civil liability under state tort law. Such a training program could include discussions of assault and battery, intentional infliction of emotional distress, invasion of privacy, loss of "consortium," tortious interference with contract, and negligent hiring and retention. A training program should be designed to teach employees about prohibited types of behavior rather than whether or not a specific type of behavior constitutes sexual harassment.

Training programs should also teach employees how to respond to informal charges that their behavior has been offensive. Christopher Hunter and Kent McClelland's (1991) study of student-to-student harassment at a small liberal arts college in the Midwest found (747–48):

> Man's verbal account for his behavior influences perceived seriousness almost as much as does the man's original behavior.
>
> . . . .
>
> Apologies and some excuses (those that focus attention on one's temporary failure to follow culturally appropriate norms) reduce the perceived seriousness.

Training programs should make efforts to teach harassers how to respond effectively to victims. The extent to which a harasser uses an excuse, justification, or apology when confronted by a victim influences the perceived seriousness of the conduct.

Conclusion

Training programs should encourage, if not require, employees to use established procedures to report specific types of conduct. Fear of retaliation for reporting should be discussed, and an incentive program for reports found valid should be considered. A training program should encourage employees to attempt informal resolution of unwanted or unwelcome sexual conduct, dispel the myths surrounding such a response, and train employees how to respond more effectively to sexual harassment on an informal basis.

Some conduct, such as requests for dates, becomes the basis for a valid hostile environment harassment charge only if the conduct persists for a period of time (i.e., it is sufficiently pervasive). It is unclear whether a contractual provision that an employee informally confront a harasser in specific circumstances within a specified period may form the basis of the dismissal of an employee who failed to do so.[12] It is clear that Title VII prohibits retaliation against an employee for filing an EEOC charge.

Chapter 14
Duty to Investigate

Judge Edith Jones has noted:

> We have so little social consensus in sexual mores nowadays that, short of incidents involving physical contact, it is impossible generally to categorize unacceptable sexual etiquette. It is likewise impossible to eradicate sexual conduct from the workplace — without unthinkable intrusiveness.[1]

The extent to which employers may intrude on the privacy of their employees for the purpose of avoiding civil liability under Title VII is unclear. An employer has a duty to conduct an investigation once allegations of sexual harassment are made known to or should have been known by the employer. Both the promptness and adequacy of the employer's response are subject to allegations of inadequacy (Lindemann and Kadue 1992).

Knowledge of Harassment Triggering Duty to Investigate

An employer is charged with knowing about sexual advances in the workplace. For example, in *Baker v. Weyerhaeuser Co.,*[2] a 25-year-old single mother brought a sexual harassment suit against her employer for failing to take action against a coworker who was sexually harassing female employees. The employee alleged that she was subjected to "repeated offensive sexual flirtations, advances, propositions, continued and repeated verbal commentaries and sexually suggestive conduct by an employee ... known to [the employer] and its agents and supervisors to be a sexual harasser."[3]

The district court held that the conduct of the coworker had been pervasive and continual for months and was so severe and continuous as to create a hostile and abusive work environment. The district court also found that the plaintiff had complained about the coworker's conduct to other coworkers and to supervisors, that the employer either knew or should have known of the sexual harassment, and that the employer was liable for sexual harassment under Title VII. The court of appeals affirmed the decision of the district court.

As a practical matter, short of developing a "snitch" system like those used in some prisons, periodic surveys asking whether employees have been subjected to sexual harassment may provide the best evidence of continuing efforts of an employer to identify and address incidents of sexual harassment. Surveys of the work force can also be used to evaluate the effectiveness of training programs designed to combat sexual harassment and to monitor the views of the work force relating to these complex issues.

In most cases, employers do not know about the alleged harassment until, or unless, the allegations are explicitly brought to the attention of the employer. Far fewer employees report sexual harassment to management through established grievance procedures than report being subjected to sexual harassment (USMSPB 1981; USMSPB 1988). Livingston (1982) found victims were more likely to take formal action when harassed by a supervisor than when harassed by a coworker. Social science research suggests that few targets of sexual harassment file formal lawsuits or complaints with the EEOC (Terpstra 1986; Maypole 1986; Terpstra and Baker 1989; Gruber 1989). This is not surprising, however, when the fact that much of what has been labeled "sexual harassment" in social science research does not state a cause of action under Title VII. Many allegations of sexual harassment however, are first brought to the attention of an employer when a formal charge is filed with the EEOC.

Once an employer knows, or should have known, of sexual harassment in the workplace, the employer has an obligation to investigate the incident. It has often been argued that an employer may enhance the likelihood of being aware of allegations of sexual harassment by enacting a policy prohibiting the conduct, disseminating the policy, and investigating all allegations of sexual harassment made under the policy. The "should have known" requirement imposes a duty to conduct an investigation into whether sexual harassment is occurring in the workplace. This general duty may best be met by conducting periodic random surveys of employees.

Duty to Conduct Investigation

When an employer learns of allegations of sexual harassment, an employer has an obligation to conduct a prompt and thorough investigation. Title VII does not appear to require a confidential procedure.[4] However, the procedures established by an employer should be followed.[5]

It may be impossible to consider fully allegations of sexual harassment without disclosing the identity of the victim to the alleged harasser because the harasser must be able to place the conduct in context to provide a meaningful explanation of the totality of the circumstances.

Choosing an Investigator

The complainant and alleged harasser should be interviewed as soon as possible after the employer is made aware of the problem. Care should be given in choosing an investigator. Hope Comisky (1992: 199) argued: "The investigation should be conducted by someone outside the concerned department, such as a personnel manager, or even outside the company, such as an outside counsel." Attorneys may be able to assert an attorney-client or "work-product" privilege for information prepared during the course of an investigation (Lindemann and Kadue 1992). If the employer is committed to combating sexual harassment and the investigation is properly conducted, however, the investigative report should be the first document provided to the EEOC or a court to justify the employer's action or inaction resulting from the investigation. Result-oriented investigations are no longer an appropriate course of action under existing laws.

Creating a Written Record

Hope Comisky (1992: 199) argues that "both the alleged harasser and his victims should be interviewed and written statements obtained." Barbara Lindemann and David Kadue (1992: 433–34) have cautioned:

> Creating a complete and accurate record can evidence that the employer took prompt and appropriate action. Creating a record that is incomplete or inaccurate, however, may undermine the adequacy of the investigation and taint the employer's response to the sexual harassment claim. . . .
> Where an employer finds that sexual harassment has occurred and takes responsive disciplinary action, the employer should record the investigation and witness statements to guard against the possibility that the alleged harasser will challenge the action taken. Similarly, if an employer finds insufficient evidence of harassment and thus has no grounds for discipline, the employer's defense to any sexual harassment suit will require full access to the statements of all witnesses to show that its decision was well-founded [footnote omitted].

If the investigation is accurate, thorough, valid, and appropriately responded to, it should be written. Other types of investigations should not be reduced to writing.

Interviewing Parties and Witnesses

Barbara Lindemann and David Kadue (1992: 431) suggest that the following questions should be answered during the first interview with a complainant: (1) when and where the incident occurred; (2) what precisely was said and done by both parties; (3) whether there were any witnesses; (4) the effects of the incident; (5) whether there are any documents containing information about the alleged incident; and (6) whether the complainant has knowledge of any other target of harassment. The complainant should be assured that he or she will not be retaliated against for cooperating in the investigation and that disclosure of the complainant's identity will be limited to the alleged harasser and those with a legitimate reason to know (Lindemann and Kadue 1992: 431–32). Any reluctance or refusal by the complainant to cooperate should be noted because "it bears on the reasonableness and scope of the employer's response" (Lindemann and Kadue 1992: 432).

Lindemann and Kadue (1992: 432) had the following comments to make about interviewing the alleged harasser after he or she has been apprised of the nature of the allegations and has been informed that the same provisions regarding confidentiality applicable to the complainant will apply to him or her:

> Ideally, the interview of the alleged harasser will disclose the time, place and circumstances of each incident as well as information on relevant witnesses and documents. If the alleged harasser believes that the complainant has a motive to lie, the facts supporting that belief should be explored. If the alleged harasser denies that the acts claimed to be harassment were "unwelcome," all facts supporting that denial should be obtained.

"Although the complainant must prove that a sexual advance was unwelcome, as a practical matter the employer may need to produce evidence that the advances were in fact welcome" (Lindemann and Kadue 1992: 140). The extent to which the unwelcomeness of conduct will be viewed by an objective or subjective standard varies among jurisdictions (Lindemann and Kadue 1992).

If the alleged harasser asserts that the conduct was welcome, the investigator may want to reinterview the complainant to inquire into actions taken by the claimant to show the conduct was unwelcome. The claimant's alleged response to the behavior in question is often used to indicate whether the conduct was unwelcome. Lindemann and Kadue have identified a scale of possible responses to unwelcome sexual advances in quid pro quo cases: "(1) outright rejection, (2) initial rejection and later acceptance, (3) initial acceptance followed by later rejection, (4) ambiguous conduct, (5) coerced submission, and (6) welcome acceptance" (Lindemann and Kadue 1992: 135).

All witnesses identified by the claimant and alleged harasser should be interviewed, and all documents identified by either party should be reviewed, copied, and made exhibits to the investigative report. Once all parties and witnesses have been interviewed and all applicable documents reviewed, the interviewer should confront the claimant with the evidence and ask for additional input or rebuttal. The harasser should then be confronted with the evidence and the claimant's input and given an opportunity to comment upon or rebut the evidence. The investigator must then weigh the motives and biases of the parties, witnesses, and evidence and draw factual conclusions about what happened. These factual conclusions then need to be analyzed under applicable law in the applicable jurisdiction.

Investigations of allegations of sexual harassment often turn to one of two issues: (1) whether the conduct was welcome; (2) whether the conduct occurred at all. Each of these investigations has the potential of being limited by other forms of potential civil liability. Investigations into whether sexual conduct is welcome may be impossible without inquiring into those areas of an employee's life that have traditionally been considered personal and beyond the scope of an employer's legitimate business concerns. Today, the extent to which an employer knows who is intimate with whom in the workplace may have an effect on an employer's ability to make effective risk-management decisions.

The extent to which such surveillance of employees should be allowed, much less required, is clearly debatable. The fear of civil liability for invasion of privacy or the moral respect for the privacy of employees may deter an employer from compiling much of the information about the sexual conduct and personal lives of employees than is required successfully to defend a lawsuit alleging hostile environment harassment. This is especially true in cases where the alleged harasser and victim socialized for a long time and came to know many facts about the other's personal life. In these types of investigations, an employee's right to privacy may be in direct conflict with an employer's obligation to determine whether conduct of a sexual nature should be perceived as welcome or unwelcome in light of what the parties knew about each other.

Employee Privacy Rights

Employees have a privacy interest in avoiding disclosure of personal information. An employee's sexual conduct is within the zone of conduct generally protected by an employee's right to privacy. Thus, an employer's investigation into allegations of sexual harassment may violate an employee's privacy rights if information relating to an employee's sexual conduct is necessary for a prompt and fair inquiry into allegations of sexual harassment. Privacy rights appear to be most implicated in cases which turn on whether the conduct was welcome or unwelcome under the circumstances.

In *Meritor Sav. Bank, FSB v. Vinson,*[6] the Supreme Court said, "The gravamen of any sexual harassment claim is that the alleged sexual advances were 'unwelcome.'"[7] The court distinguished between "involuntary" and "unwelcome":

> The fact that sex-related conduct was "voluntary," in the sense that the complainant was not forced to participate against her will, is not a defense to a sexual harassment suit brought under Title VII. . . . The correct inquiry is whether respondent by her conduct indicated that the alleged sexual advances were unwelcome, not whether her actual participation in sexual intercourse was voluntary.[8]

Conduct such as flirting and kissing may defeat a claim that sexual advances were "unwelcome."[9] A plaintiff's sexually provocative speech or dress can be relevant in determining whether he or she found particular sexual advances unwelcome.[10] The relevance of such evidence, however, may be outweighed by its potential for unfair prejudice in some cases.[11]

In some cases, an employer may not be permitted to conduct a prompt and fair investigation into whether sexual conduct is unwelcome without running the risk of being sued for invading an employee's privacy rights until a lawsuit is filed and a court orders the plaintiff to disclose needed information. On the other hand, fear of inquiry by an employer into the sexual conduct of a plaintiff is one aspect of discovery which can deter employees from pursuing valid sexual harassment claims. Some courts have refused to allow discovery of information relating to an employee's past sexual history.[12] To the extent that requested discovery relates to a plaintiff's off-duty intimate or sexual conduct, victims may resist discovery on the ground that court-ordered discovery of this information violates the victim's constitutional rights to privacy and association.[13]

In *Mitchell v. Hutchings,*[14] the plaintiffs filed a Title VII claim alleging they had been sexually harassed by the defendants. The defendants gave notice to three people who were alleged to have had personal relationships with the plaintiffs and another person alleged to have taken sexually suggestive pictures of one or more of the plaintiffs. The defendants also gave notice of their intent to take the deposition of a police officer alleged to have been held down while one of the plaintiffs fondled him. The plaintiffs moved for a protective order limiting the scope of examination in the depositions.

The defendants argued that the information sought in the depositions was relevant, in part because "sexually promiscuous plaintiffs would not be as distressed by unwanted sexual advances as would plaintiffs who are less sexually active" and "the sexual atmosphere at plaintiffs' workplace has a bearing on [defendants'] possible defense that he considered his conduct to be welcomed by the plaintiffs."

The court rejected the defendants' argument:

> In the instant case, evidence relating to the work environment where the alleged sexual harassment took place is obviously relevant, if such conduct was known to defendant. . . . This evidence can establish the context of the relationship between plaintiffs and [defendant] and may have a bearing on what conduct [defendant] thought was welcome. At the same time, evidence of sexual conduct which is remote in time or place to plaintiffs' working environment is irrelevant. [Defendant] cannot possibly use evidence of sexual activity of which he was unaware or which is unrelated to the alleged incidents of sexual harassment as evidence to support his defense. Given the annoying and embarrassing nature of this discovery, the court holds, as a matter of law, that Rule 26 of the Federal Rules of Civil Procedure preponderates against its discoverability.[15]

The *Mitchell* court limited discovery to sexual behavior in the workplace environment.

In *Weiss v. Amoco Oil Co.,*[16] an employee brought a wrongful termination case after being terminated for allegedly harassing two female employees, Jude Gustafson and Angel Streebin. Streebin sought a protective order prohibiting inquiry into her sexual history. The court noted the following facts:

> Streebin alleged that Weiss called her at home in May, 1990. Streebin and Weiss dated and saw each other socially.
> Streebin had cards pinned up at her work station which were of a sexual nature, and sent a male employee, Daryl Mosley, a birthday card which showed the torso of an adult female clad in a bikini swim suit. Streebin made jokes of a sexual nature with other employees, and discussed her sexual activities while at work.[17]

The court held the past sexual conduct of Streebin with other employees known to Weiss relevant to whether his conduct was offensive or unwelcome and to assessing the thoroughness of the employer's investigation into allegations of sexual harassment by Streebin.

Polygraphs

Sexual harassment often occurs in the absence of witnesses. In some cases, employers are confronted with making a decision regarding an allegation of sexual harassment based on conflicting views on whether the conduct complained of occurred (as opposed to whether conduct constituted sexual harassment). Employers can do little to obtain objective evidence to guide an otherwise totally subjective decision about whom to believe in many cases. The use of one imperfect tool once available in efforts to make more objective decisions, the polygraph, has been severely restricted by federal law. At the same time, the courts have held that subjective employment decisions are inherently suspect in employment discrimination cases.

The extent to which polygraph examinations can accurately reflect truth or deception is open to much debate, while both field studies and laboratory studies report that the results of polygraph examinations are sometimes incorrect (Tiner and O'Grady 1988). Tiner and O'Grady (1988: 100–102) asserted that research supports the following conclusions:

> The risks which the inaccuracy of the polygraph pose to innocent workers are exacerbated by the bias of the polygraphers who work for private employers.
>   . . . .
> Due to the inaccuracy of the polygraph itself and the potential bias of polygraphers, innocent people are more likely to be misjudged than are the guilty. In 1979, Waid and his associates conducted a study which showed that highly socialized people, i.e. people who have highly developed moral standards and consciences, tend to fail polygraph examinations even though they tell the truth. Conversely, poorly socialized people are more likely to "pass" a polygraph examination whether they tell the truth or not. [Footnotes omitted.]

Tiner and O'Grady (1988: 86, fn. 2) described the standard polygraph examination as follows:

> The standard polygraph has three components: a blood pressure cuff, a galvanic skin response indicator, and a pneumatic chest tube. The blood pressure cuff is attached to a person's upper arm to record changes in blood pressure. The galvanic skin response indicator measures changes in the skin's electrical conductivity, which increases when a person perspires. It consists of two electrodes which are attached to the index and second fingers of one hand. The pneumatic chest tube is strapped around the chest to measure changes in breathing pattern.

Changes in blood pressure, breathing pattern, and skin moisture are recorded during a polygraph examination (Weimer 1987). The chart generated during a polygraph examination is then interpreted by a polygraph examiner. Because the polygraph examiner must interpret the results of the examination to determine the subject's truthfulness, the bias or prejudice of the polygrapher can affect the results (Tiner and O'Grady 1988; Taylor 1984).

The Employee Polygraph Protection Act of 1988 greatly limited a private-sector employer's use of polygraph examinations as a tool in resolving sexual harassment complaints; 22 U.S.C. 2002 states:

> Except as provided in sections 2006 and 2007 of this title, it shall be unlawful for any employer engaged in or affecting commerce or in the production of goods for commerce —
>
> (1) directly or indirectly, to require, request, suggest, or cause any employee or prospective employee to take or submit to any lie detector test;
>
> (2) to use, accept refer to, or inquire concerning the results of any lie detector test of any employee or prospective employee;
>
> (3) to discharge, discipline, discriminate against in any manner, or deny employment or promotion to, or threaten to take any such action against —
>
> (A) any employee or prospective employee who refuses, declines, or fails to take or submit to any lie detector test, or
>
> (B) any employee or prospective employee on the basis of the results of any lie detector test; or
>
> (4) to discharge, discipline, discriminate against in any manner, or deny employment or promotion to, or threaten to take any such action against, any employee or prospective employee because —
>
> (A) such employee or prospective employee has filed any complaint or instituted or caused to be instituted any proceeding under or related to this chapter,
>
> (B) such employee or prospective employee has testified or is about to testify in any such proceeding, or
>
> (C) of the exercise by such employee or prospective employee, on behalf of such employee or another person, of any right afforded by this chapter.

The Polygraph Protection Act of 1988 does not generally prohibit polygraphs from being given to federal, state, or local government employees, contractors with the Federal Bureau of Investigation, employees of security services, and employees involved in the manufacture of drugs.[18] The Employee Polygraph Protection Act of 1988 does allow employers to conduct polygraphs in very limited circumstances as a tool in investigations.[19] The act does prohibit an employer from inquiring into an employee's "political beliefs or affiliations" or "any matter relating to sexual behavior" in a polygraph conducted during an investigation.[20]

Actions asserting a violation of the Polygraph Act of 1988 can be brought in either state or federal court within three years after the violation.[21] An employer who violates the provisions of the Polygraph Act of 1988 may be liable to the employee or prospective employee affected by such violation "for such legal or equitable relief as may be appropriate, including, but not limited to, employment, reinstatement, promotion, and the payment of lost wages and benefits.... The court, in its discretion, may allow the prevailing party (other than the United States) reasonable costs, including attorney's fees."[22]

In *New Mexico v. City of Albuquerque,*[23] a female employee filed a formal written complaint with the city of Albuquerque accusing Cleo F. Hughes of sexual harassment. Hughes was placed on administrative leave while the allegations were investigated. Hughes was given notice of the allegations against him, represented by counsel during the investigation, and allowed to testify personally and identify favorable witnesses. The investigators found evidence to support the allegations against Hughes, and he was given notice of a pretermination hearing. At the hearing, Hughes was allowed to defend against the allegations. After the hearing, Hughes was terminated.

Hughes appealed his termination to the city personnel board, which upheld the termination after another hearing. The district court reaffirmed the decision of the city personnel board, and Hughes appealed the decision to the New Mexico Court of Appeals.

In rejecting Hughes's argument regarding the admission of polygraph evidence against him, the New Mexico Court of Appeals wrote:

> At the hearing before the personnel board, Hughes contended that one basis for his termination was a polygraph examination taken by the complainant. To show that the examination should not have been used by the City in deciding to terminate him, he sought to introduce evidence that the results of the examination were misinterpreted and did not support the reliability of the accusations against him. The board refused to hear the evidence because the City had not offered the polygraph examination results in the board hearing. We find no error in this evidentiary ruling.
>
> The polygraph examination results were not a separate *ground* for the termination of Hughes. The ground for his termination was the conduct about which the complainant testified. Both the city administrators and the board needed to determine whether the complainant was telling the truth. But the basis upon which the administrators determined her veracity was not material to the board. The polygraph examination in this case served the same role as a witness testifying to the complainant's character for veracity. Even if the City considered the statement of such a character witness in deciding whether to terminate an employee, the City would not therefore have to establish the reliability of the character witness at the board hearing if the character witness was not offered as a witness at the hearing. The reliability of the polygraph examination was not material to the board hearing, and the board properly refused to hear evidence on the matter.[24]

The use of polygraph evidence alone is generally insufficient to justify an adverse employment action.[25]

While an employer may be prohibited from conducting polygraph examinations during its in-house investigation, an employee may voluntarily take a polygraph examination and seek its admission into evidence at a civil trial regarding sexual harassment. The extent to which this type of evidence is admissible in a civil trial varies from state to state.

Conclusion

It is important to remember that an employer has only so many resources to spread around and that in-house investigations can reasonably be understood only in light of an employer's resources. Investigations into employment disputes are often very expensive. In today's legal environment, more time is spent by attorneys preparing responses to discovery requests made by former employees.[26] The discovery may take the form of giving oral testimony before a court reporter (depositions) or providing written answers to questions (written interrogatories). Personnel managers who are not required to give testimony in an employment discrimination case may nevertheless be affected by such a suit by the requirement that hours be spent searching and identifying records and, sometimes, compiling statistics. However, employers often have more resources than employees who have been sexually harassed. The employer may also have staff attorneys and possession of many of the documents the employee needs to prosecute his or her case.

It should not be surprising that one of the common objections to discovery requests in employment discrimination cases is "burdensomeness." An employer's objections to discovery requests should be rejected where the employer fails to provide sufficient information to ascertain the precise burden it claims undue or oppressive.

Even where a court decides in favor of an employer's burdensomeness objections on their merits, discovery can be ordered. "In making a decision regarding burdensomeness, a court should balance the burden on the interrogated party against the benefit to the discovering party of having the information."[27] "The production of discovery materials in litigation is often a costly and burdensome enterprise. It can involve many hours of labor unrelated to any other business purpose. The resistance to discovery for those reasons will not be sustained, however, unless the discovery sought is found to be unreasonably burdensome."[28] Where an employer has not shown that it will suffer any burden not normally associated with like litigation, the objections to a former employee's discovery requests based on burdensomeness are generally rejected. Some courts have held that an interrogatory calling for research is not objectionable if the interrogated party would gather the information in the preparation of its case.[29] Real burdens can be imposed upon employers without their being defined as "unduly burdensome."

Courts generally decide cases on their merits after extensive and expensive discovery proceedings. Cases decided on their merits at trial are decided with the opportunity to hear examination of witnesses. The cost of conducting an investigation in litigation prohibits such an extensive investigation of allegations of sexual harassment every time an allegation of harassment is made in the workplace. Employers must generally make personnel decisions based on much less evidence than is presented at a trial. With the benefit of thousands of dollars in pretrial investigation and research spent on each side of a lawsuit, the court second-guesses the employer who cannot afford to conduct such a thorough investigation as a matter of course because of prohibitive costs. The court may determine that an employer knew or should have known of sexual harassment or that prompt remedial action was inappropriate based on facts unknown to the employer when making a personnel decision.

Chapter 15

Prompt Remedial Action

Although Title VII imposes an obligation on employers to take prompt remedial action, whether it is in an employer's economic best interest to terminate an employee the employer subjectively believes has engaged in sexual harassment is far from clear in many cases. Taking disciplinary action against an employee based solely on an employer's belief that an employee has engaged in sexual harassment may subject an employer to liability under an employment contract requiring "good cause" for disciplinary action.[1] An employer's liability for violating the free-speech rights of its employees when taking prompt remedial action under Title VII is likewise unclear.

Duty to Take Prompt Remedial Action

The Ninth Circuit Court of Appeals has concluded that an employer's obligation to take "appropriate corrective action" requires that some form of disciplinary action be taken against an employee found to have engaged in sexual harassment.[2] The disciplinary action must be reasonably calculated to end the harassment. While minor forms of discipline such as an oral warning and counseling may be a sufficient initial response to less severe forms of sexual harassment, more severe disciplinary action is required if initial efforts are ineffective.

In *Intlekofer v. Turnage,*[3] the female plaintiff alleged the VA was liable for a male coworker's harassment of her because the VA had actual knowledge of the harassment yet failed to take immediate and appropriate action to remedy the harassment. The district court held the conduct sexual harassment but held that the VA was not liable because it "acted promptly and reasonably in responding to plaintiff's Reports of Contact."[4] The district court found that after a consensual relationship had existed between the coworkers, the plaintiff began making complaints of sexual harassment.

The first Report of Contact, alleging harassment in the form of "touching, highly personal and private suggestions and constant pressure to enter into a totally unwanted relationship,"[5] in April 1987 first placed the VA on notice of the problem. The plaintiff's supervisor met with the plaintiff, but the plaintiff declined to provide a more detailed description of the objectionable behavior. The supervisor informed the alleged harasser that the conduct alleged by the plaintiff "was inappropriate and must stop immediately" and that "if there should be additional complaints in the future, a more severe disciplinary measure would be required."[6]

In a second Report of Contact, the plaintiff alleged that the harasser telephoned her at her home. About five months later, a third report was filed, alleging that the coworker yelled at the plaintiff in the presence of staff and patients. Although VA management told the harasser to cease the inappropriate conduct, he failed to do so. A fourth Report of Contact was filed, alleging that the harasser was monitoring the victim's telephone calls and arguing with her. In a fifth report, it was alleged that the harasser chased the victim out of the hospital and threatened her, causing her to fear for her life. A warning was issued to the alleged harasser. A sixth Report of Contact alleged that a superior had accused her of leading the harasser on. Seventh, eighth, ninth, and tenth reports were filed.

The plaintiff then filed a complaint with the EEOC. The harasser was warned to change his behavior, and an investigation was conducted. The *Intlekofer* court explained the investigation and the VA's subsequent remedial actions as follows:

> After two months of investigation, Donna Reese, the E.E.O.C. counselor for the VA, issued a report concluding that Cortez was sexually harassing Intlekofer. The report made four proposals for remedying the harassment: (1) Cortez should receive professional counseling; (2) Cortez and Intlekofer should not work the same shifts; (3) Cortez must stop discussing Intlekofer with other employees; and (4) Cortez and Intlekofer should limit their contact at work to VA business. Although the VA disagreed with the report and did not believe that Cortez's actions constituted sexual harassment, it adopted the last three courses of action. Specifically, the VA adjusted both Intlekofer and Cortez's shifts in order to reduce contact at work, and repeatedly warned both employees not to be in the Medical Center at any time other than during their respective shifts. The VA also forbade Cortez from speaking with other employees about Intlekofer, and told both employees to limit their contact at work to business matters. It declined to adopt the first recommendation, citing its lack of authority to order Cortez to seek outside help in the form of professional psychological counseling.
>
> After the VA instituted the three measures, Intlekofer filed six Reports of Contact in the next six months. Only three Reports concerned incidents between Cortez and Intlekofer, and none alleged that Cortez continued to discuss Intlekofer with other employees. The February 15, 1988 Report stated that Cortez "throws keys at me, gives me looks that could

kill, and does not give any report as to what is happening at the hospital."
On June 1, 1988, Intlekofer filed a Report stating that Cortez made an
obscene gesture at her in the employee parking lot. Finally, one of the
three Reports filed July 7, 1988 claimed that a co-worker saw Cortez draw
an obscene picture on Intlekofer's locker.

While the VA investigated Intlekofer's complaints and held continuous
counseling sessions with Cortez in which he received both oral warnings
to refrain from talking to or about Intlekofer, and threats that he would
be disciplined if he continued his behavior, the VA did not take more
severe disciplinary steps against Cortez, such as issue a formal warning
letter or impose probation or suspension. Moreover, it is unclear whether
the VA met with Cortez after each Report of Contact or sporadically.
Kehoe estimated that she had approximately ten meetings with Cortez in
response to Intlekofer's Reports of Contact, and that she spent a total of
two weeks working time attempting to solve the conflict. Although
Brown estimated that he spent approximately one hundred hours trying
to remedy the problem, he did not discipline Cortez in any manner other
than meeting with him and requesting that he stop the harassment and
that he stay away from Intlekofer.

Maryann Coffey, the Director of the VA Medical Center, met with Intlekofer at least four times starting in December of 1987. Each meeting
took approximately one to two hours. Coffey attempted to change Cortez's and Intlekofer's shifts in an effort to separate the two, but did not
meet with Cortez personally or discipline him in any other manner. Jacqueline Freeman, the Personnel Management Specialist, met with Kehoe
and Brown to discuss possible scheduling changes. She also looked for
other positions for both Intlekofer and Cortez, but could not find a
suitable position for either employee.

Brown, Coffey and Kehoe met several times after Reese submitted her
report in order to prepare a settlement agreement. Each of the three pro-
posed settlement agreements offered to continue implementing Reese's
recommendations in exchange for Intlekofer withdrawing her formal
complaint with the E.E.O.C. Intlekofer refused each proposal.[7]

The *Intlekofer* court held that the VA's efforts failed to constitute
prompt and appropriate remedial action designed to end the harassment:

> An oral rebuke may be very effective in stopping the unlawful conduct.
> At the first sign of sexual harassment, an oral warning in the context of
> a counseling session may be an appropriate disciplinary measure if the
> employer expresses strong disapproval, demands that the unwelcome
> conduct cease, and threatens more severe disciplinary action in the event
> that the conduct does not cease. I approve of this remedy in a case such
> as this where the harassing conduct is not extremely serious and the
> employer cannot elicit a detailed description concerning the occurrence
> from the victim. I stress, however, that counseling is sufficient only as a
> first resort. If the harassment continues, limiting discipline to further
> counseling is inappropriate. Instead, the employer must impose more
> severe measures in order to ensure that the behavior terminates. Again,

> the extent of the discipline depends on the seriousness of the conduct.[8]

The court held that the appropriateness of a remedy depends on (1) the seriousness of the offense, (2) the employer's ability to stop the harassment, (3) the likelihood that the remedy will end the harassment, and (4) the general deterrent effect of the remedy.[9]

To be meaningful, a remedy must address the roots of the problem. Men and women are born into a culture which includes a set of ideas and attitudes relating to sex (biological) and gender (psychological, social, and cultural) (Richardson 1988).

Sex stereotypes are learned from language, parents, schools, and the mass media long before people are responsible for supporting themselves or a family (Richardson 1988). Institutions such as religion, the law, and medical and mental health systems tend to reinforce cultural sex stereotypes (Richardson 1988). Research has consistently shown that sex discrimination results from the way citizens are socialized (Richardson 1988; Dowd 1989).

Title VII appears to require employers to terminate employees who continue to act in a manner consistent with this socialization process unless the employees are willing to change. While the fairness of imposing upon employers the obligation of changing the socialization process to the extent Title VII appears to require is debatable, fundamental fairness would seem to require that an employer be able to comply with Title VII's duty to take prompt and effective remedial action without being subjected to liability for doing so.

In *Ellison v. Brady,*[10] the Court of Appeals for the Ninth Circuit noted that "Title VII requires more than a mere request to refrain from discriminatory conduct.... Employers send the wrong message to potential harassers when they do not discipline employees for sexual harassment."[11] The *Ellison* court held that a "victim of sexual harassment should not be punished for the conduct of the harasser. We wholeheartedly agree with the EEOC that a victim of sexual harassment should not have to work in a less desirable location as a result of an employer's remedy for sexual harassment."[12] The court further stated:

> We believe that in some cases the mere presence of an employee who has engaged in particularly severe or pervasive harassment can create a hostile working environment.... To avoid liability under Title VII for failing to remedy a hostile environment, employers may even have to remove employees from the workplace if their mere presence would render the working environment hostile.
>
> ....
>
> If harassers are not removed from the workplace when their mere

presence creates a hostile environment, employers have not fully remedied the harassment. When employers cannot schedule harassers to work at another location or during different hours, employers may have to dismiss employees whose mere presence creates a hostile environment.[13]

The decision recognized that it is the harasser, rather than the victim of the harassment, whose position should be altered by the employer if such action is warranted.

In *T. L. v. Toys 'R' Us, Inc.,*[14] a 27-year-old plaintiff who had worked her way up from a file clerk to systems analyst for the purchasing department alleged that her supervisor began making remarks she found offensive and subsequently lifted the back of her shirt up over her shoulders and said, "Give them a show." The sexually offensive remarks continued, and the plaintiff witnessed her supervisor engage in offensive conduct with other employees.

The plaintiff did not report these incidents and explained she had not done so because she was afraid of her supervisor. The plaintiff eventually complained to the harasser's boss, who in part told the plaintiff to handle it herself. The plaintiff wrote a letter setting forth her harassment complaints. The plaintiff was interviewed by an employee relations manager, gave specific examples of incidents which offended her, and supplied the names of others who could substantiate the sexual harassment. The plaintiff was told that her supervisor had been spoken to.

The offensive remarks did not stop, and the plaintiff again complained. The plaintiff was being talked about and had been called paranoid by company officials. The plaintiff decided to resign and was offered a transfer within the company. The plaintiff was called into an office, and the alleged harasser was summoned. Being required to confront the harasser resulted in the plaintiff becoming hysterical.

The plaintiff designed and filed a lawsuit, in part under New Jersey's discrimination law prohibiting sexual harassment. The trial judge concluded that the plaintiff had not been discriminated against, and the plaintiff appealed. The appellate division reversed and remanded the case for further proceedings. The *T. L.* court adopted the "reasonable woman" standard articulated by the Ninth Circuit Court of Appeals in *Ellison v. Brady:*

> We are satisfied that, so long as plaintiff can demonstrate that defendant's offensive conduct was unwelcome, intentional, and sexually oriented to the extent that it would not have occurred but for the fact that plaintiff was a woman, it need not be shown that defendant intended to harass plaintiff. It may be that Baylous did not recognize that his conduct constituted sexual harassment or misconduct. We have no doubt that many actions that a reasonable woman would "find offensive are perceived by

> men to be harmless and innocent." *See Sexual Harassment Claims of Abusive Work Environment Under Title VII,* 97 Harv. L. Rev. 1449, 1451 [1984].[15]

It is now clear that some conduct men perceive as harmless and innocent can create civil liability in New Jersey. Jonathan Segal (1991: 72) has argued that "to accuse someone of sexual harassment when the person doesn't realize that the action was wrong is unlikely to bring about the desired behavioral changes." And can innocent conduct constitute good cause for disciplinary action?

Breach of Contract

Employers have been sued for discharging employees accused of sexual harassment under common-law claims alleging breach of public policy, breach of contract, and intentional infliction of emotional distress (Lindemann and Kadue 1992). For example, supervisors terminated by the Postal Service have challenged their termination resulting from allegations of sexual harassment.[16] Government employees have sued their employers for breaching their procedural due process rights in disciplinary proceedings resulting from allegations of sexual harassment (Lindemann and Kadue 1992).

Employers and employees have been sued for defamation on the basis of statements made during an investigation into allegations of harassment and for taking disciplinary action against those accused of sexual harassment (Lindemann and Kadue 1992). Persons opposing sexual harassment have been sued personally for "interference with contractual relations" where they participated in opposing sexual harassment and those efforts resulted in an employee's termination for sexual harassment (Lindemann and Kadue 1992).

For many years, state courts held that an employer could fire an employee for any reason not prohibited by law: the employment-at-will rule. This rule became an irrebuttable presumption. Employers could terminate for good cause or no cause without being subjected to civil liability (Parker 1987). One court explained the foundations of the employment-at-will rule as follows:

> That rule rests upon the concept of freedom of contract and mutuality of obligation; since an employer cannot force an employee into labor, neither should an employee have the power to force an employer to hire or retain him. This rule of mutuality apparently evolved in the nineteenth century during the industrial revolution when the employer-employee relationship became more impersonal. . . . Some authorities have sug-

gested that various social and economic factors such as the concepts of freedom of contract, free enterprise and *laissez-faire* provide the foundation for its wide acceptance.[17]

The employment-at-will rule prevailed in most American courts until the 1970s and 1980s when state courts began to create exceptions to the rule.

Many courts appear to apply a two-part test in determining whether an employee handbook constitutes an "implied" employment contract. Courts have looked at whether the handbook is definite enough for a reasonable employee to believe the provisions of the handbook control the employee-employer relationship and whether the intent of the parties can be ascertained in relation to the extent the handbook controls the employee-employer relationship.

Employee handbooks which constitute implied employment contracts often establish a binding procedure (for example, progressive discipline or a formal in-house review procedure) which must be exhausted before an employer may terminate an employee.

For example, in *Forrester v. Parker,*[18] the New Mexico Supreme Court held that a personnel policy guide controlled the employee-employer relationship in question:

> Forrester should have and did expect Parker to conform to the procedures for terminating him as spelled out in the guide. For the guide constituted an implied employment contract; the conditions and procedures provided in it bound both Forrester and Parker. The words and conduct of the parties here gave rise to this implied contract.[19]

In *Vigil v. Arzola,*[20] the court held that a probationary employee could bring an action against an employer for a termination not following procedures established in the personnel manual.

In addition to establishing procedures for the termination of employees, some employee handbooks provide that employees may be terminated only for "good cause" or "just cause." As with termination procedures, limitations placed upon the reasons for discharge by an implied employment contract are enforceable in many states. For example, in *Danzer v. Professional Insurors, Inc.,*[21] the New Mexico Supreme Court recognized that an employee handbook can create a "standard" for termination. The court adopted the definition of "good cause" announced by the court of appeals of the state of Washington in *Comfort & Fleming Insurance Brokers, Inc. v. Hoxsey:*[22]

> Termination for good cause shown is a restriction on the employer's right to discharge an employee at will. Such a provision is an employment condition guaranteeing tenure and job security against the whim or caprice

> of an employer allowing discharge only for legal cause, i.e., some causes inherent in and related to the qualifications of the employee or a failure to properly perform some essential aspect of the employee's job function.[23]

A breach of an implied employment contract by an employer may give rise to a breach of contract lawsuit by an employee for damages. It appears clear that employers must comply with the provisions of employee handbooks (definite enough to constitute an implied employment contract) to avoid civil liability under the theory that the employer breached an implied contract by taking prompt remedial action to eliminate sexual harassment.

For example, in *Kestenbaum v. Pennzoil Co.,*[24] the New Mexico Supreme Court framed the positions of the parties:

> [Plaintiff] claimed that, without fair investigation and consideration of the allegations and his response, he was terminated on the grounds of sexual harassment for which he was innocent. Pennzoil denied [plaintiff's] claim and affirmatively asserted that [plaintiff] was an employee at will and was dischargeable for any or no reason. Alternatively, if a good reason was required to discharge [plaintiff], Pennzoil asserted that it had reasonable grounds to believe that sufficient cause existed to justify its actions.[25]

The court held that the employer must prove good cause under an objective standard of reasonable belief, as opposed to a subjective good-faith belief. The court found the following evidence insufficient to justify the termination of an employee for good cause:

> In her deposition, Pennzoil's investigator admitted on cross-examination that her summary was not intended to stand alone, that it failed to differentiate between first-hand knowledge, attributed hearsay, or mere gossip or rumor, and no attempt was made to evaluate the credibility of the persons interviewed. Nevertheless, the only document reviewed by [the vice president] before he fired [the employee] was his investigator's summary of interviews. Moreover, he did not take a close look at the way the investigation had been handled, but relied upon the professionalism of his investigators. At trial, [the employee] presented an expert who testified that Pennzoil's investigators did not observe the standards of good investigative practice and who identified numerous deficiencies in the investigation.[26]

The *Kestenbaum* court held that where an employer knew of the improper conduct and the conduct represented a company practice, the employer could not rely on the conduct as grounds for terminating an employee.

Where a practice of harassment exists, an employer could be subjected to liability under an implied employment contract theory for taking action against an employee who can show that the conduct has traditionally been allowed. This fear of civil liability may deter employers with sexually charged workplaces from discharging that first employee in an effort to change the workplace environment.

In *Western-Southern Life Ins. Co. v. Fridley,*[27] the court explained the facts before it as follows:

> Western-Southern's business is selling life insurance. Fridley, a nine-year employee at the time of his discharge, was its district sales manager assigned to the Cincinnati-East office. He was employed in that capacity pursuant to an agreement dated July 1, 1985. Between October 1986 and February 1987, Fridley carried on an extramarital sexual affair with Mallien Walker Cobb, whom he hired in September 1986 as a Western-Southern sales representative. Fridley admitted that he had sexual relations with Cobb on four different occasions while he was her supervisor. On June 17, 1987, Cobb told her immediate sales manager that she was quitting because she could not take any more sexual harassment from Fridley. Fridley, who knew why she quit, concealed the reasons from his superiors, but on August 3, 1987, upon learning of Fridley's conduct with Cobb, Western-Southern discharged him.[28]

The court held that because an employer could be subjected to liability under Title VII for a consensual sexual affair between a coworker and subordinate, the supervisor's extramarital affair could constitute *immoral conduct* and justify termination for *good cause* as those terms applied to Ohio's unemployment compensation laws.

In *Stroehmann Bakeries v. Local 776,*[29] the court recognized that an arbitrator's reinstatement of an employee accused of harassment without determining whether the harassment actually occurred undermines an employer's ability to prevent and correct sexual harassment in the workplace.[30] While suits by alleged harassers are generally unsuccessful (Conte 1990), litigation is expensive — win, lose, or draw.

The conflict between being sued under state law for taking prompt remedial action and the duty to take prompt remedial action under Title VII places employers in a catch-22 in many instances. In this environment, it is not unreasonable for an employer to weigh the potential economic exposure for violating state law or federal law in making personnel decisions. Employers are being required to absorb the risk of civil liability (if nothing else, in litigation expenses) for complying with Title VII's prompt remedial action requirement as interpreted by many courts. Employers are in essence being required to absorb the cost of litigating a "right" to take prompt remedial action.

Free Speech

Title VII also raises substantial concerns regarding the extent to which it infringes on First Amendment rights of employers[31] and employees alike. Some types of speech are clearly not protected by the First Amendment. For example, "fighting words"[32] are not entitled to First Amendment protection. Hate speech directed toward a particular group, however, appears to constitute protected speech.[33] Public employers can be sued for violating the First Amendment rights of their employees and can be sued under Title VII in some jurisdictions for failing to take remedial action against employees who exercise their First Amendment rights in a manner which offends women.[34]

In cases where a public employee alleges a free-speech violation, the interests of the employee as a citizen must be balanced against the government's interest in promoting the efficiency of the public services it performs through its employees.[35] "The threshold question in applying this balancing test is whether [the employee's] speech may be 'fairly characterized as constituting speech on a matter of public concern.'"[36] The *Connick* Court held:

> When a public employee speaks not as a citizen upon matters of public concern, but instead as an employee upon matters only of personal interest, absent the most unusual circumstances, a federal court is not the appropriate forum in which to review the wisdom of a personnel decision taken by a public agency allegedly in reaction to the employee's behavior.[37]

It appears clear that the extent to which government should regulate sexual conduct in the workplace, whether women should be in the workplace, comments about pornography in nationally distributed magazines, comments about locally shown movies, comments about AIDS, and comments about one's sexual orientation could all be considered comments about matters of public concern while at the same time creating a hostile environment prohibited by Title VII. The extent to which employees perceive their right to free speech in the workplace as subordinate to, or superior to, the right to be free from a hostile environment when those two rights conflict is unclear. Likewise, it is unclear what an employer is supposed to do when confronted with these conflicting rights.

Legislative restraints on free speech can be challenged as violating the First Amendment's guarantee of free speech. It has been argued that women's interest in achieving equal employment opportunities outweighs the First Amendment's guarantee of free speech in most cases involving sexist or sexually degrading comments (Strauss 1990).

Conclusion

Employers must attempt to determine whether the risk of liability in a wrongful-discharge case or a free-speech case outweighs the potential for liability under Title VII when deciding what remedial action to take in a given situation. The prompt remedial action required by Title VII, a federal law, may conflict with an employer's contractual duties under state law. An employee's right to be free from adverse employment decisions, absent good cause under state law, may fall in cases involving allegations of sexual harassment because Title VII may preempt state law.[38]

Chapter 16
Costs

The 1980 U.S. Merit Systems Protection Board study suggests that the costs of sexual harassment decrease as the severity of the conduct increases. That is, the less severe forms of sexual harassment may cause more loss in quantity and quality of work, time off, and emotional or physical injury than more severe forms of harassment (*see* Table 16.1).

However, it is the less severe harassment about which there is the least consensus and over which employers have the least legitimate business interests. The least severe (and most costly) forms of sexual harassment also appear to be the most often reported forms of sexual harassment to which federal employees are subjected.

Many of the costs included in the cost of sexual harassment in studies, such as recruiting and replacement costs, continue to be incurred by employers making efforts to comply with Title VII. The costs of replacement have little to do with whether the former employee was a victim or a harasser. It costs an employer money to litigate an unemployment case on the ground that an employee engaged in sexual harassment and is therefore not entitled to benefits. It also costs money to litigate a case about whether sexual harassment constituted good cause for quitting employment under unemployment laws. It costs employers money to litigate sexual harassment cases and wrongful-discharge cases.

While the costs of sexual harassment are great (*see* Figure 16.1), our present approach to combating sexual harassment in the workplace does not appear to be cost-effective.

The costs of efforts to combat sexual harassment are great. In fact, the costs of combating sexual harassment may exceed the damages caused by sexual harassment were we to stop regulating it. Every American taxpayer has a financial stake in the extent to which government spends its money regulating sexual harassment rather than educating children, providing cheaper health care, or engaging in some other activity. While more money can be generated by raising taxes, we simply do not have enough money to do everything everyone would like government to do. We must elect between competing interests.

Table 16.1. Percentage of Narrators Who Indicated These Aspects of Their Lives Became Better or Were Not Affected by the Sexual Harassment

CONDUCT	MOST SEVERE		SEVERE		LESS SEVERE		TOTAL NARRATORS	
	WOMEN	MEN	WOMEN	MEN	WOMEN	MEN	WOMEN	MEN
Feelings About Work								
Had no effect	39%	73%	58%	80%	76%	81%	64%	80%
Became Better	0%	0%	0.3%	1%	0.2%	1%	0.3%	1%
Total Respondents	3,600	1,500	134,800	48,900	66,600	37,100	207,600	89,100
Emotional or Physical Condition								
Had no effect	18%	31%	62%	77%	78%	81%	66%	78%
Became Better	0%	16%	1%	2%	1%	2%	1%	2%
Total Respondents	3,800	1,300	128,800	48,900	64,700	34,000	199,400	87,700
Ability to Work with Others								
Had no effect	63%	57%	82%	83%	89%	84%	84%	83%
Became Better	6%	19%	1%	1%	1%	1%	1%	2%
Total Respondents	3,600	1,400	123,200	46,600	64,200	35,000	193,000	84,400
Time and Attendance at Work								
Had no effect	49%	72%	86%	91%	95%	90%	88%	90%
Became Better	3%	5%	0.3%	1%	0.4%	2%	0.4%	2%
Total Respondents	3,600	1,300	123,100	47,200	62,400	34,000	191,000	84,000
The Quantity of Work								
Had no effect	66%	62%	87%	87%	94%	90%	89%	88%
Became Better	6%	28%	0.4%	1%	1%	2%	1%	2%
Total Respondents	3,200	1,300	120,700	47,100	62,000	33,900	187,800	83,800
The Quality of Work								
Had no effect	73%	60%	88%	87%	95%	92%	90%	87%
Became Better	6%	34%	1%	1%	1%	2%	1%	2%
Total Respondents	3,400	1,400	121,400	47,500	62,200	33,400	188,900	83,800

Source: USMSPB 1981: D-16.

Many costs are quietly incurred by taxpayers, such as the costs of administrative agencies to address sexual harassment complaints and the costs of courts to hear lawsuits involving harassment.[1] One of the many costs incurred in the present approach to regulating sexual harassment is the cost of a justice system to respond to harassment suits. Justice is expensive, and it's not getting any cheaper:

> Federal, State, and local governments in the United States spent $74 billion in fiscal year 1990 for civil and criminal justice, an increase of 21% since 1988, the last year comparable data were collected.
>
> . . . .
>
> In October 1990, the Nation's civil and criminal justice system employed 1.7 million persons, with a total October payroll of almost $4.3 billion [Lindgren 1992].

Figure 16.1

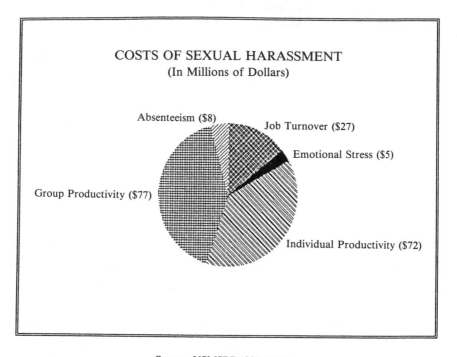

COSTS OF SEXUAL HARASSMENT
(In Millions of Dollars)

Absenteeism ($8)

Job Turnover ($27)

Emotional Stress ($5)

Group Productivity ($77)

Individual Productivity ($72)

Source: USMSPB 1981: 76–79.

The September 28, 1992 issue of *Fair Employment Practices* reported the following about the EEOC's budget: "The Bush administration asked Congress for $245 million for fiscal 1993. . . . The House cut the request to $218 million and the Senate voted $212 million." The EEOC states that budget constraints will seriously hamper effective case processing. This may be especially true in light of increasing numbers of discrimination charges being filed with the EEOC. The September 14, 1992 issue of *Fair Employment Practices* reported:

> In the third quarter of fiscal year 1992 — between April 1 and the end of June — EEOC received 51,367 discrimination charges, an 11.3 percent increase from the same period a year ago the agency reports. . . . Of the charges filed, 35,667 were brought under Title VII. . . . EEOC collected $72.5 million through conciliation and settlement and about $23.5 million in court actions during the quarter.

Costs incurred by employers to comply with government regulations are passed on to the consumer. Although an employer may not be able to prevent some forms of sexual harassment in the workplace, employers are penalized for the socialization process resulting in these forms of sexual harassment. These costs are simply another cost of doing business over which the employer has no control. The cost of doing business must be figured into the cost of a product or service when prices to the consumer are calculated. The consumer most often pays the bill. The employer runs the risk that the costs of its product or service will become so expensive that it is no longer competitive with products or services offered by those not required to comply with America's employment discrimination laws. When an employer can no longer make a profit and closes its doors, its employees, men and women alike, lose their jobs. Enough Americans will buy lower-cost foreign products rather than higher-priced American products (prices due in large part to the high costs of complying with laws protecting employees) that employers are encouraged to move abroad and hire employees in other countries.

Chapter 17
Theories of Liability Under Common Law

"In sexual harassment actions, intentional infliction of emotional distress is the most litigated common-law theory of recovery" (Lindemann and Kadue 1992: 352; *see also* Conte 1990: 267). Other types of common-law tort claims based on conduct labeled sexual harassment include assault, battery, invasion of privacy, and negligent retention or hiring. Private employers may also be sued under common-law tort theories for workplace conduct which has been labeled sexual harassment in some jurisdictions. Other jurisdictions have held that claims for intentional infliction of emotional distress based on conduct which also constitutes sexual harassment are barred by state workers' compensation laws or state laws explicitly prohibiting sexual harassment.

Intentional Infliction of Emotional Distress

Prior to the enactment of the Civil Rights Act of 1991, emotional distress damages were not available in Title VII employment discrimination cases. Because emotional distress damages were not available, many employees brought claims for intentional infliction of emotional distress concurrently with claims for employment discrimination in an effort to obtain compensation for the emotional distress inflicted upon them by discriminatory conduct in the workplace.

State common-law claims for intentional infliction of emotional distress are designed to protect citizens regardless of their sex. Intentional infliction of emotional distress has been defined as follows:

> One who by extreme and outrageous conduct intentionally or recklessly causes severe emotional distress to another is subject to liability for such emotional distress, and if bodily harm to the other results from it, for such bodily harm.[1]

150

The four elements of the tort of intentional infliction of emotional distress:

1. the conduct of defendant was extreme and outrageous.

2. the conduct of defendant was intentional and reckless.

3. the conduct of defendant caused plaintiff emotional distress.

4. the emotional distress suffered by plaintiff as a direct and proximate result of defendant's actions was severe.[2]

Conduct Extreme and Outrageous

The test to determine whether conduct is outrageous is whether a reasonable person, upon hearing the events, would react by exclaiming "Outrageous!"[3] A court must determine "whether the [defendant's] conduct may reasonably be regarded as so extreme and outrageous as to permit recovery, or whether it is necessarily so."[4] "Where reasonable minds may differ the jury must decide whether the conduct 'is so outrageous in character, and so extreme in degree, as to go beyond all possible bounds of decency, and to be regarded as atrocious, and utterly intolerable in a civilized community.'"[5]

In *Hogan v. Forsyth Country Club Co.,*[6] three former female employees of a country club brought a sexual harassment suit. April Cornatzer alleged that the club's chef, Pfeiffer, shouted at her, used profanity, interfered with her duties, threatened her, made sexual advances toward her, made sexually derogatory remarks about her, and placed her in fear of bodily harm.[7] The court held:

> No person should have to be subject to nonconsensual sexual touchings, constant suggestive remarks and on-going sexual harassment such as that testified to by Cornatzer, without being afforded remedial recourse through our legal system. Such conduct, if found by a jury to have actually existed, is beyond the "bounds usually tolerated by decent society" and would permit Cornatzer to recover, at least as against Pfeiffer.[8]

The court held the following conduct sufficiently outrageous to submit Cornatzer's emotional distress claim to the jury:

> The evidence with respect to April Cornatzer's claim for intentional infliction of emotional distress, taken in the light most favorable to her, tends to show that in September 1982, Hans Pfeiffer began making sexual advances towards her. At her deposition, and in an affidavit, Cornatzer maintained that Pfeiffer made sexually suggestive remarks to her while she was working, coaxing her to have sex with him and telling her that

he wanted to "take" her. He would brush up against her, rub his penis against her buttocks and touch her buttocks with his hands. When she refused his advances, he screamed profane names at her, threatened her with bodily injury, and on one occasion, advanced toward her with a knife and slammed it down on a table in front of her. As a result of Pfeiffer's actions toward her, Cornatzer maintains that she became very nervous, anxious, humiliated and depressed, to the extent that she was required to seek medical treatment for ulcers.[9]

The court also rejected the employer's argument that it could not be held liable for the chef's conduct under the doctrine of *respondeat superior.* The evidence showed that Cornatzer had complained to the general manager but nothing had been done to prevent the chef from continuing the sexual harassment.[10]

In *Hogan,* Marlene Hogan alleged that Pfeiffer shouted at her, used profanity, interfered with employees under her supervision, threatened her, and threw objects at her.[11] In discussing Hogan's case, the court held:

> Hogan's evidence tends to show that Pfeiffer screamed and shouted at her, called her names, interfered with her supervision of waitresses under her charge, and on one occasion threw menus at her. She also testified that she shouted back at Pfeiffer. This conduct lasted during the period from 22 June 1983 until her termination on 24 July 1983. The general manager, Clifford Smith, received complaints from both Hogan and Pfeiffer concerning the temper of the other. His attempt to discuss the situation with both employees was unsuccessful because Pfeiffer walked out.
>
> . . . .
>
> We hold Pfeiffer's conduct, as shown by Hogan's forecast of evidence, was not such as to be reasonably regarded as "extreme and outrageous" so as to permit Hogan to recover for intentional infliction of mental distress.[12]

The court held that Hogan failed to show extreme and outrageous conduct. The effect of Hogan's yelling back at Pfeiffer on the court's decision is unclear.

Most conduct labeled sexual harassment consists of words or gestures. Some courts have held that each member of society has a duty to refrain from inflicting emotional distress upon others by insulting or abusive language.[13] For example, in *Tuggle v. Wilson,*[14] the court held:

> In Georgia, there is no tort of obscenity as such. . . . However, there is authority to sanction recovery in tort where the defendant has willfully and wantonly caused emotional upset to the plaintiff through the use of abusive or obscene language.
>
> . . . .

> We agree with the plaintiff that in this case there exists a jury issue on the question of his intent to harm the defendant through use of the language uttered over the telephone.[15]

In *Coleman v. Housing Auth. of Americus,*[16] the court held abusive or obscene language amounting to sexual harassment sufficient for a claim of emotional distress:

> The workplace is not a free zone in which the duty not to engage in wilfully and wantonly causing emotional distress through the use of abusive or obscene language does not exist. Actually, by its very nature, it provides an environment more prone to such occurrences because it provides a captive victim who may fear reprisal for complaining, so that the injury is exacerbated by repetition, and it presents a hierarchy of structured relationships which cannot easily be avoided. The opportunity for commission of the tort is more frequently presented in the workplace than in casual circumstances involving temporary relationships.[17]

"Florida recognizes a cause of action for insulting and abusive language resulting in mental distress if the conduct was sufficient to cause severe emotional distress to one of ordinary sensibilities."[18] In *Russo v. Iacono,*[19] the court held a claim of intentional infliction stated where it was alleged that another person "on three separate occasions shouted vile, objectionable and obscene language at her."

Harassment of an employee for making allegations of sexual harassment or opposing the sexual harassment of women in the workplace can also constitute sufficiently extreme and outrageous conduct to create liability for intentional infliction of emotional distress.[20]

Intentional and Reckless Conduct

The *Restatement (Second) of Torts,* Section 46, Comment i:

> The rule stated in this Section applies where the actor desires to inflict severe emotional distress, and also where he knows that such distress is certain, or substantially certain, to result from his conduct. It applies also where he acts recklessly . . . in deliberate disregard of a high degree of probability that the emotional distress will follow.

"Intent or recklessness can be inferred from the outrageousness of the acts."[21] "The essence of 'recklessness' is 'an indifference whether wrong is done or not—an indifference to the rights of others.'"[22]

In *Ford v. Revlon, Inc.,*[23] the court held that even if an employer does not intend to cause emotional distress, an employer's reckless disregard of allegations of sexual harassment can form the basis of liability for intentional infliction of emotional distress of a subordinate by a supervisory employee.[24] The court held the failure to take appropriate remedial action sufficient in itself to support a claim for intentional infliction of emotional distress.[25] The failure of an employer to follow its own policies when conducting an investigation of allegations of sexual harassment may also give rise to a claim for intentional infliction of emotional distress.[26]

Caused Severe Emotional Distress

In *Morrison v. Sandell,*[27] the court held intensity and duration of the distress are factors to be considered in determining the severity of the emotional distress.[28]

Abuse of Employee-Employer Relationship

"Extreme and outrageous conduct most often arises from abuse of a position of power over the plaintiff or some relationship between the parties."[29] "The extreme and outrageous character of conduct may also arise from the actor's knowledge that the plaintiff is peculiarly susceptible to mental distress by reason of some physical or mental condition."[30] Courts place great emphasis on the relationship between the parties in determining whether the conduct of one party constitutes extreme and outrageous conduct likely to result in emotional distress.

Assault

The *Restatement (Second) of Torts,* Section 21 (1) (1965) defines assault as follows:

> An actor is subject to liability to another for assault if
> (a) he acts intending to cause a harmful or offensive contact with the person of the other or a third person, or an imminent apprehension of such a contact, and
> (b) the other is thereby put in such imminent apprehension.

"To make the actor liable for an assault under the rule stated in § 21, it is not necessary that the actor be inspired by personal hostility or desire to offend."[31] To make the actor liable for an assault, the other must be put in apprehension of an imminent contact with his own person[32] by the actor or another.[33] "In order that the other may be put in the apprehension necessary to make the actor liable for an assault, the other must believe that the act may result in imminent contact unless prevented from so resulting by the other's self-defensive action or by his flight or by the intervention of some outside force."[34]

The *Restatement (Second) of Torts,* Section 31 (1965), states:

> Words do not make the actor liable for assault *unless together with other acts or circumstances* they put the other in reasonable apprehension of an imminent harmful or offensive contact with his person. [Emphasis added.]

While "mere words do not constitute an assault,"[35] "words which accompany or precede acts known to the other and understood by him may be decisive evidence of the actor's intention to commit the assault and of the other's apprehension."[36] *Acts or circumstances* which can put another in reasonable apprehension of imminent harmful or offensive contact with his person include gestures, attitude, and other nonverbal behavior. *Restatement (Second) of Torts,* Section 31, Comment d (1965), recognizes that verbal behavior does not exist in a vacuum:

> Even apart from such cases where the words indicate the intent of an act, there may be other situations in which the words themselves, without any accompanying gesture, are sufficient under the circumstances to arouse a reasonable apprehension of imminent bodily contact. Words are never spoken in a vacuum, and they cannot be utterly divorced from past conduct, or from the accompanying circumstances. An entirely motionless highwayman, standing with a gun in his hand and crying "Stand and deliver!" creates quite as much apprehension as one who draws the gun; and any rule which insists upon such a gesture as essential to liability is obviously quite artificial and unreasonable.

It is clear that words alone can cause a person to be placed in fear.[37]

In *Baca v. Velez,*[38] the court held:

> For there to be an assault, there must have been an "act, threat or menacing conduct which causes another person to reasonably believe that he is in danger of receiving an immediate battery." NMSA 1978, § 30-3-1 (B) (Repl. Pamp. 1984).[39]

The *Baca* court concluded that because there was no evidence that plaintiff felt frightened before the touching took place, "there was no genuine issue of material fact whether, under these circumstances, an assault actually occurred."[40]

In *Johnson v. Bollinger,*[41] the plaintiff alleged the following facts in a claim for assault:

> Briefly, plaintiff's complaint alleged plaintiff owned a gas station in the City. Defendant was employed by the City as an animal warden....

Plaintiff further alleged that defendant "approached plaintiff ... in an angry, hostile and threatening manner" at the Cleveland County Law Enforcement Center, "shook his hand in the plaintiff's face and said in a loud, rude and offensive manner..., 'You are a liar,' and stated further 'I will get you.'" Defendant wore his City uniform and carried a pistol during the incident. Persons were present in the Law Enforcement Center during defendant's statements.[42]

The *Johnson* court held that the plaintiff had stated a good cause of action for assault:

Plaintiff could reasonably expect imminent offensive contact under these circumstances.... Under the circumstances alleged in the complaint, we find no legal insufficiency or defect in plaintiff's allegation of assault. Plaintiff's allegations clearly give rise to certain facts which, if proved, would support plaintiff's claim.... The trial court erroneously dismissed plaintiff's claim of assault.[43]

In *Jung-Leonczynska v. Steup,*[44] the plaintiff alleged the following facts to support a claim for assault:

Leonczynska's complaint ... asserted the material allegations that Steup, as a faculty member of the University of Wyoming, engaged in intentional tortious conduct against her, as his student, during class hours of the class he was teaching in a classroom at the University. Allegedly, he ran toward her in a fit of anger, yelling at her and shaking his fist in her face; he pounded the table in front of her as well as her personal belongings on the table. She alleges that his intention was to create in her fear and apprehension of imminent bodily contact by him and that as a result of his conduct she was in fear of and apprehensive about imminent unconsented bodily contact by him.[45]

The *Jung-Leonczynska* court agreed that claims for assault, battery, and intentional infliction of emotional distress had been stated by the plaintiff:

In our review of the intentional torts pleaded by Leonczynska, we find that the elements of civil assault, as recognized in *Restatement (Second) of Torts* §§ 21, 24, 26, 27, 28, 31, 33 and 34 (1965), are stated, and the technical elements of civil battery, as recognized in *Restatement (Second) of Torts* §§ 18–20, are stated. Also stated are the elements of intentional infliction of emotional harm.[46]

In cases where the conduct which could be labeled sexual harassment consists of language intended to place a reasonable person in fear of bodily harm and causes the victim such fear, a claim for assault appears to exist in some jurisdictions.

Negligent Hiring and Retention

In *Hogan v. Forsyth Country Club Co.,*[47] the court held claims for negligent retention were not barred by North Carolina's Workers' Compensation Act, noting: "Sexual harassment is not a risk to which an employee is exposed because of the nature of the employment but is a risk to which the employee could be equally exposed outside the employment."[48] When an employer hires or retains an employee known to have a history of or propensity for sexual harassment and that employee subsequently sexually harasses a coworker or supervisor, the employer may be held liable for the sexual harassment under the theory of *negligent hiring* or *negligent retention.*[49] An employer may also be held liable for negligent supervision in some jurisdictions.[50]

Conclusion

In addition to claims under Title VII, victims of sexual harassment may sue the harasser and employer under state law. Tort actions may have more deterrent effect than Title VII because the harasser can be held personally liable. Remember, however, that state law varies from state to state.

Chapter 18
Curbing False Accusations

Victims of wrongful allegations of sexual harassment may consider suing the wrongdoer personally (for money damages) for *invasion of privacy, intentional infliction of emotional distress, defamation, negligent misrepresentations by words,* or *civil conspiracy.* In cases where administrative or judicial proceedings alleging sexual harassment are brought for illegitimate purposes or to obtain an unfair advantage, a wrongfully accused person should consider filing suit for *abuse of process* or *malicious prosecution.*

Invasion of Privacy

In *Phillips v. Smalley Maintenance Services,*[1] the court said:

> It is generally accepted that the invasion of privacy tort consists of four distinct wrongs: (1) the intrusion upon the plaintiff's physical solitude or seclusion; (2) publicity which violates the ordinary decencies; (3) putting the plaintiff in a false, but not necessarily defamatory, position in the public eye; and (4) the appropriation of some element of the plaintiff's personality for a commercial use [footnote omitted].[2]

In *Phillips,* the court held that "one's emotional sanctum is certainly due the same expectations of privacy as one's physical environment."[3]

The *Restatement (Second) of Torts,* Section 652E (1977), defines invasion of privacy resulting from publicly placing a person in a false light, as follows:

> One who gives publicity to a matter concerning another that places the other before the public in a false light is subject to liability to the other for invasion of his privacy, if
>
> (a) the false light in which the other was placed would be highly offensive to a reasonable person, and
>
> (b) the actor had knowledge of or acted in reckless disregard as to the falsity of the publicized matter and the false light in which the other would be placed.

A claim for invasion of privacy also exists for publicly invading the personal life of another (*Restatement [Second] of Torts,* Section 652D [1977]).

Defamation

Although it is generally recognized that in most instances the law does not prohibit someone from speaking his or her opinions, "the law should protect only those who act reasonably and with a reasonable belief of the truth of their remarks" (*Salazar v. Bjork,* 85 N.M. 94, 509 P. 2d 569 (Ct. App. 1973). Defamatory statements are defined in the *Restatement (Second) of Torts,* Section 559:

> A communication is defamatory if it tends so to harm the reputation of another as to lower him in the estimation of the community or to deter third persons from associating with him.

An employer may be held liable for an employee's unauthorized slanderous statements made within the scope and course of employment (unless the employer if found to have immunity). As a general rule, statements made in administrative and judicial proceedings enjoy immunity and cannot form the basis of a defamation action.

Abuse of Process

In cases where administrative proceedings or lawsuits are filed for improper reasons, such as to get even with someone or to gain an undue advantage in a promotion decision, the victim may consider a claim against the wrongdoer for abuse of process. A claim for abuse of process requires that a suit be groundless or brought solely for an improper purpose. The *Restatement (Second) of Torts,* Section 682 (1977), defines abuse of process generally as follows:

> One who uses a legal process, whether criminal or civil, against another primarily to accomplish a purpose for which it is not designed, is subject to liability to the other for harm caused by the abuse of process.

Because it is a state-law claim, the recognition of the tort under a given set of circumstances and the elements necessary to prevail on such a claim will vary among states.

Negligent Misrepresentations

The *Restatement (Second) of Torts,* Section 552 (1977), states:

> (1) One who in the course of his business, profession or employment, or in any other transaction in which he has a pecuniary interest, supplies false information for the guidance of others in their business transactions, is subject to liability for pecuniary loss caused to them by their justifiable reliance upon the information, if he fails to exercise reasonable care or competence in obtaining or communicating the information.

> (2) Except as stated in Subsection (3), the liability stated in Subsection (1) is limited to loss suffered
>   (a) by the person or one of a limited group of persons for whose benefit and guidance he intends to supply the information or knows that the recipient intends to supply it; and
>   (b) through reliance upon it in a transaction that he intends the information to influence or knows that the recipient so intends or in a substantially similar transaction.

> (3) The liability of one who is under a public duty to give the information extends to loss suffered by any of the class of persons for whose benefit the duty is created, in any of the transactions in which it is intended to protect them.

Claims for negligent misrepresentation may be available to a person wrongfully accused of harassment where another makes misrepresentations regarding allegations of sexual harassment or fails to disclose information in a harassment investigation for the purpose of causing harm.

Civil Conspiracy

In some cases, a wrongfully accused person may have a claim for civil conspiracy. In *Morris v. Dodge Country, Inc.,*[4] the court said:

> For a conspiracy to exist there must be a common design or a mutually implied understanding; an agreement. *First National Bank of Dodge City, Kansas v. Perschbacher,* 335 F. 2d 442 (10th Cir. 1964); *Hedrick v. Perry,* 102 F. 2d 802 (10th Cir. 1939); *State v. Deaton,* 74 N.M. 87, 390 P. 2d 966 (1964); *State v. Farris,* 81 N.M. 589, 470 P. 2d 561 (Ct. App. 1970). A conspiracy may be established by circumstantial evidence; generally, the agreement is a matter of inference from the facts and circumstances, including the acts of the persons alleged to be conspirators. *State v. Deaton,* supra. The question is whether the circumstances, considered as a whole, show that the parties united to accomplish the fraudulent scheme. *Hedrick v. Perry,* supra.[5]

In *Las Luminarias of the N.M. Council v. Isengard,*[6] the court said:

> To constitute an actionable civil conspiracy, there must be a combination by two or more persons to accomplish an unlawful purpose or to accomplish a lawful purpose by unlawful means. *Bourland v. State,* 528 S.W. 2d 350 (Tex. Civ. App. 1975); *International Bankers Life Insurance Company v. Holloway,* 368 S.W. 2d 567 (Tex. 1963); *Boman v. Gibbs,* 443 S.W. 2d 267 (Tex. Civ. App. 1969); 16 Am Jur. 2d Conspiracy 43 (1964). Civil conspiracy is not of itself actionable; the gist of the action is the damage arising from the acts done pursuant to the conspiracy. *Armijo v. National Surety Corp.,* 58 N.M. 166, 268 P. 2d 339 (1954); *Lindbeck v. Bendziunas,* 84 N.M. 21, 498 P. 2d 1364 (Ct. App. 1972); *Barber's Super Markets, Inc. v. Stryker,* 84 N.M. 181, 500 P. 2d 1304 (1972), cert. denied, 84 N.M. 180, 500 P. 2d 1303 (1972). Generally, to state a cause of action for conspiracy, the complaint must allege: (1) the existence of the conspiracy; (2) the wrongful act or acts done pursuant to the conspiracy; and (3) the damage resulting from such act or acts.... The existence of the conspiracy must be pled either by direct allegations or by allegation of circumstances from which a conclusion of the existence of a conspiracy may be reasonably inferred.[7]

A claim for civil conspiracy may be available to a target of an agreement to make false charges of sexual harassment to cause the discharge or removal of the target.

Malicious Prosecution

An action for malicious prosecution based on the initiation of judicial proceedings is defined generally by the *Restatement (Second) of Torts,* Section 674 (1977), as follows:

> One who takes an active part in the initiation, continuation or procurement of civil proceedings against another is subject to liability to the other for wrongful civil proceedings if
> (a) he acts without probable cause, and primarily for a purpose other than that of securing the proper adjudication of the claim in which the proceedings are based, and
> (b) except when they are ex parte, the proceedings have terminated in favor of the person against whom they are brought.

To support a claim of malicious prosecution, the sexual harassment case must have been brought "without probable cause." Probable cause is defined by the *Restatement (Second) of Torts,* Section 675 (1977):

> One who takes an active part in the initiation, continuation or procurement of civil proceedings against another has probable cause for doing

so if he reasonably believes in the existence of the facts upon which the claim is based, and either

(a) correctly believes that under those facts the claim may be valid under applicable law, or

(b) believes to this effect in reliance upon the advice of counsel, sought in good faith and given after full disclosure of all relevant facts within his knowledge and information.

And the sexual harassment suit must have been brought for an improper purpose. The *Restatement (Second) of Torts,* Section 676 (1977), explains:

To subject a person to liability for wrongful civil proceedings, the proceedings must have been initiated or continued primarily for a purpose other than that of securing the proper adjudication of the claim on which they are based.

The probable-cause and improper-purpose requirements may bar recovery in many cases where a person has wrongfully been accused of sexual harassment.

Conclusion

There is no uniform definition of sexual harassment. Thus, employees contemplating filing a sexual harassment case and employers contemplating defending a sexual harassment case are in large part guessing whether a judge or jury will consider some conduct labeled sexual harassment to be based on sex, unwelcome, and sufficiently severe or pervasive to alter the conditions of employment.

It is clear that some of the conduct labeled sexual harassment should be regulated by law. However, including conduct which constitutes traditionally acceptable dating or courting behavior requires employers to become judges of morality regarding when conduct such as requests for a date is socially acceptable. A simple request for a date, a smile, or a comment about the attractiveness of a coworker will generally not give rise to civil liability under Title VII.

Targets of this type of behavior, however, do have available a range of informal personal responses which have proven effective in many cases. If the offensive conduct continues after informal responses have been tried, these facts should be reported to the employer. Reporting any type of sexual harassment to an employer prior to filing a formal charge with the EEOC or a court appears to enhance the likelihood of the plaintiff prevailing.

Both civil and criminal law have traditionally provided remedies against those who without justification or consent physically touch, assault, or rape another person. Including such serious conduct in the definition of sexual harassment tends to exaggerate the seriousness of suggestive looks and requests for dates while trivializing rape and sexual assault. A question of validity is raised in the minds of some jurors when charges of rape or sexual assault are not reported to the police.

Employees contemplating filing a formal harassment suit should be prepared to have their backgrounds checked and all personal information disclosed to the harasser. Employers will often argue that other events such as divorce, menopause, loss of a loved one, or some other event caused the plaintiff to suffer emotional distress rather than the alleged sexual

163

harassment. Many personal matters may become an issue once a lawsuit is filed. Even if an employee convinces the judge or jury that sexual harassment occurred, was unwelcome, and created an offensive or abusive work environment, the employer may be relieved of liability if the employer takes prompt, effective corrective action. And there is no uniform definition about what constitutes sufficiently prompt, effective remedial action.

It is important to point out that the geographic location of the court can have a substantial impact on whether some types of sexual harassment are actionable under Title VII. "'Substantive' law of course is regularly established in cases brought before the Court."[1] The U.S. Court of Appeals for the Second Circuit explained: "The existence of divergent results in different circuits, however, does not amount to a violation of equal protection. Certainly there is a rational justification for the division of the federal system into separate and independent circuits."[2]

The Delaware Supreme Court has held: "The equal protection clause does not require uniformity of judicial decisions."[3] In *Trujillo v. City of Albuquerque*,[4] the court stated:

> So long as the state chooses to provide particular rights to litigants, it must allow litigants to exercise these rights in a manner that comports with principles of equal protection and equal access to the courts, and it may not limit the exercise of such rights selectively unless the limitation is justified by a counterbalanced state interest of sufficient weight.[5]

Both employees and employers must be careful not to rely on cases from other jurisdictions when deciding whether to pursue a sexual harassment case. The decisions in the jurisdiction where the case will be brought will govern. Substantive law relating to an employer's liability for hostile environment sexual harassment and definitions of that conduct have been established by the courts. Employers should consider their potential liability under Title VII and accompanying costs before setting up shop in new jurisdictions.

Title VII imposes upon employers an obligation to make efforts to monitor and change behavior that most agree is caused by the socialization process.[6] Our socialization process also produces many who are unable to feel comfortable with conduct traditionally considered normal dating and social behavior. Because traditional behavior will most likely continue to offend some and courts have taken up the task of deciding the extent to which traditional social and dating behavior must be changed, an end to litigation about the appropriate boundaries of such behavior does not seem foreseeable. What is foreseeable is many employees who have problems with authority, sexuality, intimacy, or working with people of one sex or the other.

Child sexual abuse, a major problem in America, often results in supersensitive and sexually dysfunctional workers. In *Study Findings: National Study of the Incidence and Severity of Child Abuse and Neglect* (1981: 28–29), it was found that

> in the area of sexual abuse, girls are victimized more often than boys at all age levels. The problem is not unique to girls, however. Overall, 17 percent of sex abuse victims are boys. . . . As many female sex abuse victims are under age 12 (50 percent of the total) as are in the 12–17 age range. . . . The risk in the years before puberty is only somewhat lower than it is after puberty, for girls as well as boys.

The dark figure of child abuse, the number of cases which go undiscovered and unreported, is unknown. Some suspect the dark figure is very high because it usually occurs in the privacy of a home (Broadhurst 1984).

Reported sexual abuse cases had tripled from the 1980 incident rate by 1986 (1988 *Executive Summary*). As noted in *A Report to the Congress* (1986: 1), increases in reported rates of child abuse or neglect "may be attributed to greater public awareness, the strengthening of state laws, the implementation of 24-hour hotlines, and the improvement of state data collection systems." A portion of the increase in reported incidents of child sexual abuse may result from false reports. Allegations of sexual abuse often occur in custody disputes. Many of the allegations of sexual abuse made in custody disputes are later held "unfounded" (*Research Symposium on Child Sexual Abuse* 1988).

A portion of the increase in reports of child abuse may also be attributed to increased numbers of single mothers exercising their right to work. *A Report to the Congress* (1986: 1) concluded that "of the total number of families in the United States with children under age 18, 19% are headed by single females. However, within the reported statistics of child abuse and neglect, 40% of the cases occur in families headed by single females." As the number of single parents in the work force has increased, the function of the public school system has changed. For many single parents, public schools have become the equivalent of free day care, and the education of children seems to have taken a back seat. The physical and sexual abuse of children in America's schools has reached sickening proportions.[7]

When children leave home because they were abused or otherwise dissatisfied with the home environment, they may still be sexually abused or exploited. *Report to the Congress* (1986: 1) concluded that America "has an estimated 1 million runaways and 225,000 to 500,000 homeless youth, many of whom are particularly vulnerable to prostitution, pornography, or other sexual exploitation." The sexual exploitation of children and youths, such as engaging young people in prostitution and child pornography, has emerged as a social problem (*see Research Symposium on Child Sexual Abuse* 1988).[8] Diane Broadhurst (1984: 6) has noted that "child abuse and neglect are often as damaging emotionally as they are physically."

Jenkins, Salus, and Schultze (1979: 6) have noted that

> abused or neglected children may be impaired in self-concept, ego competency, reality testing, defensive functioning and overall thought processes. They also often have a higher level of aggression, anxiety, low impulse control, and self-destructiveness. These characteristics can cause abused or neglected children to display high levels of antisocial behavior as they get older.

The adverse effects of child sexual abuse can be very long-lasting. For example,

> Sequelae of abuse, however, can be extensive and do not always appear immediately. Post-Traumatic Stress syndrome is now associated with some sexual abuse victims. Not infrequently, 8 to 14 years after the onset or disclosure of abuse, physical or mental problems may arise. Victims seek treatment for disorders such as anxiety, depression, sleep disturbances, eating disorders, and problems of intimacy, not realizing that they are symptomatic of their unresolved experiences as a victim of child sexual abuse [*Research Symposium on Child Sexual Abuse* 1988: 4].

The antisocial behavior exhibited by some survivors of childhood sexual abuse includes the inability to cope with authority and the inability to establish intimate relationships. Others may suffer from depression, anxiety, sleep disturbances, and eating disorders, not realizing that these symptoms result from childhood sexual abuse.

The antisocial behavior exhibited by some adult survivors of child sexual abuse may result in supervisors and coworkers disliking the survivor's personality traits. The symptoms of sexual abuse which occurred long ago can easily be attributed to a stressful job by survivors. An adult survivor may be more sensitive to sexual issues and advances by a person of the same sex as the perpetrator of the childhood abuse both in and out of the workplace. Adult survivors presently exist in the American work force in substantial numbers. Reports of the number of children being sexually abused today suggests that American employers will be confronted with persons exhibiting survivor behavior for many years to come.

Because it appears that child abuse, among other social problems, will continue to create large numbers of future workers who are uncomfortable with traditional behavior, the end of litigation about what is offensive, sexual, or appropriate in the workplace is not likely in the near future. The rules, however, should be changed to require that (1) victims of nonphysical sexual harassment ask the harasser to stop the offensive conduct or take some other appropriate informal action at the time the unwelcome conduct occurs; (2) victims of sexual harassment involving physical contact and recurring nonphysical sexual harassment report the conduct to their employer immediately; (3) harassers be held personally liable; and (4) state legal barriers deterring full compliance with an employer's obligations under Title VII be removed.

Employers need to explore the legal implications of mandatory reporting policies in jurisdictions where they are doing business. To avoid the "cuing" effect, employers should consider asking questions related to specific harassment conduct in recorded exit interviews. Courts must proceed with more caution when determining what management should have known. Once an employer has knowledge of harassment, it has a duty to conduct an investigation. While some employees argue that they should not be required to disclose their dating and sexual activity to employers, Title VII requires an employer to investigate the dating and sexual behavior of employees and to monitor these activities. Employees and courts need to determine the extent to which employees are willing to give up enough of their privacy rights to allow employers to comply with Title VII.

Another issue which needs to be addressed is the conflict between employees' right to free speech and employees' right to be free from verbal communication they find offensive. Much harassment occurs without witnesses, and most employers are prohibited from using polygraphs in harassment investigations. Employers are required by Title VII to take prompt remedial action yet can be sued for doing so under state law. Placing employers in a legal environment in which it may be impossible to avoid high insurance premiums or litigation costs and civil liability when allegations of harassment are made does not seem to be an incentive for continuing to do business in America. The catch-22s need to be resolved, one way or another.

Perhaps our limited resources (both governmental and private) would be better spent on programs designed to address the socialization of children and decrease the number of future workers who have problems dealing with authority, personal and social relationships, and members of one gender or the other.

Appendix A:
Baker v. New Mexico Division of Vocational Rehabilitation

BEFORE THE HUMAN RIGHTS COMMISSION
OF THE STATE OF NEW MEXICO

PAMELA JO BAKER,	)	
Complainant,	)	
vs.	)	HRD No. 90-03-21-0698
	)	
NEW MEXICO DIVISION OF	)	
VOCATIONAL REHABILITATION,	)	
	)	
Respondent.	)	

Decision and Order

Beginning on June 15, 1992, and continuing on June 17, 1992, this matter came before the Human Rights Commission. A panel of three Commissioners, Ms. Dorothy Clark, Mr. Nicklos E. Jaramillo and Mr. Joe D. Marquez, heard case number 90-03-21-0698, Baker v. Department of Vocational Rehabilitation, in the New Mexico Tech Building located at 2808 Central, N.E., Albuquerque, New Mexico. Both Ms. Pamela Jo Baker ("Baker") and the Department of Vocational Rehabilitation ("DVR") were represented by counsel. The panel heard testimony and received exhibits from both parties. After fully considering the record established, the Human Rights Commission enters the following:

Findings of Fact

1. Baker, a female, resides in Tijeras, New Mexico.
2. DVR is a division of the New Mexico Department of Education

and employs more than four (4) employees. The facts that give rise to the allegations occurred at the DVR (Disability Determination Services) office in Albuquerque, New Mexico.

3. Ms. Joan Benvenuti is an employee of DVR and was Baker's immediate supervisor from September 1986 until late March 1990.

4. Baker has been employed by DVR since 1981, and is still employed by DVR. Baker is employed as a typist/word processor.

5. Baker alleges that DVR violated Section 28-1-7 (A) of the Human Rights Act when Ms. Benvenuti on numerous occasions sexually harassed Baker. The unwanted sexual advances began in 1987 and ended in 1989.

6. Baker testified that the physical sexual contact by Ms. Benvenuti included: "grabbing and touching her buttocks"; "kissing her on the neck by the ear"; "attempting to fondle her breasts"; "asking her out on dates"; and "grabbing her knee."

7. Baker testified that the advances were discouraged and unwelcome.

8. The unwanted sexual advances by Ms. Benvenuti towards Baker did not stop after Baker asked Ms. Benvenuti to stop "touching her."

9. Mr. David B. Larison, an employee who worked at DVR from August 1985 until May 1988, testified that Ms. Benvenuti touched Baker in a sexual manner on the "but" [sic] and that the touching appeared to be unwelcome.

10. Mrs. Liz Olds-Lucero, an employee who worked at DVR from 1981 until May 2, 1992, testified that Ms. Benvenuti pinched Baker on the "but" [sic] and that Ms. Benvenuti "sat real close to her (Baker)." Ms. Olds-Lucero further testified that the pinching was unwelcome.

11. Ms. Betty Hatfield, an employee who worked for DVR from June 1986 and is currently employed by DVR, testified that Ms. Benvenuti "patted her (Baker) on the rear-end." Ms. Hatfield heard Baker ask Ms. Benvenuti to "stop that."

12. It was widely known that Ms. Benvenuti used abusive language, including expletives, in the work place towards employees.

13. Baker received exemplary evaluations ("greatly surpassed") from March 25, 1985 until the present. Baker has never received a substandard evaluation as a result of the sexual advances towards her by Ms. Benvenuti.

14. Ms. Benvenuti evaluated Baker from November 26, 1986 until February 6, 1990.

15. On or around December 28, 1989, Baker complained to Ms. Judy Fisher, Ms. Benvenuti's supervisor, about the abusive work environment at DVR.

16. Ms. Fisher did not take any action against Ms. Benvenuti for Ms. Benvenuti's use of abusive language in the work place.

17. On January 10, 1990, Ms. Fisher reprimanded, in writing, Baker for insubordination towards Ms. Benvenuti. Ms. Fisher's decision to reprimand Baker came after a heated discussion between Ms. Benvenuti and Baker. Ms. Benvenuti claimed Baker had falsified work sheets. In response to the allegations against Baker, Baker shouted "put up or shut up."

18. On January 30, 1990, Baker filed a grievance against Ms. Benvenuti, requesting that Ms. Benvenuti refrain from "use of profanity" and that Baker's personnel file be purged of the written reprimand.

19. On March 17, 1990, Mr. Ross E. Sweat, Director of DVR, reassigned Baker to the word processing unit at DVR. Baker received the same pay as she did in her previous job classification. Baker accepted the reassignment and did not file a grievance in protest of the transfer.

20. On March 20, 1990, Baker filed a charge of sexual discrimination/harassment with DVR.

21. On March 22, 1990, Mr. Sweat responded to Baker's grievance. Mr. Sweat concluded that the work sheets had never been falsified and directed that Baker's record be "expunged" of the written reprimand. Mr. Sweat "admonished" Ms. Benvenuti for using profanity in the work place.

22. In response to the sexual harassment claim filed by Baker, Mr. Sweat directed that Ms. Pauline Romero, the equal employment affirmative action coordinator conduct an investigation to determine whether the allegations by Baker were true.

23. Ms. Romero conducted an investigation and issued a report on April 2, 1990, with her findings. Ms. Romero spoke with 17 witnesses, Baker and Ms. Benvenuti, and concluded that:

> Ms. Benvenuti did indeed sexually harassment [sic] Ms. Baker in as much as she made physical advances of a sexual nature by grabbing Ms. Baker and/or patting her on the buttocks, touching, and kissing Ms. Baker on the neck. Ms. Benvenuti also made verbal comments regarding Ms. Baker's use of sweaters and how nice she looked in them.

24. Ms. Romero's report also concluded that at least on one other occasion another employee, Ms. Stephanie Blackwell, had been sexually harassed by Ms. Benvenuti, and that Ms. Fisher was aware of the incident.

25. Ms. Benvenuti has never been transferred to another position. She received a written reprimand from Mr. Sweat only after Ms. Romero's report to Mr. Sweat.

26. The sexual advances towards Baker by Ms. Benvenuti occurred during working hours and it was widely known by the staff that Ms. Benvenuti was making sexual advances towards Baker.

27. Further Ms. Fisher knew prior to the grievance filed by Baker that Ms. Benvenuti had sexually harassed another employee, Ms. Blackwell.

Ms. Fisher took no measures to reprimand Ms. Benvenuti for sexually harassing Ms. Blackwell or Baker.

28. Ms. Fisher admitted to Ms. Romero that she was aware of Ms. Benvenuti's use of profanity towards employees she supervised. Ms. Fisher has never reprimanded Ms. Benvenuti for the use of inappropriate language in the work place.

29. Baker testified that she had applied for a position as administrative secretary in late 1990 (after she filed her sexual harassment claim) by asking Ms. Emily Griego, personnel officer for DVR, to place her on the list for administrative secretary and by giving Ms. Griego her application for employment. Ms. Griego testified that she did not remember talking to Baker about placing Baker on the list for administrative secretary. Further Baker testified that she did not take any further steps to make sure she was on the list of qualified applicants. Baker did not introduce evidence to support her claim that she was qualified or was more qualified for the position of administrative secretary, a position which was two (2) grades higher than her present position. Ms. Joyce Cox was eventually hired for that position.

30. Baker testified that DVR has taken few remedial actions since Baker filed her complaint. Since filing the sexual harassment claim, Baker overheard a female supervisor, Ms. Mary Fisher, laughing about the topic of sexual harassment. Since filing the complaint, DVR has conducted sexual harassment training only for the supervisors and not all of its employees as it contended at the hearing.

31. Baker has suffered emotional distress as a direct and proximate result of the sexual harassment by Ms. Benvenuti.

32. Baker became physically ill as a result of the work environment at DVR. Her medical expenses, including sick leave, amount to $3257.19. Baker incurred medical expenses of $653.04, including $84.00 for prescribed medication (after subtracting the insurance co payment); $30.00 for visits to doctors (after subtracting the insurance co payment); $445.00 for mental health counseling (after subtracting the insurance co payment); and $94.04 in related costs for mileage.

Baker's hourly wage at DVR is $8.50 per hour. Baker used approximately 315.25 hours of sick leave to attend counseling seasons [sic] and recuperate from the work environment at DVR, amounting to $2604.15 in lost sick leave.

33. Baker used 40 hours of annual leave to prepare for the hearing which is the subject matter herein, at a cost of $340.00 (40 hours × $8.50 per hour) in annual leave.

34. Baker retained an attorney to defend her lawsuit against DVR.

35. The attorney for Baker submitted an affidavit in the amount $14,057.63, including $13,461.98 in attorney's fees and $595.65 in costs.

Conclusions of Law

1. The New Mexico Human Rights Commission has jurisdiction over the parties and the subject matter herein.

2. At the time the allegations arose, Baker was an employee of DVR as defined in NMSA 1978, §28-1-2 (E) (Repl. Pamp. 1991).

3. DVR is an employer as defined in NMSA 1978, §28-1-2 (B) (Repl. Pamp. 1991).

4. Ms. Benvenuti is an employer as defined by §28-1-2 (B) (Repl. Pamp. 1991), which states that an employer is "any person acting for any employer." Ms. Benvenuti was acting for DVR with DVR's full consent and knowledge when Ms. Benvenuti used profanity in the work place and sexually harassed Baker and at least one other employee, Ms. Blackwell. The sexual harassment took place during working hours in full view of the staff and Ms. Fisher. Ms. Benvenuti was acting for DVR and within scope of her employment when she sexually harassed Baker. *See Hirschfeld v. New Mexico Corrections Dept.,* 916 F. 2d 572 (10th Cir. 1990).

5. Under *Carrero v. New York City Housing Authority,* 668 F. Supp. 196 (S.D.N.Y. 1987), *aff'd in part, rev'd in part,* 890 F. 2d 569 (2nd Cir. 1989), where an employer fails to investigate a charge, and further incidents of harassment occur, then the employer is liable for the actions of its employees. DVR knew or should have known about Ms. Benvenuti's inappropriate sexual conduct in the work place. Ms. Fisher knew that Ms. Benvenuti used profanity in the work place and knew that Ms. Benvenuti had sexually harassed Ms. Blackwell. DVR failed to investigate Ms. Blackwell's charge and did not investigate Baker's charge until Baker filed a "formal complaint" with DVR.

6. Ms. Benvenuti created a "hostile work environment" by making sexual unwanted advances towards Baker and by making sexual verbal comments to Baker in violation of NMSA 1978, §28-1-7 (A) (Repl. Pamp. 1991). *See Meritor Savings Bank, FSB v. Vinson,* 477 U.S. 57 (1986). Baker did not suffer a tangible job detriment as a result of the sexual harassment.

The preponderance of the evidence shows that Ms. Benvenuti repeatedly made unwanted sexual advances towards Baker during working hours in full view of the staff. Further that Ms. Fisher knew and DVR knew or should have known that Ms. Benvenuti was making unwanted sexual advances towards Baker. Ms. Fisher further knew that Ms. Benvenuti used profanity in the work place towards employees Ms. Benvenuti supervised. Ms. Fisher took no remedial steps to correct or alleviate the problem at DVR.

7. Baker was damaged as a result of DVR's discriminatory practices and incurred reasonable attorney's fees.

8. Under the Human Rights Act, NMSA 1978, §28-1-11 (E) (Repl. Pamp. 1991), Baker is entitled to receive actual damages and attorney's fees.

9. The Human Rights Commission shall only award *actual damages.* NMSA 1978, §28-1-11 (E) (Repl. Pamp. 1991). While the panel ruled that it customarily does not award damages for emotional distress, upon reconsideration the panel reverses its decision not to award damages for emotional distress. The Human Rights Commission has the authority to award damages for emotional distress. In *Behrmann v. Phototron Corp.,* 110 N.M. 323, 795 P. 2d 1015 (1990), the court held that compensatory and actual damages are synonymous. Compensatory damages include damages for pain and suffering. *See Alber v. Nolle,* 98 N.M. 100, 645 P. 2d 456 (1982). Baker's actual damages are **$17,985.95**, i.e., sick and annual leave $2944.15, medical expenses $653.04 and $14,388.76 for emotional distress.

10. Under the Human Rights Act, NMSA 1978, §28-1-11 (E) (Repl. Pamp. 1991), DVR shall pay Baker's attorney's fees and costs in the amount of **$14,057.63.**

11. Baker is not entitled to received [sic] any compensation related to the lost job opportunity. Those damages are too speculative. Further, Baker failed to prove by a preponderance of the evidence that she was qualified for the position of administrative secretary and even if she was on the list of applicants that she was more qualified than Ms. Cox.

Order

The New Mexico Human Rights Commission concludes that Baker proved by a preponderance of the evidence that Ms. Benvenuti made unwelcomed sexual advances towards Baker and used profanity in the work place creating a "hostile work environment" for Baker. Further that DVR knew or should have known that Ms. Benvenuti created a "hostile work environment" in which Baker was unable to do her job. Ms. Benvenuti was acting within the scope of employment at the time of the harassment.

IT IS THEREFORE ORDERED that Baker be awarded actual damages in the amount of **$17,985.95.**

IT IS FURTHER ORDERED that DVR be responsible for Baker's attorney's fees and costs in the amount of $14,057.63.

NEW MEXICO HUMAN RIGHTS COMMISSION

By: [signed] Joe D. Marquez _____
Entered on: 08-28-1992

Appendix B: Glossary

Biological Sex: The anatomical sex of a person at birth: male or female.

Case Law: Decisions made by courts, often published and relied upon as precedent in future cases.

Common Law: The long-standing customs and principles of our civilization, some of which are explicitly recognized in case law.

Compensatory Damages: Damages awarded by a court to compensate a victim for actual loss resulting from the illegal conduct of another.

Constructive Discharge: A type of Title VII case in which the employee alleges the working conditions to which he or she was subjected were so intolerable that any reasonable person would have quit under the circumstances.

Gender: Men and women are socialized to be either masculine or feminine. The term *gender* is often used to refer to the biological sex of a party by the courts.

Harasser: In this book, the term is generally used to refer to those whom victims perceive as engaging in sexual harassment.

Hostile Work Environment Sexual Harassment: A type of Title VII claim in which the employee alleges he or she was subjected to unwelcome conduct labeled sexual harassment, generally because of his or her sex, which was sufficiently severe or pervasive to create an abusive or hostile working environment.

Organizational Power: The use of one's position in an organization to cause another to act in accordance with one's wishes.

Power: The ability to cause another to act in accordance with one's wishes. Power is attributed or inferred and cannot be measured or observed.

Prima Facie Case: A case sufficient to prove the matter sought to be proved in the absence of contradictory evidence.

Punitive Damages: Damages awarded by a court for the purpose of punishing the offender rather than making the victim whole.

Quid Pro Quo Sexual Harassment: A type of Title VII claim in which an employee alleges that submission to sexual advances or other forms of conduct labeled sexual harassment was made a condition of continued employment, promotion, or other job benefits.

Respondeat Superior: A legal doctrine which holds an employer liable for the wrongful conduct of its employees toward those to whom the employer owes a duty, when the employee is acting in the course of his or her employment.

Retaliatory Discharge: A type of Title VII claim in which the employee alleges he or she was retaliated against for complaining about discrimination or assisting others in complaining about discrimination prohibited by Title VII.

Sexual Harassment: A broad label given to conduct which includes most normal dating and courting behavior, most sex-related crimes against women, and much conduct in between the two. This term tells us little about behavior.

Sexual Power: The ability to use sex to cause another to act in accordance with one's wishes. Sexual power often involves the use of sex to obtain money, status, or information.

Title VII: Title VII of the Civil Rights Act of 1964, as amended by the Civil Rights Act of 1991, is a federal law which prohibits employers from discriminating against employees because of their sex.

Tort: A private or civil injury or wrong, other than a breach of contract, in which the plaintiff argues that the defendant breached a duty owed the plaintiff and the breach caused the plaintiff to suffer damages.

Victim: In this book, the term is generally used to refer to those who perceive themselves as subjected to sexual harassment.

Notes

Introduction

1. *See generally,* Annot., *Cause of Action for Clergy Malpractice,* 75 A.L.R. 4th 750; Annot., *Liability of Religious Association for Damages for Intentionally Tortious Conduct in Recruitment, Indoctrination, or Related Activity,* 40 A.L.R. 4th 1062; Annot., "Liability for Sexual Abuse: The Anomalous Immunity of Churches," *Law and Equality,* Vol. 9, No. 1, pp. 133-61; *Destefano v. Grabrian,* 763 P.2d 275 (Colo. 1988).

2. 232 Cal. Rptr. 685 (Cal. App. 2 Dist. 1986). *See also Jeffrey Scott E. v. Central Baptist Church,* 243 Cal. Rptr. 128 (Cal. App. 4 Dist. 1988) (sexual abuse by Sunday school teacher found to be independent self-serving acts for which church could not be held liable).

3. *See, e.g., Byrd v. Faber,* 565 N.E.2d 584 (Ohio 1991); *Miller v. Everett,* 576 So.2d 1162 (La. App. 3 Cir. 1991); *Broderick v. King's Way Assembly of God,* 808 P.2d 1211 (Alaska 1991).

4. *Haehn v. City of Hoisington,* 702 F. Supp. 1526 (D. Kan. 1988) (police officer); *Mitchell v. Hutchings,* 116 F.R.D. 481 (D. Utah 1987) (police officer); *Scott v. City of Overland Park,* 595 F. Supp. 520 (D. Kan. 1984) (police officer); *Henson v. City of Dundee,* 682 F.2d 897 (11th Cir. 1982) (police dispatcher); *Brown v. City of Guthrie,* 22 FEP Cases (BNA) 1627 (W.D. Okl. 1980) (police meter attendant); *Roybal v. City of Albuquerque,* 653 F. Supp. 102 (D.N.M. 1986) (city police department employee); *Arnold v. City of Seminole, Okl.,* 614 F. Supp. 853 (D.C. Okl. 1985) (city police officer); *Watts v. New York City Police Dept.,* 724 F. Supp. 99 (S.D.N.Y. 1989) (probationary police officer attending police academy); *Collins v. City of San Diego,* 841 F.2d 337 (9th Cir. 1988) (city police officer); *Kelsey-Andrews v. City of Philadelphia,* 713 F. Supp. 760 (E.D. Pa. 1989), *aff'd in part, rev'd in part, Andrews v. City of Philadelphia,* 895 F.2d 1469 (3d Cir. 1990) (members of police accident investigation division); *Sanchez v. City of Miami Beach,* 720 F. Supp. 974 (S.D. Fla. 1989) (city police officer); *Sapp v. City of Warner Robins,* 655 F. Supp. 1043 (M.D. Ga. 1987) (city police officer); *Dwyer v. Smith,* 867 F.2d 184 (4th Cir. 1989) (city police officer); *Froyd v. Cook,* 681 F. Supp. 669 (E.D. Cal. 1988) (police dispatcher).

5. *Simmons v. Lyons,* 746 F.2d 265 (5th Cir. 1984) (sheriff's employees); *Gray v. Lacke,* 885 F.2d 399 (7th Cir. 1989) (sheriff's communications officer).

6. *Vermett v. Hough,* 627 F. Supp. 587 (W.D. Mich. 1986) (state police officer).

7. *Bennett v. New York City Dept. of Corrections,* 705 F. Supp. 979 (S.D.N.Y. 1989) (city corrections officer).

8. *Carter v. Sedgwick County, Kan.,* 705 F. Supp. 1474 (D. Kan. 1988) (office associate at county corrections department).

9. *Hirschfeld v. New Mexico Corrections Dept.,* 916 F.2d 572 (10th Cir. 1990) (typist at medium security prison); *Valerio v. Dahlberg,* 716 F. Supp. 1031 (S.D. Ohio 1988) (technical typist for state corrections department); *Eastwood v. Dept. of Corrections of State of Okl.,* 846 F.2d 627 (10th Cir. 1988) (state corrections employee); *Minteer v. Auger,* 844 F.2d 569 (8th Cir. 1988) (state prison guard).

Sexual harassment cases have also been filed by employees of organizations providing medical and mental health services in state prisons. *See, e.g., Porras v. Montefiore Medical Center,* 742 F. Supp. 120 (S.D.N.Y. 1990).

Federal corrections employees have also sued for sexual harassment. *Bundy v. Jackson,* 641 F.2d 934 (D.C. Cir. 1981) (vocational rehabilitation specialist at federal department of corrections).

1. The Rise of Sexual Harassment as a Social Issue: 1964–1980

1. *Meritor Sav. Bank, FSB v. Vinson,* 477 U.S. 57, 106 S. Ct. 2399, 2404, 91 L.Ed.2d 49 (1986). *See also* Freeman 1991.

2. Title 42 U.S.C. Section 2000e-2(a). Although the original purpose of Title VII was to provide women with equal access to job opportunities, Title VII litigation is now used primarily as a method to challenge wrongful discharges from employment (Donohue and Siegelman 1991).

3. For purposes of Title VII, an *employer* is "a person engaged in an industry affecting commerce who has fifteen or more employees for each working day in each of twenty or more calendar weeks in the current or preceding calendar year, and any agent of such a person," with some exceptions. Title 42 U.S.C. Section 2000e(b).

4. Title 42 U.S.C. Section 2000e-3(a).

5. *See Roybal v. City of Albuquerque,* 653 F. Supp. 102, 104 (D.N.M. 1986).

6. 42 U.S.C. 2000e-16(a).

7. 42 U.S.C. 2000e-5(a) and 2000e-16(b).

8. To the extent rape, attempted rape, and other sexual misconduct which had been labeled criminal prior to the 1970s were later renamed sexual harassment, sexual harassment was recognized as a social problem prior to the 1970s. It has been argued that sexual assault in the workplace is a serious problem (Schneider 1991). Title VII can be seen as protecting the interests of those in power by creating a civil remedy for acts which were previously, and for poor people still are, considered criminal in nature.

9. Others have argued that "not only were unions absent from the forefront of claims-making activities, but they have not subsequently shown much support" (Weeks et al. 1986: 437).

10. Speakouts, a tactic also used in the women's liberation movement during the 1960s and early 1970s, are large gatherings of people where people share their experiences. By gathering people with shared problems together to talk about them, speakouts can result in the problem being seen as a class problem.

11. To support these claims, many studies were conducted of groups of people not representative of the general population (convenience samples and random

sampling within selected environments), a wide variety of operational definitions of sexual harassment were used, and important information was ignored in analyzing the data (Gillespie and Leffler 1987).

12. 390 F. Supp. 161 (D. Ariz. 1975).

13. *Id*. at 163.

14. 413 F. Supp. 654 (D.D.C. 1976).

15. *Id*. at 655–56.

16. *Id*. at 656.

17. *Id*. at 657.

18. *Id*. at 658.

19. *Id*. at 659.

20. *Williams v. Bell,* 587 F.2d 1240 (D.C. Cir. 1978).

21. *Burns v. Terre Haute Regional Hospital,* 581 F. Supp. 1301, 1308 (S.D. Ind. 1983); *Boyd v. James S. Hayes Living Health Care Agency,* 671 F. Supp. 1155, 1164–67 (W.D. Tenn. 1987); *Silverberg v. Baxter Healthcare Corp.,* 52 FEP Cases (BNA) 1848, 1852–54 (N.D. Ill. 1990).

22. *DeCintio v. Westchester County Medical,* 807 F.2d 304 (2nd Cir. 1986). The EEOC regulations, however, provide that "where employment opportunities or benefits are granted because of an individual's submission to the employer's sexual advances or requests for sexual favors, the employer may be held liable for unlawful sex discrimination against other persons who were qualified for but denied that employment opportunity or benefit." 29 C.F.R. 1604.11(g).

23. *Meritor Sav. Bank, FSB v. Vinson,* 477 U.S. 57, 106 S. Ct. 2399, 91 L. Ed. 2d 49 (1986); 29 C.F.R. 1604.11(a)(3); *Boczar v. Manatee Hospitals,* 52 FEP Cases (BNA) 321, 324–25 (M.D. Fla. 1990).

24. Popular media attention of sexual harassment was not surprising since "circulation and viewership are increased by sensationalism, and sexual harassment stories exhibit several ingredients that make them appealing for this purpose, i.e., they may be perceived as titillating, controversial, or humorous" (Weeks et al. 1986: 441).

25. The AASC and WWI relied on donations from members and supporters to fund their activities. In 1984 the AASC ceased operations due to budget constraints. By 1986, the WWI had to significantly decrease its activities due to lack of funding (Weeks et al. 1986).

26. The women to whom the survey was sent were randomly selected out of a phone book and worked for different firms.

27. Many studies appear to infer erroneously that when a female reports sexual harassment in a survey, the initiator is male.

28. In 1986, it was asserted that the enactment of the EEOC guidelines was probably "the single most important event" in the process of legitimizing sexual harassment as a social issue (Weeks et al. 1986: 444).

29. *Morgan v. Massachusetts General Hosp.,* 901 F.2d 186, 192 (1st Cir. 1990). Most social sciences studies fail to make an effort to distinguish between what constitutes sexual harassment in the opinion of the respondents and what constitutes sexual harassment prohibited by Title VII. Grieco's (1987) survey study of nurses (LPNs and RNs) is an exception. Grieco (1987: 264) found that while reports of "sexual harassment" were widespread, "legal violations were relatively infrequent."

30. 29 C.F.R. 1604.11(a) (1990).

31. 29 C.F.R. 1604.11(b) (1990).

32. 29 C.F.R. 1604.11(c) (1990).

33. 29 C.F.R. 1604.11(d) (1990).

34. 29 C.F.R. 1604.11(e) (1990). In considering sexual harassment by nonemployees, "the Commission will consider the extent of the employer's control and any other legal responsibility which the employer may have with respect to the conduct of such nonemployees." *Id.*

35. 29 C.F.R. 1604.11(f) (1990).

36. *Id.*

37. *Kestenbaum v. Pennzoil Co.,* 108 N.M. 20, 766 P.2d 280 (1989).

38. *Id.*

39. *Lawson v. Boeing Co.,* 58 Wash. App. 261, 792 P.2d 545 (Wash. App. 1990).

2. U.S. Merit Systems Protection Board Studies

1. The OPM definition of sexual harassment used by the Merit Systems Protection Board: "deliberate or repeated unsolicited verbal comments, gestures or physical contact of a sexual nature which are unwelcome" (USMSPB 1981: E-8).

2. The Merit Systems Protection Board cautioned that "in reading this report and interpreting the data, some issues should be kept in mind. First, the incidence data is based upon the number of respondents who personally indicated that they had received what they believed to be uninvited and unwanted sexual attention. Thus, the method of identifying victims for this report involved a self-defining process on the part of the respondents" (USMSPB 1981: 23).

3. The 1988 Merit Systems Protection Board report cautioned: "Since the EEOC guidelines were issued, a body of legal precedents, including a 1986 Supreme Court decision, has provided legal clarification as to what constitutes sexual harassment. For purposes of this report, however, the Board relies upon the expressed views of Federal employees for its definition. If a respondent to the Board's survey stated that he or she had received uninvited or unwanted sexual attention during the preceding 24 months, that was counted as an incident of sexual harassment even though not every incident, if fully investigated, would necessarily meet the legal definition of sexual harassment" (USMSPB 1988: 2).

4. The sexual orientation of the respondents is unknown.

5. The sex of the harasser was not requested in the 1987 survey (USMSPB 1988: 20).

6. This finding suggests that not all respondents who reported being subjected to behavior labeled sexual harassment by the researchers perceived the conduct as constituting sexual harassment, i.e., unwanted or uninvited behavior.

7. Title VII generally provides no remedy for false allegations of sexual harassment.

8. Title VII does not require proof that the person engaging in the behavior intended to be offensive.

3. Supreme Court Decisions and Recent Events in Congress

1. 477 U.S. 57, 106 S. Ct. 2399, 91 L. Ed. 2d 49 (1986).

2. *Id.,* 106 S. Ct. at 2402.

3. *Id.*

4. *Id.*

5. *Id.* at 2405, *quoting Henson v. City of Dundee,* 682 F. 2d 897, 904 (11th

Cir. 1982). The EEOC regulations provide that when "determining whether alleged conduct constitutes sexual harassment, the Commission will look at the record as a whole and at the totality of the circumstances, such as the nature of the sexual advances and the context in which the alleged incidents occurred. The determination of the legality of a particular action will be made from the facts, on a case by case basis." 29 C.F.R. 1604.11(b) (1990).

6. *Meritor,* 106 S. Ct. at 2406.

7. *Id.*

8. *Id.*

9. *Id.* at 2406–7.

10. *Id.* at 2408.

11. The fact that Thomas was poor, to the extent he was, and made it to the Supreme Court may encourage other poor people to work hard.

12. Sexual harassment is not an issue limited to the relationship between men and women, and is not a problem which is limited to the workplace. Both men and women have been sexually harassed in the workplace (USMSPB 1981; USMSPB 1988). One big difference between men and women is that many men still perceive sexual harassment as a private problem requiring a private solution. Many believe it is more acceptable for a woman to complain about sexual harassment than it is for a man to do so. This may change as more women begin to supervise men.

13. Melvin Anchell (1992: 41) has defined *pseudology* as "a psychological phenomenon (seen especially in women patients) which consists of pathological lying in speech or writing. The lies consist of elaborate and often fantastic accounts of a patient's sensual or other exploits which are completely false but which the patient believes are true."

14. The substance of the video is unknown, and therefore whether the conduct of the teaching assistant in question would constitute sexual harassment under Title VII is unknown.

15. This study suggests that an employee training program which attaches the label sexual harassment to conduct perceived as "rude," "unprofessional," or "demeaning" may increase the number of allegations of harassment made by female employees.

16. Punitive damages cannot, however, be awarded against a government agency or political subdivision under the 1991 Act.

17. *See, e.g., Coriz by and Through Coriz v. Martinez,* 915 F. 2d 1469 (10th Cir. 1990); *Garcia by Garcia v. Miera,* 817 F. 2d 650 (10th Cir. 1987).

18. Depending upon the age of the student, the sexual abuse of students may constitute child sexual abuse under state criminal laws.

19. *Cannon v. University of Chicago,* 441 U.S. 677, 99 S. Ct. 1946, 60 L. Ed. 2d 560 (1979).

20. *North Haven Bd. of Ed. v. Bell,* 456 U.S. 512, 102 S. Ct. 1912, 72 L. Ed. 2d 299 (1982).

21. 112 S. Ct. 1028 (1992).

22. *Id.* at 1031.

23. *Franklin v. Gwinnett Cty. Public Schools,* 911 F. 2d 617 (11th Cir. 1985).

24. *Franklin v. Gwinnett County Public Schools,* 112 S. Ct. 1028, 1038 (1992).

25. For a discussion of when a person acts under color of state law, *see West v. Atkins,* 108 S. Ct. 2250 (1988); *Slater v. Bangor Communications,* 58 FEP Cases (BNA) 1486 (D. Maine 1992) (state regulation of private industry insufficient).

26. A violation of Title VII is insufficient, in itself, to support a claim under Section 1983.

27. For a discussion of gender discrimination as a violation of the Fourteenth Amendment, *see Forester v. White,* 108 S. Ct. 538 (1988), in which the court held a state court judge does not have absolute immunity from suit under Section 1983 for his decision to demote and dismiss a court probation officer.

28. 782 F. Supp. 1573 (S.D. Ohio 1990).

29. *Id.* at 1579.

30. *Memphis Community School Dist. v. Stachura,* 106 S. Ct. 2537 (1986).

31. *Id.* Compensatory damages must be obtained before punitive damages can be awarded.

32. The Merit Systems Protection Board surveys indicate that the majority of both male and female respondents thought that sexual remarks, suggestive looks, pressure for sexual favors and dates, letters and calls, and deliberate touching can constitute sexual harassment when that conduct is uninvited or unwelcome.

4. Natural Attraction as a Cause of Sexual Harassment

1. *Miller v. Bank of America,* 418 F. Supp. 233 (N.D. Cal. 1976), *rev'd,* 600 F. 2d 211 (9th Cir. 1979).

2. *Tomkins v. Public Service Elec. & Gas Co.,* 422 F. Supp. 553, 557 (D.N.J. 1976), *rev'd,* 568 F. 2d 1044 (3d Cir. 1977).

3. 422 F. Supp. at 556.

4. Researchers have inquired into the notion that sexual harassment results from the natural attraction between people in the workplace, sometimes referred to as the natural or biological model (Tangri et al. 1982). The natural or biological model focuses on the natural motivation of the harasser (Tangri et al. 1982). MacKinnon (1979: 91) noted that "not all women experience sexual attraction to all men, not all men to all women."

5. 29 C.F.R. 1604.11(g) (1990).

6. 975 F. 2d 588 (9th Cir. 1992).

7. *Id.* at 590.

8. *Id.*

9. 807 F. 2d 304 (2d Cir. 1986).

10. *Id.* at 306–7.

11. 569 A. 2d 793, 117 N.J. 539 (1990).

12. *Id.*

13. The central issue in *Erickson* was intentional sex discrimination rather than sexual harassment.

14. *Erickson,* 569 A. 2d at 801.

15. *Id.* at 802.

16. 904 F. 2d 853 (3d Cir. 1990).

17. *Id.* at 855.

18. *Id.* at 861.

19. *Id.*

20. *Id.* at 862.

21. *Id.*

22. *Id.* at 861. *See also Nicolo v. Citibank New York State, N.A.,* 554 N.Y.S. 2d 795 (Sup. 1990).

23. 710 F. Supp. 328 (N.D. Ga. 1988).

24. *Id.* at 331. *See also Nix v. WLCY Radio/Rahall Communications,* 738 F.

2d 1181, 1187 (11th Cir. 1984) ("The employer may fire an employee for a good reason, a bad reason, a reason based on erroneous facts, or for no reason at all, as long as its action is not for a discriminatory reason").

25. *Id.* at 331. *See also DeCintio v. Westchester County Medical Center,* 807 F. 2d 304, 306-7 (2d Cir. 1986) ("The proscribed differentiation under Title VII ... must be a distinction based on a person's sex, not on his or her sexual affiliations").

26. 908 F. 2d 902 (11th Cir. 1990).

27. 794 F. 2d 602, 610 (10th Cir. 1986).

28. *Id.* at 610. *See also DeCintio v. Westchester County Medical Center,* 807 F. 2d 304, 307 (2d Cir. 1986) ("We can adduce no justification for defining 'sex,' for Title VII purposes, so broadly as to include an ongoing, voluntary, romantic engagement").

5. Power

1. Sexual harassment is a problem in the workplace for men and women alike. It is a problem which needs to be studied in much more depth than in the past. Terms used in studies and in the literature need to be developed or operationally defined so that they can be objectively measured.

2. *Dominguez v. Stone,* 97 N.M. 211, 213, 638 P. 2d 423 (Ct. App. 1981), *citing Castaneda v. Partida,* 430 U.S. 482, 97 S. Ct. 1272, 51 L. Ed. 2d 498 (1977).

3. Lesbians exist in substantial numbers in America: "In 1982 it was estimated that there were over two million lesbian mothers in the United States. . . . An estimated 10% of women in the United States are lesbians" (DiLapi 1989: 103).

4. 30 FEP Cases (BNA) 223 (N.D. Ill. 1980).

5. "A nationwide telephone poll by Gordon S. Black Corp. of 758 adults conducted 6-9 p.m. EDT Sunday. The poll has a margin of error of 3.5%. A total of 204 blacks were interviewed for comparisons between blacks and whites, with the poll weighted to accurately represent the percentage of blacks nationwide" (*USA Today,* October 14, 1991: 2A).

6. Radical feminism may have been one of the most successful negative campaigns in American history.

7. "Sexual sadism is a persistent pattern of becoming sexually excited in response to another's suffering" (Hazelwood et al. 1992: 12).

8. *Tomkins v. Public Service Elec. & Gas Co.,* 422 F. Supp. 553, 556 (D.N.J. 1976).

9. For example, norms, sex roles, rules about behavior, home-work conflict, work roles, shared tasks, shared goals, continuity, hours of work, biological differences between men and women, etc.

10. *See Barlow v. Northwestern Memorial Hosp.,* 30 FEP Cases (BNA) 223 (N.D. Ill. 1980).

11. *Wright v. Methodist Youth Services, Inc.,* 511 F. Supp. 307 (N.D. Ill. 1981).

12. *Huebschen v. Dept. of Health and Social Services,* 716 F. 2d 1167 (7th Cir. 1983); Annot., *Sexual Advances by Employee's Superior as Sex Discrimination Within Title VII of Civil Rights Act of 1964, as Amended (42 USCS §§ 2000e et seq.),* 46 A.L.R. Fed 224 (1980).

13. Because it is presumed that women have an equal opportunity to work,

women may be less likely to receive alimony or may receive less in child support judgments, resulting in their being forced into the labor market when they would have preferred to stay home and raise their children.

14. References to page numbers are to the *Marx-Engels Reader,* where Marx's work is reprinted.

15. *Freeman v. Continental Technical Services, Inc.,* 710 F. Supp. 328 (N.D. Ga. 1988); *DeCintio v. Westchester County Medical,* 807 F. 2d 304 (2d Cir. 1986). *See also Polk v. Pollard,* 539 So. 2d 675 (La. App. 3 Cir. 1989) (construing Louisiana antidiscrimination statute); *Erickson v. Marsh & McLennan Co.,* 569 A. 2d 793, 117 N.J. 539 (1990) (construing New Jersey antidiscrimination statute); *Nicolo v. Citibank New York State, N.A.,* 554 N.Y.S. 2d 795 (Sup. 1990).

16. *Drinkwater v. Union Carbide Corp.,* 904 F. 2d 853 (3d Cir. 1990); *Miller v. Aluminum Co. of America,* 679 F. Supp. 495 (W.D. Pa. 1988); *Candelore v. Clark County Sanitation Dist.,* 752 F. Supp. 956 (D. Nev. 1990).

6. The Process of Evaluating Sexual Harassment Claims

1. Are rape and suggestive looks similar enough to be lumped into the same category and treated alike? The conduct labeled sexual harassment needs to be dissected and closely scrutinized.

2. Most research using survey data and interview data reports the views of people at this stage of the process.

3. *See, e.g., Sorlucco v. New York City Police Dept.,* 703 F. Supp. 1092 (S.D.N.Y. 1989).

4. *E.E.O.C. v. Commercial Office Products Co.,* 108 S. Ct. 1666 (1988).

5. *Id.*

6. *Id.* Federal law controls in determining whether an administrative claim is timely filed for pursuing a claim under Title VII.

7. *See Jensen v. Bd. of County Com'rs for Sedgwick County,* 636 F. Supp. 293 (D. Kan. 1986); *Jiron v. Sperry Rand Corp. (Sperry-Univac),* 423 F. Supp. 155 (D. Utah 1975).

8. *See Borumka v. Rocky Mountain Hosp.,* 599 F. Supp. 857 (D. Colo. 1984); *Gupta v. East Texas State University,* 654 F. 2d 411 (5th Cir. 1981).

9. *See Romero v. Union Pac. RR.,* 615 F. 2d 1303 (10th Cir. 1980).

10. *Hicks v. Gates Rubber Co.,* 928 F. 2d 966 (10th Cir. 1991).

11. *Jarrell v. United States Postal Service,* 753 F. 2d 1088 (D.C. Cir. 1985).

12. *Antoine v. United States Postal Service,* 781 F. 2d 433 (5th Cir. 1986) (sex and race discrimination).

13. *Cooper v. United States Postal Service,* 740 F. 2d 714 (9th Cir. 1984) (sex discrimination).

14. *See, e.g., Batson v. Kentucky,* 476 U.S. 79, 106 S. Ct. 1712, 90 L. Ed. 2d 69 (1986).

15. In *Ellison v. Brady,* 924 F. 2d 872, 879 fn. 11 (9th Cir. 1991), the court held that "where male employees allege that coworkers engage in conduct which creates a hostile environment, the appropriate victim's perspective would be that of a reasonable man."

16. *Id.* at 878, 879 (footnote omitted).

17. *Newsweek,* October 21, 1991b: 36.

18. *Id.*

7. The Process of Litigating a Sexual Harassment Case

1. *Scheuer v. Rhodes,* 416 U.S. 232, 236, 94 S. Ct. 1683, 40 L. Ed. 2d 90 (1974).

2. *Miree v. DeKalb County, Ga.,* 433 U.S. 25, 27 n. 2, 97 S. Ct. 2490, 2492 n. 2, 53 L. Ed. 2d 557 (1977). *See also Cruz v. Beto,* 405 U.S. 319, 322, 92 S. Ct. 1079, 1081, 31 L. Ed. 2d 263 (1972); *Papasan v. Allain,* 106 S. Ct. 2932, 2943 (1986).

3. *Scheuer v. Rhodes,* 416 U.S. 232, 236, 94 S. Ct. 1683, 40 L. Ed. 2d 90 (1974).

4. *Conley v. Gibson,* 355 U.S. 41, 78 S. Ct. 99, 102, 2 L. Ed. 2d 80 (1957) (footnote omitted).

5. *Henderson v. National R.R. Passenger Corp.,* 113 F.R.D. 502 (N.D. Ill. 1986).

6. *Oppenheimer Fund, Inc. v. Sanders,* 437 U.S. 340, 98 S. Ct. 2380, 57 L. Ed. 2d 253 (1978).

7. *Flanagan v. Travelers Ins. Co.,* 111 F.R.D. 42, 46 (W.D.N.Y. 1986).

8. *Morrison v. City & Cty. of Denver,* 80 F.R.D. 289, 292 (D. Colo. 1978).

9. *Henderson v. National R.R. Passenger Corp.,* 113 F.R.D. 502 (N.D. Ill. 1986).

10. *Flanagan v. Travelers Ins. Co.,* 111 F.R.D. 42 (W.D.N.Y. 1986); *Orbovich v. Macalester College,* 119 F.R.D. 411 (D. Minn. 1988).

11. *Cf. Rich v. Martin Marietta Corporation,* 522 F. 2d 333, 342–45 (10th Cir. 1975).

12. 621 F. 2d 1080 (10th Cir. 1980).

13. *Id.* at 1083.

14. *Cf. Henderson v. National R.R. Passenger Corp.,* 113 F.R.D. 502 (N.D. Ill. 1986).

15. 894 F. 2d 1150, 1156 (10th Cir. 1990).

16. *Id.*

17. *Hicks v. Gates Rubber Co.,* 833 F. 2d 1406, 1416 (10th Cir. 1987).

18. *Hicks v. Gates Rubber Co.,* 928 F. 2d 966 (10th Cir. 1991).

19. *Anderson v. Liberty Lobby, Inc.,* 477 U.S. 242, 106 S. Ct. 2505, 2509–10, 91 L. Ed. 2d 202 (1986).

20. *Adickes v. S. H. Kress and Company,* 398 U.S. 144, 90 S. Ct. 1598, 26 L. Ed. 2d 142 (1970).

21. *Anderson,* 106 S. Ct. at 2511.

22. *Celotex Corp. v. Catrett,* 106 S. Ct. 2548, 2553 (1986).

23. *Anderson,* 106 S. Ct. at 2511.

24. *Id.* at 2514.

8. Theories of Liability Under Title VII

1. 639 F. Supp. 1199 (D. Utah 1986).

2. *Id.* at 1204.

3. 833 F. 2d 1406 (10th Cir. 1987).

4. *Id.* at 1409.

5. *Id.* at 1410.

6. *Id.*

7. *Id.* at 1414.

8. *Kwiatkowski v. Bolger,* 39 FEP Cases (BNA) 1740 (N.D. Ill. 1985).

See also Young v. Sedgwick County, Kan., 660 F. Supp. 918 (D. Kan. 1987).

9. 106 S. Ct. 2399 (1986).

10. *Id.* at 2405.

11. *Rabidue v. Osceola Refining Co.,* 805 F. 2d 611 (6th Cir. 1986), *cert. denied,* 107 S. Ct. 1983 (1987).

12. 702 F. Supp. 1526 (D. Kan. 1988).

13. *Id.* at 1529.

14. *Hicks v. Gates Rubber Co.,* 928 F. 2d 966 (10th Cir. 1991).

15. *Wright v. Methodist Youth Services,* 511 F. Supp. 307 (N.D. Ill. 1981); *Joyner v. AAA Cooper Transp.,* 597 F. Supp. 537 (M.D. Ala. 1983), *aff'd,* 749 F. 2d 732 (11th Cir. 1984); *Barlow v. Northwestern Memorial Hospital,* 30 FEP Cases (BNA) 223 (N.D. Ill. 1980).

16. *Smith v. Liberty Mut. Ins. Co.,* 569 F. 2d 325 (5th Cir. 1978).

17. *Sommers v. Budget Marketing, Inc.,* 667 F. 2d 748 (8th Cir. 1982).

18. *Parton v. GTE North, Inc.,* 971 F. 2d 150 (8th Cir. 1992).

19. *Hendrix v. Fleming Companies,* 650 F. Supp. 301, 302 (W.D. Okla. 1986). *See also E.E.O.C. v. F & D Distributing, Inc.,* 728 F. 2d 1281 (10th Cir. 1984).

20. *Hendrix v. Fleming Companies,* 650 F. Supp. 301 (W.D. Okla. 1986).

21. *Id.*

22. 477 U.S. 57, 106 S. Ct. 2399, 2408, 91 L. Ed. 2d 49 (1986).

23. *Flowers v. Rego,* 691 F. Supp. 177 (E.D. Ark. 1988) (one without supervisory authority cannot be held liable under Title VII).

24. An employer's liability for hostile work environment sexual harassment is not limited to sexual harassment engaged in by its employees; 29 C.F.R. 1604.11 (e) states:

> An employer may also be responsible for the acts of non-employees, with respect to sexual harassment of employees in the workplace, where the employer (or its agents or supervisory employees) knows or should have known of the conduct and fails to take immediate and appropriate corrective action. In reviewing these cases the Commission will consider the extent of the employer's control and any other legal responsibility which the employer may have with respect to the conduct of such non-employees.

25. *Hicks v. Gates Rubber Co.,* 833 F. 2d 1406 (10th Cir. 1987).

26. 916 F. 2d 572 (10th Cir. 1990).

27. The inmate was placed in administrative detention.

28. The demotion was invalidated by the New Mexico State Personnel Board as a result of the loss or destruction of tapes of the interviews.

29. 916 F. 2d at 575. Both male and female correctional officers have reported being the targets of incidents in which an inmate used "his body or an object to touch the officer in an overtly sexual manner" (Light 1991).

30. *Hirschfeld,* 916 F. 2d 572 (10th Cir. 1990).

31. *Id.*

32. *Id.* at 577, *quoting, EEOC v. Hacienda Hotel,* 881 F. 2d 1504, 1516 (9th Cir. 1989). The EEOC regulations provide that "with respect to conduct between fellow employees, an employer is responsible for acts of sexual harassment in the workplace where the employer (or its agents or supervisory employees) knows or should have known of the conduct, unless it can show that it took immediate and appropriate corrective action." 29 C.F.R. 1604.11(d) (1990).

33. In *Meritor,* the Court rejected the employer's argument that "the mere

existence of a grievance procedure and a policy against discrimination, coupled with [the employer's] failure to invoke that procedure, must insulate [the employer] from liability" (106 S. Ct. at 2408). The *Meritor* Court pointed out that the policy before it did not specifically address sexual harassment and required the employee to report the incident to the employee's supervisor, the alleged harasser. The Court held the employer's position "might be substantially stronger if its procedures were better calculated to encourage victims of harassment to come forward" (*Id.*).

34. The *Hirschfeld* court held that "an employer notified that an employee is engaging in hostile work environment sexual harassment is not obligated to discharge or demote the harasser in every case. While there may be egregious cases where such action is the only option for an employer, in less serious cases a reprimand, brief suspension, or other remedial steps may be sufficient to remedy the situation" (916 F. 2d at 579, fn. 6).

35. 916 F. 2d at 579, *quoting Restatement (Second) of Agency,* Section 219 (2) (d) (1958).

36. *Hirschfeld,* 916 F. 2d at 579.

37. *Brown v. City of Guthrie,* 22 FEP Cases (BNA) 1627 (W.D. Okla. 1980).

38. *Hirschfeld,* 916 F. 2d at 580, *quoting Derr v. Gulf Oil Corp.,* 796 F. 2d 340, 343 (10th Cir. 1986).

39. *Id.*

40. *Downum v. City of Wichita, Kan.,* 675 F. Supp. 1566 (D. Kan. 1986).

41. *Babcock v. Frank,* 59 FEP Cases (BNA) 410, 411 (S.D.N.Y. 1992).

42. *See, e.g., Burrus v. United Telephone Co. of Kansas,* 683 F. 2d 339 (10th Cir. 1982).

43. *Zowayyed v. Lowen Co., Inc.,* 735 F. Supp. 1497 (D. Kan. 1990).

44. 58 FEP Cases (BNA) 310 (2d Cir. 1992).

45. *Id.* at 314.

46. *Sahs v. Amarillo Equity Investors, Inc.,* 702 F. Supp. 256, 259 (D. Colo. 1988).

47. *Pedreyra v. Cornell Prescription Pharmacies,* 465 F. Supp. 936, 948 (D. Colo. 1979).

9. *From Whose Eyes Do We Look?*

1. *See, e.g., Rabidue v. Osceola Refining Co.,* 805 F. 2d 611 (6th Cir. 1986).

2. 819 F. 2d 630 (6th Cir. 1987).,

3. *Babcock v. Frank,* 59 FEP Cases (BNA) 410 (S.D.N.Y. 1992).

4. Babcock refused to identify the male manager.

5. *Babcock v. Frank,* 59 FEP Cases (BNA) 410, 415 (S.D.N.Y. 1992).

6. *Id.* at 416.

7. *Id.* at 416–17.

8. *Id.* at 417.

9. *Id.* at 418.

10. *Id.*

11. 58 FEP Cases (BNA) 1171 (N.D. Ill. 1992).

12. *Id.* at 1177.

13. *See, e.g., Steele v. Offshore Shipbuilding, Inc.,* 867 F. 2d 1311, 1317 (11th Cir. 1989) (no constructive discharge where harassment ended 12 days before plaintiff resigned); *Benton v. Kroger,* 640 F. Supp. 1317 (S.D. Tex. 1986) (no constructive discharge where last act of harassment was one month before plaintiff resigned). *See also Stockett v. Tolin,* 58 FEP Cases (BNA) 1441, 1453 (S.D. Fla. 1992)

(resignation before harasser returns from trip supports constructive discharge where harasser tells employee, "I'll see you when I return" coupled with explicit ultimatum that plaintiff have sex or be fired).

14. *Saxton* at 1176.
15. 924 F. 2d 872 (9th Cir. 1991).
16. *Id.* at 873.
17. *Id.* at 874.
18. *Id.*
19. *Id.*
20. *Id.*
21. *Id.* (footnote omitted).
22. *Id.* at 874 fn. 1.
23. *Id.* at 874.
24. *Id.*
25. *Id.* at 875.
26. *Id.*
27. 924 F. 2d 872, 880 (9th Cir. 1991) (footnote omitted).
28. *Id.* at 879. The Ninth Circuit has asserted that the "reasonable woman standard does not establish a higher level of protection for women than men" (*Id.*).
29. *Id.* at 879 fn. 12.

10. Sexual Teasing, Jokes, Gifts, Remarks, or Questions

1. *See, e.g., Rabidue v. Osceola Ref. Co.,* 805 F. 2d 611 (6th Cir. 1986), *cert. denied,* 481 U.S. 1041 (1987) (coworker's references to women as "cunts" and "pussies" held permissible, given crude behavior of men at worksite).
2. *Robinson v. Jacksonville Shipyards, Inc.,* 760 F. Supp. 1486, 1525–27 (M.D. Fla. 1991) ("social context" defense inconsistent with Title VII's goal of opening the workplace to women).
3. *See, e.g., Sahs v. Amarillo Equity Investors, Inc.,* 702 F. Supp. 256, 260 (D. Colo. 1988).
4. *Id.* at 260.
5. 106 S. Ct. 2399 (1986).
6. *Id.* at 2406.
7. *Stockett v. Tolin,* 58 FEP Cases (BNA) 1441, 1453 (S.D. Fla. 1992).
8. 57 FEP Cases (BNA) 1373 (8th Cir. 1992).
9. As it relates to appearance management, the symbolic-interactionist perspective asserts that clothing provides the wearer with a sense of identity, that people manage their appearances as a method of creating their own realities, and that people interpret their situation in the world through symbols (Kaiser 1990).
10. *See Drinkwater v. Union Carbide Corp.,* 904 F. 2d 853, 863 (3d Cir. 1990).
11. *Id.; Miller v. Aluminum Co. of America,* 679 F. Supp. 495, 502 (W.D. Pa. 1988) (single comment about employee's breasts insufficient to create hostile working environment).
12. 647 F. Supp. 957 (E.D. Va. 1986).
13. *Id.* at 958.
14. *Marentett v. Michigan Host, Inc.,* 506 F. Supp. 909, 912 (E.D. Mich. 1980).
15. *Smolsky v. Consolidated Rail Corp.,* 785 F. Supp. 71, 73 (E.D. Pa. 1992).

16. 788 F. Supp. 1336 (S.D.N.Y. 1992).

17. *Id.* at 1349.

18. *See, e.g., Ebert v. Lamar Truck Plaza,* 878 F. 2d 338 (10th Cir. 1989).

19. *Ebert v. Lamar Truck Plaza,* 715 F. Supp. 1496, 1499 (D. Colo. 1987), *aff'd,* 878 F. 2d 338 (10th Cir. 1989).

20. *Id.*

21. *Id.,* 715 F. Supp. at 1499.

22. 584 F. Supp. 419, 430 (E.D. Mich. 1984), *aff'd,* 805 F. 2d 611 (6th Cir. 1986).

23. 58 FEP Cases (BNA) 1218 (Me. Sup. Jud. Ct. 1992).

24. *Id.* at 1220.

25. *Id.*

26. *Id.* at 1221.

27. 742 F. Supp. 120 (S.D.N.Y. 1990).

28. *Id.* at 123.

29. *Id.*

30. *Id.* at 124.

31. *Id.* at 126 (footnote omitted).

32. 106 S. Ct. 2399, 2405 (1986).

33. 59 FEP Cases (BNA) 1077 (S.D.N.Y. 1989).

34. *Id.* at 1079.

35. 805 F. 2d 611, 620 (6th Cir. 1986). The Sixth Circuit subsequently adopted a reasonable woman standard.

36. *Id.*

37. *Porras v. Montefiore Medical Center,* 742 F. Supp. 120 (S.D.N.Y. 1990).

38. *Id.* at 127.

39. *Id.* at 126.

40. *Bowen v. Department of Human Services,* 58 FEP Cases (BNA) 1218 (Me. Sup. Jud. Ct. 1992).

41. 675 F. Supp. 1566 (D. Kan. 1986).

42. *Id.* at 1570.

43. *Id.*

44. *Id.*

45. 58 FEP Cases (BNA) 310 (2d Cir. 1992).

46. *Id.* at 311.

47. *Id.*

48. *Id.*

49. *Id.* at 312.

50. *Id.* at 313.

51. *Id.*

52. 881 F. 2d 1504 (9th Cir. 1989).

11. Letters, Calls, and Pressure for Dates or Sexual Favors

1. (1) Most men and women identified uninvited pressure for sexual favors could constitute sexual harassment; (2) the percentage of men and women identifying this conduct as sexual harassment increased between 1980 and 1987.

2. This increase may reflect a slight increase in the opportunity for female supervisors to harass male subordinates. The USMSPB studies did not control for the opportunity to harass subordinates of the opposite sex.

3. 59 FEP Cases (BNA) 1085 (N.Y. Super. Ct., N.Y. Cty. 1990).

4. Plaintiff did make a minor appearance in the initial shooting of *Caligula*.

5. *Id.* at 1087.

6. *Id.*

7. *Id.*

8. *Id.* at 1088.

9. *Thoreson v. Penthouse International,* 59 FEP Cases (BNA) 1092 (N.Y. Sup. Ct., App. Div., 1st Dept. 1992).

10. 57 FEP Cases (BNA) 1373 (8th Cir. 1992).

11. E.g., "Have you been playing with yourself in there?"

12. E.g., Ludvik allegedly told other employees that Burns did not douche and that Burns was dating the owner.

13. *Burns,* at 1375.

14. *Id.* at 1376.

15. 760 F. Supp. 1486 (M.D. Fla. 1991).

16. *Valdez v. Mercy Hosp.,* 961 F. 2d 1401 (8th Cir. 1992) (circulation of handwritten "Mexican Sex Manual" and "Polish Sex Manual" to male employee insufficiently severe or pervasive "to demonstrate a discriminatorily hostile work environment," at 1403).

12. *Deliberate Touching, Assault, Actual or Attempted Rape*

1. 962 F. 2d 120 (1st Cir. 1992).

2. *Id.* at 125.

3. 59 FEP Cases (BNA) 1077 (S.D.N.Y. 1989).

4. *Id.* at 1079.

5. *Id.*

6. 770 F. Supp. 1479 (D. Kan. 1991).

7. *Id.* at 1486 (footnote omitted).

8. *Id.* at 1486.

9. 916 F. 2d 572 (10th Cir. 1990).

10. The inmate was placed in administrative detention.

11. The demotion was invalidated by the New Mexico State Personnel Board as a result of the loss or destruction of tapes of the interviews.

12. 916 F. 2d at 575. Both male and female correctional officers have reported being the targets of incidents in which an inmate used "his body or an object to touch the officer in an overtly sexual manner" (Light 1991).

13. *58* FEP Cases (BNA) 692 (7th Cir. 1992).

14. *Id.* at 692 fn. 1.

15. *Id.* at 693.

16. 7 Cal. Rptr. 2d 418 (Cal. App. 3 Dist. 1992).

17. *Id.* at 419.

18. 58 FEP Cases (BNA) 1523 (M.D. Tenn. 1992).

19. *Id.* at 1525.

20. *Id.* at 1527.

21. *Id.* at 1528.

22. *Id.*

23. 924 F. 2d 872 (9th Cir. 1991).

24. *Id.* at 879 (footnote omitted).

25. *Id.* at 879 fn. 10.

26. While rape is generally perceived as a man raping a woman, women do rape others. For example, the *Sourcebook of Criminal Justice Statistics—1990* reflects 366 women arrested for rape in the United States during 1989. As with rape, sexual assault is generally viewed as men assaulting women. However, some women do sexually assault men or other women. The *Sourcebook of Criminal Justice Statistics—1990* reports that during 1989, 47,459 women were arrested for aggravated assault and another 120,726 for other assaults.

27. In criminal cases, the allegations against the offender are prosecuted by the state or federal government on behalf of the people against the defendant (Reid 1987). In criminal cases, the victim often contacts law-enforcement officials or the prosecuting attorney's office and requests that charges be brought against the defendant. An investigation generally occurs, and an attorney for the government decides which cases will be prosecuted. Few cases of rape reported to the police and referred to the government attorney charged with deciding which cases to prosecute are actually prosecuted (LaFree 1989). Those cases prosecuted are generally cases in which the defendant is poor (Reid 1988; Reid 1987).

28. *See, e.g.,* U.S. Merit Systems Protection Board (1981); *Meritor Sav. Bank, FSB v. Vinson,* 106 S. Ct. 2399 (1986).

29. The legal provision of civil sanctions for those in power for conduct for which poor people are criminally prosecuted is not limited to the offenses discussed here. *See, e.g.,* Kairys (1982).

13. Duty to Take General Preventive Measures: Policy Statements and Training Programs

1. 29 CFR 1604.11(b); *Price v. Lawhon Furniture Co.,* 24 FEP Cases (BNA) 1506 (N.D. Ala. 1978); *Miller v. Bank of America,* 418 F. Supp. 233 (N.D. Cal. 1976), *rev'd,* 600 F. 2d 211 (9th Cir. 1979).

2. 483 N.W. 2d 481 (Minn. App. 1992).

3. *Id.* at 482–83.

4. *Id.* at 484.

5. *Id.*

6. In *Spicuzza v. Fonseca,* 537 So. 2d 272, 275 (La. App. 4 Cir. 1988), the court held: "We find that there is no constitutional violation in treating the class of professional rescuers differently from non-professional rescuers. We find that the classification serves a legitimate purpose. It is reasonable for the courts to discourage proprietors from taking matters into their own hands and placing the safety of the public at risk."

7. 57 FEP Cases (BNA) 1416 (N.M. Ct. App. 1991).

8. The personnel board's findings of fact and conclusions of law established that Hughes had engaged in behavior *construed* as sexual harassment by the alleged victims. The Court of Appeals held the phrasing "raises a question as to whether the board found that the most egregious of the alleged conduct actually occurred." *Id.* at 1420.

9. *Id.*

10. *Id.* at 1421 (footnote omitted).

11. Some argue that people act in accordance with society's expectations.

12. Such a policy could arguably be based on the legitimate business activities of decreasing the incidence of pervasive sexual harassment and decreasing exposure for civil liability.

14. Duty to Investigate

1. *Waltman v. International Paper Co.,* 875 F. 2d 468, 484, 50 FEP Cases (BNA) 179, 192 (5th Cir. 1989) (footnotes omitted).

2. 903 F. 2d 1342 (10th Cir. 1990).

3. *Id.* at 1343.

4. *Whitaker v. Carney,* 778 F. 2d 216 (5th Cir. 1985), *cert. denied,* 107 S. Ct. 64 (1986).

5. *Yates v. Avco Corp.,* 819 F. 2d 630 (6th Cir. 1987).

6. 106 S. Ct. 2399 (1986).

7. *Id.* at 2406.

8. *Id.*

9. *Reichman v. Bureau of Affirmative Action,* 536 F. Supp. 1149 (M.D. Pa. 1982). *See also Koster v. Chase Manhattan Bank,* 687 F. Supp. 848 (S.D.N.Y. 1988).

10. *Meritor,* at 2406.

11. *Cf.* 2406–7.

12. *Priest v. Rotary,* 98 F.R.D. 755 (N.D. Cal. 1983).

13. A plaintiff's lawful off-duty sexual conduct implicates the right to be free, except in very limited circumstances, from unwanted governmental intrusions into one's privacy. *Stanley v. Georgia,* 394 U.S. 557, 564, 89 S. Ct. 1243, 1247, 22 L. Ed. 2d 542 (1969); *Whisenhunt v. Spradlin,* 464 U.S. 965, 971, 104 S. Ct. 404, 408, 78 L. Ed. 2d 345 (1983) (Justice Brennan, with whom Justices Marshall and Blackmun joined, dissenting from denial of certiorari).

Likewise, a plaintiff's lawful off-duty sexual conduct may be protected by plaintiff's associational rights. *Hollenbaugh v. Carnegie Free Liberty,* 439 U.S. 1052, 99 S. Ct. 734, 58 L. Ed. 2d 713 (1978) (Justice Marshall, dissenting from denial of certiorari).

14. 116 F.R.D. 481 (D. Utah 1987).

15. *Id.* at 484.

16. 58 FEP Cases (BNA) 1352 (S.D. Iowa 1992).

17. *Id.* at 1353 (footnote omitted).

18. 22 U.S.C. 2006.

19. 29 U.S.C. 2006 (d).

20. 29 U.S.C. 2007 (b).

21. 29 U.S.C. 2005 (c).

22. *Id.*

23. 57 FEP Cases (BNA) 1416 (N.M. Ct. App. 1991).

24. *Id.* at 1418–19.

25. 29 U.S.C. 2007 (a).

26. Although not the original intent of Title VII of the Civil Rights Act of 1986, 42 U.S.C. 2000e *et seq.,* today Title VII is primarily used to challenge wrongful discharges from employment rather than discrimination in hiring (Donohue and Siegelman 1991).

27. *Hoffman v. United Telecommunications, Inc.,* 117 F.R.D. 436, 438 (D. Kan. 1987).

28. *Orbovich v. Macalester College,* 119 F.R.D. 411, 416 (D. Minn. 1988).

29. *Hoffman v. United Telecommunications, Inc.,* 117 F.R.D. 436, 438 (D. Kan. 1987), *citing Flour Mills of America, Inc. v. Pace,* 75 F.R.D. 676, 680–81 (E.D. Okla. 1977) and cases cited therein.

15. *Prompt Remedial Action*

1. Of course, an employer must remember not to discriminate against someone because of race while prohibiting another from being discriminated against because of sex. In *EEOC v. Mount Vernon Mills,* 58 FEP Cases (BNA) 73 (N.D. Ga. 1992), a black male employee, Mr. Adams, alleged he was discriminated against when he was terminated for making remarks that a white female employee, Ms. Turner, allegedly found offensive. Ms. Turner immediately reported the incident to her female supervisor, who told her to "shake it off." The next day, Ms. Turner reported the incident to her supervisor's male supervisor, Mr. Kellett. Mr. Kellett and his supervisor investigated the incident and terminated Mr. Adams for violating a company policy against sexual harassment. Mr. Adams filed a suit alleging he was treated differently than white employees.

2. *Intlekofer v. Turnage,* 59 FEP Cases (BNA) 929, 932 (9th Cir. 1992).

3. 59 FEP Cases (BNA) 929 (9th Cir. 1992).

4. *Id.* at 933.

5. *Id.* at 930.

6. *Id.*

7. *Id.* at 931 (footnotes omitted).

8. *Id.* at 934.

9. *Id.* at 933.

10. 924 F. 2d 872 (9th Cir. 1991).

11. *Id.* at 882.

12. *Id.*

13. *Id.* at 883 and fn. 19.

14. 605 A. 2d 1125 (N.J. Super. A.D. 1992).

15. *Id.* at 1135.

16. *Carosella v. U.S. Postal Service,* 816 F. 2d 638 (Fed. Cir. 1987); *Snipes v. U.S. Postal Service,* 677 F. 2d 375 (4th Cir. 1982).

17. *Vigil v. Arzola,* 102 N.M. 682, 686, 699 P. 2d 613 (Ct. App. 1983), *reversed on other grounds,* 101 N.M. 687, 687 P. 2d 1038 (1984).

18. 93 N.M. 781, 606 P. 2d 191 (1980).

19. *Id.* at 782.

20. 101 N.M. 687, 687 P. 2d 1038 (1984).

21. 101 N.M. 178, 679 P. 2d 1276 (1984).

22. 26 Wash. App. 172, 613 P. 2d 138 (1980).

23. *Id.* at 177.

24. 108 N.M. 20, 766 P. 2d 280 (1989).

25. *Id.* at 22.

26. *Id.* at 28.

27. 590 N.E. 2d 325 (Ohio App. 1 Dist. 1990).

28. *Id.* at 327.

29. 59 FEP Cases (BNA) 249 (3d Cir. 1992).

30. The arbitrator found that the sexual harassment policy at issue failed to meet "industrial due process" requirements.

31. "A statute is presumptively inconsistent with the First Amendment if it imposes a financial burden on speakers because of the content of their speech." *Simon & Schuster v. New York Crime Victims Bd.,* 112 S. Ct. 501, 508 (1991).

32. "Fighting words" are words which can cause a person to be placed in fear. *State v. James M.,* 111 N.M. 473, 476, 806 P. 2d 1063 (Ct. App. 1990), *cert. denied,* 111 N.M. 529, 807 P. 2d 227 (1991) ("fuck you" and "fuck you, you don't know who

I am" constitute fighting words); *Chaplinsky v. State of New Hampshire,* 315 U.S. 568 (1942); *Brandenberg v. Ohio,* 395 U.S. 444 (1969); *Norwell v. City of Cincinnati, Ohio,* 414 U.S. 15 (1973); *Gooding v. Wilson,* 405 U.S. 518 (1972).

33. *See R.A.V. v. City of St. Paul, Minnesota,* 112 S. Ct. 2538 (1992) (content-based regulation of hate speech violates First Amendment).

34. One need only review feminist journals to see remarks as derogatory toward men as remarks used in Title VII litigation as evidence of an employer's "sexist" attitude.

35. *Connick v. Myers,* 461 U.S. 139, 142, 103 S. Ct. 1684, 1687, 75 L. Ed. 2d 708 (1983) (state assistant district attorney). *See also Rankin v. McPherson,* 107 S. Ct. 2891, 2896 (1987).

36. *Rankin v. McPherson,* 107 S. Ct. at 2897 (1987), *quoting, Connick,* 461 U.S. at 146, 103 S. Ct. at 1689.

37. *Connick v. Myers,* 103 S. Ct. at 1690.

38. *Cf. International Union, UAW v. Johnson Controls,* 111 S. Ct. 1196, 1208–09 (1991) (discussing but not deciding whether Title VII would preempt state tort law claim).

16. Costs

1. The Supreme Court has held that "the extra cost of employing members of one sex [women] . . . does not provide an affirmative defense for a discriminatory refusal to hire members of this gender. . . . We, of course, are not presented with, nor do we decide, a case in which costs would be so prohibitive as to threaten the survival of the employer's business." *International Union, UAW v. Johnson Controls,* 111 S. Ct. 1196, 1209 (1991).

17. Theories of Liability Under Common Law

1. *Restatement (Second) of Torts,* Section 46 (1) (1965).

2. For general cases discussing this tort, *see American Road Serv. Co. v. Inmon,* 394 So. 2d 361 (Ala. 1981) (in reaching its conclusion that an unorganized investigation was not outrageous and thus tort was not available, the court said: "It should be sufficient to observe that an employer, by virtue of his position, possesses no roving license to treat his employee in an extreme and outrageous manner, whether before, during or after their relationship"); *Chuy v. Philadelphia Eagles Football Club,* 595 F. 2d 1265 (3d Cir. 1979) (football player successfully sued former employer for defamation and intentional infliction of emotional distress due to false statement that employee had fatal disease); *Agis v. Howard Johnson Company,* 355 N.E. 2d 315 (Mass. 1976) (firing employees in alphabetical order because someone was stealing stated claim for intentional infliction of emotional distress); *Dominguez v. Stone,* 97 N.M. 211, 638 P. 2d 423 (Ct. App. 1981) (statements at a public meeting to the effect that plaintiff was not suited for her employment with the village of Central because she was a Mexican sufficient allegation to require jury to decide whether conduct was sufficient to constitute extreme and outrageous conduct). A collection of cases in which courts have found conduct constituting sexual harassment under Title VII to state a claim for intentional infliction of emotional distress is found at Annot., *Liability of Employer, Supervisor, or Manager for Intentionally or Recklessly Causing Employee Emotional Distress,* 52 A.L.R. 4th 853, Section 7 (a).

A spouse who works in family businesses or for the same employer may not have the same protection from the intentional infliction of emotional distress from a spouse as from the conduct of a stranger. *See Hakkila v. Hakkila,* 112 N.M. 172, 812 P. 2d 1320 (Ct. App.), *cert. denied,* 112 N.M. 77, 811 P. 2d 575 (1991) (husband's insults and outbursts failed to meet the heightened legal standard of outrageousness required in cases where one spouse sues the other spouse for intentional infliction of emotional distress).

3. *Restatement (Second) of Torts,* Section 46, Comment d (1965).

4. *Salazar v. Furr's Inc.,* 629 F. Supp. 1403, 1411 (D.N.M. 1986), *quoting Restatement (Second) of Torts,* Section 46, Comment h (1965).

5. *Salazar v. Furr's Inc.,* 629 F. Supp. at 1411, *quoting Restatement (Second) of Torts,* Section 46, Comment d (1965). One only need compare the cases collected at Annot., *Modern Status of Intentional Infliction of Mental Distress as Independent Tort; "Outrage,"* 38 A.L.R. 4th 998 and Annot., *Civil Liability for Insulting or Abusive Language — Modern Status,* 20 A.L.R. 4th 773 (1983 and 1991 Supp.), to conclude that reasonable people, including judges, disagree about what types of conduct may reasonably be regarded as so extreme and outrageous as to permit recovery for intentional infliction of emotional distress.

6. 340 S.E. 2d 116 (N.C. App. 1986). The North Carolina Court of Appeals held the plaintiffs' claims for intentional infliction of emotional distress were not barred by North Carolina's Workers' Compensation Act. *Id.* at 119-21. In *Loges v. Mack Trucks,* 58 FEP Cases (BNA) 1009, 1010 (S.C. 1992), the court held claims for intentional infliction of emotional distress were barred by South Carolina's workers' compensation laws.

7. *Id.* at 118.

8. *Id.* at 121.

9. *Id.*

10. *Id.* at 121-22.

11. *Id.* at 118.

12. *Id.* at 122-23.

13. *See, e.g.,* 74 Am. Jur. 2d, Torts Section 32; Annot., *Civil Liability for Insulting or Abusive Language — Modern Status,* 20 A.L.R. 4th 773, Section 3 [a].

14. 282 S.E. 2d 110 (Ga. 1981).

15. *Id.* at 111, 112. *See also Brown v. Manning,* 764 F. Supp. 183 (M.D. Ga. 1991).

16. 381 S.E. 2d 303 (Ga. App. 1989). The *Coleman* court held Title VII's analysis inapplicable to a common-law claim for intentional infliction of emotional distress.

17. *Id.* at 306.

18. *Singleton v. Foreman,* 435 F. 2d 962, 971 (5th Cir. 1970).

19. 423 N.Y.S. 2d 253, 254 (N.Y. Super Ct., App. Div., 2nd Dept. 1980). *See also Zalnis v. Thoroughbred Datsun Car Co.,* 645 P. 2d 292 (Colo. App. 1982).

20. *Sauls v. Union Oil Co. of California,* 750 F. Supp. 783, 789-90 (E.D. Tex. 1990).

21. *Howard University v. Best,* 484 A. 2d 958, 985 (D.C. App. 1984).

22. *Laughinghouse v. Risser,* 58 FEP Cases (BNA) 778, 781 (D. Kan. 1992), *quoting Blackburn v. Colvin,* 191 Kan. 239, 380 P. 2d 432, 437 (1963). The *Laughinghouse* court held the claim for intentional infliction of emotional distress not barred by Kansas' discrimination law prohibiting sexual harassment.

23. 153 Ariz. 38, 734 P. 2d 580 (Ariz. 1987). The *Ford* court held the plaintiff's claims not barred by the Arizona workers' compensation law. *Id.,* 734 P. 2d at 586.

24. *Id.,* 734 P. 2d at 585–86.

25. *Id.* at 586. *See also Baker v. Weyerhaeuser Co.,* 903 F. 2d 1342, 1347 (10th Cir. 1990) and *Marshall v. Nelson Elec.,* 766 F. Supp. 1018, 1029 (N.D. Okl. 1991).

26. *Marshall v. University of Hawaii,* 821 P. 2d 937, 947 (Hawaii App. 1991).

27. 446 N.E. 2d 290, 112 Ill. App. 3d 1057, 68 Ill. Dec. 556 (Ill. App. 4 Dist. 1983).

28. *Id.* at 291. *See also Restatement (Second) of Torts,* Section 46, Comment j, at 77 (1965).

29. Acosta, "The Tort of 'Outrageous Conduct' in New Mexico: Intentional Infliction of Emotional Harm Without Physical Injury," 19 N.M.L.R. 425, 441 (1989).

30. Acosta at 443.

31. *Restatement (Second) of Torts,* Section 34 (1965).

32. *Id.,* Section 26, 29 (1).

33. *Id.,* Section 25.

34. *Id.,* Section 24.

35. *Id.,* Section 31, Comment a; *Romero v. Kendricks,* 74 N.M. 24, 27, 390 P. 2d 269 (1964).

36. *Restatement (Second) of Torts,* Section 31, Comment b (1965).

37. *See, e.g., State v. James M.,* 111 N.M. 473, 806 P. 2d 1063 (Ct. App. 1990), *cert. denied,* 111 N.M. 529, 807 P. 2d 227 (1991); *State v. Wade,* 100 N.M. 152, 667 P. 2d 459 (Ct. App. 1983); *Rael v. Cadena,* 93 N.M. 684, 604 P. 2d 822 (Ct. App. 1979); *Griego v. Wilson,* 91 N.M. 74, 570 P. 2d 612 (Ct. App. 1977); *Mead v. O'Conner,* 66 N.M. 170, 344 P. 2d 478 (1959).

38. 31 N.M.S.B.B. 691 (Ct. App., filed May 13, 1992, published in July 9, 1992 issue).

39. *Id.* at 691.

40. *Id.* A civil action for battery requires an intentional unpermitted contact which is harmful or offensive. *Sanford v. Presto Mfg. Co.,* 92 N.M. 746, 747, 594 P. 2d 1202 (Ct. App. 1979). New Mexico cases do not clearly distinguish between a cause of action for assault and a cause of action for battery. The terms *assault* and *battery* are often used collectively. "While assault and battery are closely related, one may exist without the other." *Baca v. Velez,* 31 N.M.S.B.B. 691.

41. 356 S.E. 2d 378 (N.C. App. 1987).

42. *Id.* at 380.

43. *Id.* at 381.

44. 782 P. 2d 578 (Wyo. 1989), *opinion on appeal after remand,* 803 P. 2d 1358 (Wyo. 1990).

45. 782 P. 2d at 581–82.

46. *Id.* at 583.

47. 340 S.E. 2d 116 (N.C. App. 1986).

48. *Id.* at 124.

49. *See, e.g., Radice v. Meritor Savings Bank,* 58 FEP Cases (BNA) 1006 (E.D. Pa. 1992).

50. *See, e.g., Loges v. Mack Trucks,* 58 FEP Cases (BNA) 1009 (S.C. 1992). The *Loges* court held a claim for negligent supervision not barred by South Carolina's workers' compensation law.

18. Curbing False Accusations

1. 435 So. 2d 705 (Ala. 1983).
2. *Id.* at 708.
3. *Id.* at 711.
4. 85 N.M. 491, 513 P. 2d 1273 (Ct. App.), *cert. denied,* 85 N.M. 483, 513 P. 2d 1265 (1973).
5. *Id.,* 85 N.M. at 492.
6. 92 N.M. 297, 587 P. 2d 444 (Ct. App. 1978).
7. *Id.,* 92 N.M. at 300.

Conclusion

1. *Busik v. Levine,* 307 A. 2d 571 (N.J. 1973).
2. *Valtsakis v. C.I.R.,* 801 F. 2d 622, 624 (2d Cir. 1986).
3. *Moyer v. State,* 452 A. 2d 948, 950 (Del. Supr. 1982).
4. 110 N.M. 621, 798 P. 2d 571 (1990).
5. *Id.* at 627.
6. In one light, Title VII can be seen as addressing the symptom of the problem (sexual harassment) rather than the problem (the socialization process).
7. *See, e.g., Coriz by and Through Coriz v. Martinez,* 915 F. 2d 1469 (10th Cir. 1990); *Garcia by Garcia v. Miera,* 817 F. 2d 650 (10th Cir. 1987); Roesler (1990, 1989).
8. Today, most youngsters engage in consensual sexual intercourse before they become adults. In 1991, the Children's Defense Fund noted that "a majority of both boys and girls are sexually active by eleventh grade.... According to 1988 data, by age 15, 27 percent of girls and 33 percent of boys had engaged in sexual intercourse; 50 percent of girls and 66 percent of boys had intercourse by age 17" (*State of America's Children* 1991: 93).

Bibliography

Aaron, Titus, Edward Dry, and James L. Porter. (1990) "The Grey Box in Employee Relations," *Cornell Hotel and Restaurant Administration Quarterly,* Vol. 31, No. 1, pp. 112–17.

Abbey, Antonia. (1987) "Misperceptions of Friendly Behavior as Sexual Interest: A Survey of Naturally Occurring Incidents," *Psychology of Women Quarterly,* Vol. 11, No. 2, pp. 173–94.

_____, and Christian Melby. (1986) "The Effects of Nonverbal Cues on Gender Differences in Perceptions of Sexual Intent," *Sex Roles,* Vol. 15, Nos. 5, 6, pp. 283–98.

Abramson, Jill. (1991) "Thomas-Hill Hearing Will Take Place in a Congress That Itself Isn't Unfamiliar with Sex and Harassment," *Wall Street Journal,* October 11, p. A-12.

Adams, Todd. (1991) "Universalism and Sexual Harassment," *Oklahoma Law Review,* Vol. 44, No. 4, pp. 683–94.

Adler, Jerry, and Peter Annin. (1991) "A Tale of Sex, Lies and Audiotape," *Newsweek,* October 21, p. 38.

Alston, Chuck. (1991) "Political Fallout from Thomas Vote . . . Could Cut Any Number of Ways," *Congressional Quarterly,* Vol. 49, No. 42, pp. 3028–29.

_____, and Beth Donovan. (1991) "Thomas Controversy Highlights . . . Gender Gulf on Capitol Hill," *Congressional Quarterly,* Vol. 49, No. 41, pp. 2950–51.

Alter, Jonathan. (1991) "Why There Isn't a Better Way," *Newsweek,* October 21, p. 45.

Anchell, Melvin. (1992) "A Psychoanalytic Look at the *Hill-Thomas Affair,*" *Social Justice Review,* Vol. 83, Nos. 3, 4, pp. 41–44.

Anderson, Claire, and Caroline Fisher. (1991) "Male-Female Relationships in the Workplace: Perceived Motivations in Office Romance," *Sex Roles,* Vol. 25, Nos. 3, 4, pp. 163–80.

Backhouse, Constance, and Leah Cohen. (1981) *Sexual Harassment on the Job,* Englewood Cliffs, NJ: Prentice-Hall.

Bahls, Jane Easter. (1988) "Stopping Sexual Harassment," *Business Credit,* July-August, p. 53.

Bailey, F. Lee. (1992) "Where Was the Crucible? The Cross-Examination That Wasn't," *ABA Journal,* Vol. 78, January, pp. 46–49.

Baker, Douglas, David Terpstra, and Kinley Larntz. (1990) "The Influence of Individual Characteristics and Severity of Harassing Behavior on Reactions to Sexual Harassment," *Sex Roles,* Vol. 22, Nos. 5, 6, pp. 305–25.

Baldridge, Kathy, and Gary McLean. (1980) "Sexual Harassment: How Much of a Problem Is It . . . Really?" *Journal of Business Education,* Vol. 56, pp. 294–97.

Barrett, Paul, and Jeffrey Birnbaum. (1991) "New Allegations Against Thomas Being Reviewed," *Wall Street Journal,* October 11, p. A-12.

_____, and Jill Abramson. (1991) "Even If Confirmed, Judge Thomas Will Be Under a Heavy Cloud," *Wall Street Journal,* October 14, pp. A-1, A-6.

Beauvais, Kathleen. (1986) "Workshops to Combat Sexual Harassment: A Case Study of Changing Attitudes," *Signs: Journal of Women in Culture and Society,* Vol. 12, No. 1, pp. 130–45.

Bell, Derrick. (1989) "The Effects of Affirmative Action on Male-Female Relationships Among African Americans," *Sex Roles,* Vol. 21, Nos. 1, 2, pp. 13–24.

Benson, Donna, and Gregg Thomson. (1982) "Sexual Harassment on a University Campus: The Confluence of Authority Relations, Sexual Interest and Gender Stratification," *Social Problems,* Vol. 29, No. 3, pp. 236–51.

Benson, Katherine. (1984) "Comment on Crocker's 'An Analysis of University Definitions of Sexual Harassment,'" *Signs: Journal of Women in Culture and Society,* Vol. 9, No. 3, pp. 516–19.

Bernikow, Louise. (1992) "Jessica Lange Down to Earth," *TV Guide,* Vol. 40, No. 5, pp. 5–9.

Biskupic, Joan. (1991a) "Deflecting Tough Questions, Thomas Stumps Senators," *Congressional Quarterly,* Vol. 49, No. 37, pp. 2619–23.

_____. (1991a1) "Minuet with Congress," *Congressional Quarterly,* Vol. 49, No. 37, p. 2622.

_____. (1991b) "Thomas Hearings Illustrate Politics of the Process," *Congressional Quarterly,* Vol. 49, No. 38, pp. 2688–89, 2692.

_____. (1991c) "With a Split Vote Over Thomas, Panel Sends Bush a Message," *Congressional Quarterly,* Vol. 49, No. 39, pp. 2786–87.

_____. (1991d) "Thomas Picks Up Support as Senate Nears Vote," *Congressional Quarterly,* Vol. 49, No. 40, p. 2867.

_____. (1991e) "Thomas Drama Engulfs Nation; Anguished Senate Faces Vote," *Congressional Quarterly,* Vol. 49, No. 41, pp. 2948–49, 2952–53, 2957.

_____. (1991f) "Thomas' Victory Puts Icing on Reagan–Bush Court," *Congressional Quarterly,* Vol. 49, No. 42, pp. 3026, 3030, 3032–33.

_____. (1991f1) "A Process Under Scrutiny," *Congressional Quarterly,* Vol. 49, No. 42, p. 3031.

Blumer, Herbert. (1971) "Social Problems as Collective Behavior," *Social Problems,* Vol. 18, No. 3, pp. 298–306.

BNA. (1981) *Sexual Harassment and Labor Relations: A BNA Special Report,* Bureau of National Affairs, Washington, D.C.

Borger, Gloria, Kenneth Walsh, Jeannye Thornton, and Ted Gest. (1991) "Judging Thomas," *U.S. News & World Report,* October 21, pp. 32–36.

Boxill, Bernard. (1980) "Sexual Blindness and Sexual Equality," *Social Theory and Practice,* Vol. 6, No. 3, pp. 281–98.

Brandenburg, Judith Berman. (1982) "Sexual Harassment in the University: Guidelines for Establishing a Grievance Procedure," *Signs: Journal of Women in Culture and Society,* Vol. 8, No. 2, pp. 320–36.

Bratton, Eleanor. (1987) "The Eye of the Beholder: An Interdisciplinary Examination of Law and Social Research on Sexual Harassment," *New Mexico Law Review,* Vol. 17, pp. 91–114.

Brewer, Marilynn. (1982) "Further Beyond Nine to Five: An Integration and Future Directions," *Journal of Social Issues,* Vol. 38, No. 4, pp. 149–58.

_____, and Richard Burk. (1982) "Beyond Nine to Five: Introduction," *Journal of Social Issues,* Vol. 38, No. 4, pp. 1–4.

Briscoe, David. (1992) "Men Perform Few Domestic Chores," *Albuquerque Journal,* September 7, 1992, p. B11.

Broadhurst, Diane. (1984) *The Role of Law Enforcement in the Prevention and Treatment of Child Abuse and Neglect,* U.S. Department of Health and Human Services, Washington, D.C., Publication No. OHDS 84-30193.

Brooks, Linda, and Annette Perot. (1991) "Reporting Sexual Harassment," *Psychology of Women Quarterly,* Vol. 15, pp. 31-47.

Bularzik, Mary. (1978) "Sexual Harassment at the Workplace," *Radical America,* Vol. 12, No. 4, pp. 25-43.

Burleigh, Nina. (1992) "Now That It's Over: Winners and Losers in the Confirmation Process," *ABA Journal,* Vol. 78, January, pp. 50-53.

Burstein, Paul, and Kathleen Monaghan. (1986) "Equal Employment Opportunity and the Mobilization of Law," *Law and Society Review,* Vol. 20, p. 356.

Byers, E. Sandra, and Paula Wilson. (1985) "Accuracy of Women's Expectations Regarding Men's Responses to Refusals of Sexual Advances in Dating Situations," *International Journal of Women's Studies,* Vol. 8, No. 4, pp. 376-87.

Cammaert, Lorna. (1985) "How Widespread Is Sexual Harassment on Campus?" *International Journal of Women's Studies,* Vol. 8, No. 4, pp. 388-97.

Caudill, Donald, and Regina Donaldson. (1986) "Is Your Climate Ripe for Sexual Harassment," *MW,* July-August, p. 26.

Cohen, Aaron Groff, and Barbara Gutek. (1985) "Dimensions of Perceptions of Social-Sexual Behavior in a Work Setting," *Sex Roles,* Vol. 13, Nos. 5, 6, pp. 317-27.

Coles, Frances. (1986) "Forced to Quit: Sexual Harassment Complaints and Agency Response," *Sex Roles,* Vol. 14, Nos. 1, 2, pp. 81-95.

Collins, Eliza, and Timothy Blodgett. (1981) "Sexual Harassment . . . Some See It . . . Some Won't," *Harvard Business Review,* Vol. 59, No. 2, pp. 76-95.

Comisky, Hope. (1992) "'Prompt and Effective Remedial Action?' What Must an Employer Do to Avoid Liability for 'Hostile Work Environment' Sexual Harassment?" *The Labor Lawyer,* Vol. 8, No. 2, pp. 181-201.

Conte, Alba. (1990) *Sexual Harassment in the Workplace: Law and Practice,* New York: John Wiley.

Daniels, Tom, and Barry Spiker. (1987) *Perspectives on Organizational Communication,* Dubuque, IA: Wm. C. Brown.

Deutsch, Francine, Dorothy LeBaron, and Maury March Fryer. (1987) "What Is in a Smile?" *Psychology of Women Quarterly,* Vol. 11, No. 3, pp. 341-51.

Dhooper, Surjit, Marlene Huff, and Carrie Schultz. (1989) "Social Work and Sexual Harassment," *Journal of Sociology and Social Welfare,* Vol. 16, No. 3, pp. 125-38.

DiLapi, Elena Marie. (1989) "Lesbian Mothers and the Motherhood Hierarchy," *Journal of Homosexuality,* Vol. 18, Nos. 1, 2, pp. 101-21.

DiVasto, Peter, Arthur Kaufman, Lynn Rosner, Rebecca Jackson, Joan Christy, Sally Pearson, and Terry Burgett. (1984) "The Prevalence of Sexually Stressful Events Among Females in the General Population," *Archives of Sexual Behavior,* Vol. 13, No. 1, pp. 59-67.

Dodier, Grace. (1987) "Meritor Savings Bank v. Vinson: Sexual Harassment at Work," *Harvard Women's Law Journal,* Vol. 10, pp. 203-24.

Donohue, John, and Peter Siegelman. (1991) "The Changing Nature of Employment Discrimination Litigation," *Stanford Law Review,* Vol. 43, No. 5, pp. 983-1033.

Duldt, Bonnie. (1982) "Sexual Harassment in Nursing," *Nursing Outlook,* Vol. 30, No. 6, pp. 336–43.

Elson, John, Sophfronia Scott Gregory, and Elaine Shannon. (1991) "When Reporters Make News," *Time,* October 28, p. 30.

Emerson, Robert, and Sheldon Messinger. (1977) "The Micro-Politics of Trouble," *Social Problems,* Vol. 25, No. 2, pp. 121–34.

Engel, Paul. (1985) "Sexual Harassment: Victims Talk, Management Listens," *Industry Week,* June 24, p. 57.

Epp, Charles. (1990) "Connecting Litigation Levels and Legal Mobilization: Explaining Interstate Variation in Employment Civil Rights Litigation," *Law and Society Review,* Vol. 24, p. 57.

Epstein, Cynthia Fuchs. (1989) "Workplace Boundaries: Conceptions and Creations," *Social Research,* Vol. 56, No. 3, pp. 571–90.

Esser, John, and David Trubek. (1990) "From 'Scientism Without Determinism' to 'Interpretation Without Politics': A Reply to Sarat, Harrington and Yngvesson," *Law and Social Inquiry,* Vol. 15, No. 1, pp. 171–80.

Executive Summary: Study of National Incidence and Prevalence of Child Abuse and Neglect: 1988, U.S. Department of Health and Human Services, Washington, D.C.

Fain, Terri, and Douglas Anderton. (1987) "Sexual Harassment: Organizational Context and Diffuse Status," *Sex Roles,* Vol. Nos. 5, 6, pp. 291–311.

Fein, Bruce. (1991) "The Thomas Hearings," *ABA Journal,* Vol. 77, December, p. 42.

Fitzgerald, Louise, Lauren Weitzman, Yael Gold, and Mimi Ormerod. (1988a) "Academic Harassment: Sex and Denial in Scholarly Garb," *Psychology of Women Quarterly,* Vol. 12, pp. 329–40.

————, Sandra Shullman, Nancy Bailey, Margaret Richards, Janice Swecker, Yael Gold, Mimi Ormerod, and Lauren Weitzman. (1988b) "The Incidence and Dimensions of Sexual Harassment in Academia and the Workplace," *Journal of Vocational Behavior,* Vol. 32, No. 2, pp. 152–75.

————, and Alayne Ormerod. (1991) "Perceptions of Sexual Harassment: The Influence of Gender and Academic Context," *Psychology of Women Quarterly,* Vol. 15, pp. 281–94.

Foner, Philip. (1980) *Women and the American Labor Movement: From World War I to the Present,* New York: Free Press.

Free, Marvin. (1990) "Demographic Organizational and Economic Determinants of Work Satisfaction: An Assessment of Work Attitudes of Females in Academic Settings," *Sociological Spectrum,* Vol. 10, pp. 79–103.

Freeman, Jo. (1991) "How 'Sex' Got into Title VII: Persistent Opportunism as a Maker of Public Policy," *Law & Inequality,* Vol. 9, No. 2, pp. 163–84.

Frieder, Mia. (1991) "The Most Powerful Trap," *Student Lawyer,* Vol. 20, No. 3, pp. 34–39.

Gartrell, Nanette, Judith Herman, Silvia Olarte, Michael Feldstein, and Russell Localio. (1986) "Psychiatric-Patient Sexual Contact: Results of a National Survey, I: Prevalance," *Am. J. Psychiatry,* Vol. 149, No. 9, pp. 1126–31.

————, ————, ————, ————, and ————. (1987) "Reporting Practices of Psychiatrists Who Knew of Sexual Misconduct by Colleagues," *American Journal of Orthopsychiatry,* Vol. 57, No. 2, pp. 287–95.

Garwin, Arthur. (1992) "Lawyers in Love . . . and in Conflict," *ABA Journal,* Vol. 78, September 1992, p. 94.

Gest, Ted, Amy Saltzman, Betsy Carpenter, and Dorian Friedman. (1991)

"Harassment: Men on Trial," *U.S. News & World Report,* October 21, pp. 38–40.

Gibson, Eunice. (1981) "Sexual Harassment," *Wisconsin Bar Bulletin,* March, pp. 21–23, 76–79.

Gillespie, Dair, and Ann Leffler. (1987) "The Politics of Research Methodology in Claims-Making Activities: Social Science and Sexual Harassment," *Social Problems,* Vol. 34, No. 5, pp. 490–501.

Glass, Becky. (1988) "Workplace Harassment and the Victimization of Women," *Women's Studies Int. Forum,* Vol. 11, No. 1, pp. 55–67.

Goffman, Erving. (1977) "The Arrangement Between the Sexes," *Theory and Society,* Vol. 4, No. 3, pp. 301–31.

Goldberg, Stephanie. (1991) "Hostile Environments," *ABA Journal,* Vol. 77, pp. 90–92.

Goodman, Sheilah. (1991) "Trying to Undo the Damage: The Civil Rights Act of 1990," *Harvard Women's Law Journal,* Vol. 14, pp. 184–221.

Grauerholz, Elizabeth. (1989) "Sexual Harassment of Women Professors by Students: Exploring Dynamics of Power, Authority, and Gender in a University Setting," *Sex Roles,* Vol. 21, Nos. 11, 12, pp. 789–801.

Grieco, Alan. (1984) "Suggestions for Management of Sexual Harassment of Nurses," *Hospital and Community Psychiatry,* Vol. 35, No. 2, pp. 171–72.

_____. (1987) "Scope and Nature of Sexual Harassment in Nursing," *The Journal of Sex Research,* Vol. 23, No. 2, pp. 261–66.

Gruber, James. (1989) "How Women Handle Sexual Harassment: A Literature Review," *Sociology and Social Research,* Vol. 74, No. 1, pp. 3–9.

_____, and Lars Bjorn. (1982) "Blue-Collar Blues: The Sexual Harassment of Women Autoworkers," *Work and Occupations,* Vol. 9, No. 3, pp. 271–98.

_____, and _____. (1986) "Women's Responses to Sexual Harassment: An Analysis of Sociocultural, Organizational, and Personal Resource Models," *Social Science Quarterly,* Vol. 67, No. 4, pp. 814–26.

Gutek, Barbara. (1985) *Sex and the Workplace,* San Francisco: Jossey-Bass.

_____, and Bruce Morasch. (1982) "Sex-Ratios, Sex-Role Spillover, and Sexual Harassment of Women at Work," *Journal of Social Issues,* Vol. 38, No. 4, pp. 55–74.

_____, _____, and Aaron Groff Cohen. (1983) "Interpreting Social-Sexual Behavior in a Work Setting," *Journal of Vocational Behavior,* Vol. 22, No. 1, pp. 30–48.

Harassment and Compensation: Today's Sex Discrimination Issues. (1983) Chicago: Commerce Clearing House.

Harrington, Christine, and Barbara Yngvesson. (1990) "Interpretive Sociolegal Research," *Law and Social Inquiry,* Vol. 15, No. 1, pp. 135–48.

Harwood, John, and Jackie Calmes. (1991) "Defense of the Nominee Uses Two-Prong Attack," *Wall Street Journal,* October 14, p. A-6.

Hazelwood, Robert, Park Elliot Dietz, and Janet Warren. (1992) "The Criminal Sexual Sadist," *FBI Law Enforcement Bulletin,* Vol. 61, No. 2, pp. 12–20.

Hemming, Heather. (1985) "Women in a Man's World: Sexual Harassment," *Human Relations,* Vol. 38, No. 1, pp. 67–79.

"Hill Passes Test on Lie Detector." (1991a) *Salt Lake Tribune,* October 14, p. A-1.

Hinkin, Timothy, and Chester Schriesheim. (1990) "Relationships Between Subordinate Perceptions of Supervisor Influence Tactics and Attributed Bases of Supervisory Power," *Human Relations,* Vol. 43, No. 3, pp. 221–37.

Hiscott, Robert, and Peter Cannop. (1989) "Job Stress and Occupational Burnout:

Gender Differences Among Mental Health Professionals," *Sociology and Social Research,* Vol. 74, No. 1, pp. 10–15.

Hoffmann, Frances. (1986) "Sexual Harassment in Academia: Feminist Theory and Institutional Practice," *Harvard Educational Review,* Vol. 56, No. 2, pp. 105–21.

Holroyd, Jean, and Annette Brodsky. (1977) "Psychologists' Attitudes and Practices Regarding Erotic and Nonerotic Physical Contact with Patients," *American Psychologist,* Vol. 32, pp. 843–49.

Hughes, John, and Larry May. (1980) "Sexual Harassment," *Social Theory and Practice,* Vol. 6, No. 3, pp. 249–80.

Hunter, Christopher, and Kent McClelland. (1991) "Honoring Accounts for Sexual Harassment: A Factorial Survey Analysis," *Sex Roles,* Vol. 24, Nos. 11, 12, pp. 725–52.

Jaggar, Alison. (1983) *Feminist Politics and Human Nature,* Totowa, NJ: Rowman & Allenheld.

James, Jennifer. (1981) "Sexual Harassment," *Public Personnel Management Journal,* Vol. 10, No. 4, pp. 402–07.

Janman, Karen. (1989) "One Step Behind: Current Stereotypes of Women, Achievement and Work," *Sex Roles,* Vol. 21, Nos. 3, 4, pp. 209–30.

Jaschik, Mollie, and Bruce Fretz. (1991) "Women's Perceptions and Labeling of Sexual Harassment," *Sex Roles,* Vol. 25, Nos. 1, 2, pp. 19–23.

Jenkins, James, Marsha Salus, and Gretchen Schultze. (1979) *Child Protective Services: A Guide for Workers,* U.S. Department of Health, Education, and Welfare, Washington, D.C., DHEW Publication No. OHDS 79-30203.

Jensen, Inger, and Barbara Gutek. (1982) "Attributions and Assignment of Responsibility in Sexual Harassment," *Journal of Social Issues,* Vol. 38, No. 4, pp. 121–36.

Johnson, Sharen. (1991) "Lie Detector Test: Powerful, but Imperfect," *USA Today,* October 14, p. 3A.

Kairys, David. (1982) *The Politics of Law,* New York: Pantheon Books.

Kaiser, Susan. (1990) *The Social Psychology of Clothing: Symbolic Appearances in Context,* New York: Macmillan.

Kann, Peter. (1991) "A Modest Proposal for Ending Senate's Circus," *Wall Street Journal,* October 14, p. A-12.

Kantrowitz, Barbara, Todd Barrett, Karen Springen, Mary Hager, Lynda Wright, Ginny Carroll, and Debra Rosenberg. (1991) "Striking a Nerve," *Newsweek,* October 21, pp. 34–40.

Kaplan, David, Bob Cohn, Vern Smith, Howard Manly, Carolyn Friday, Karen Springen, Todd Barrett, Lydia Denworth, Elizabeth Ann Leonard, and Alden Cohen. (1991) "Supreme Mystery," *Newsweek,* September 16, pp. 18–23, 25–27, 30–31.

————, ————, Ann McDaniel, and Peter Annin. (1991) "Anatomy of a Debacle," *Newsweek,* October 21, pp. 26–32.

Kardener, Sheldon. (1974) "Sex and the Physician-Patient Relationship," *Am. J. Psychiatry,* Vol. 131, No. 10, pp. 1134–36.

————, Marielle Fuller, and Ivan Mensh. (1973) "A Survey of Physicians' Attitudes and Practices Regarding Erotic and Nonerotic Contact with Patients," *Am. J. Psychiatry,* Vol. 130, No. 10, pp. 1077–81.

Kenealy, Kathleen. (1992) "Sexual Harassment and the Reasonable Woman Standard," *The Labor Lawyer,* Vol. 8, No. 2, pp. 203–10.

Kenig, Sylvia, and John Ryan. (1986) "Sex Differences in Levels of Tolerance and

Attribution of Blame for Sexual Harassment on a University Campus," *Sex Roles,* Vol. 15, Nos. 9, 10, pp. 535–49.

Kollias, Karen. (1975) "Class Realities: Create a New Power Base," *Quest,* Vol. 1, No. 3, pp. 28–43.

Kuntz, Phil. (1991) "Mired in Procedural, Political Mess . . . Senate Scrambled to Delay Vote," *Congressional Quarterly,* Vol. 49, No. 41, pp. 2954–55.

LaFree, Gary. (1989) *Rape and Criminal Justice: The Social Construction of Sexual Assault,* Belmont, CA: Wadsworth.

Ledgerwood, Donna, and Sue Johnson-Dietz. (1980) "The EEOC's Foray into Sexual Harassment: Interpreting the New Guidelines for Employer Liability," *Labor Law Journal,* December, pp. 741–44.

Lenhoff, Donna. (1981) "Sexual Harassment: No More Business as Usual," *Trial,* July, pp. 42–45, 78–79.

Leo, John. (1991) "Harassment's Murky Edges," *U.S. News & World Report,* October 21, p. 26.

Light, Stephen. (1991) "Assaults on Prison Officers: Interactional Themes," *Justice Quarterly,* Vol. 8, No. 2, pp. 243–61.

Lindemann, Barbara, and David Kadue. (1992) *Sexual Harassment in Employment Law,* Bureau of National Affairs, Washington, D.C.

Lindgren, Sue. (1992) "Federal Justice Spending Increases Twice as Fast as Federal Government Spending for All Activities from 1988 to 1990," *Bureau of Justice Statistics National Update,* U.S. Department of Justice, Office of Justice Programs, Bureau of Justice Statistics, Washington, D.C.

Littler-Bishop, Susan, Doreen Seidler-Feller, and Robert Opaluch. (1982) "Sexual Harassment in the Workplace as a Function of Initiator's Status: The Case of Airline Personnel," *Journal of Social Issues,* Vol. 38, No. 4, pp. 137–48.

Livingston, Joy. (1982) "Responses to Sexual Harassment on the Job: Legal, Organizational, and Individual Actions," *Journal of Social Issues,* Vol. 38, No. 4, pp. 5–22.

Loden, Marilyn, and Judy Rosener. (1991) *Workforce America! Managing Employee Diversity as a Resource,* Homewood, IL: Business One Irwin.

Lott, Bernice, Mary Ellen Reilly, and Dale Howard. (1982) "Sexual Assault and Harassment: A Campus Community Case Study," *Signs: Journal of Women in Culture and Society,* Vol. 8, No. 2, pp. 296–319.

Loy, Pamela, and Lea Stewart. (1984) "The Extent and Effects of the Sexual Harassment of Working Women," *Sociological Focus,* Vol. 17, No. 1, pp. 31–44.

Lublin, Joann. (1991) "Companies Try a Variety of Approaches to Halt Sexual Harassment on the Job," *Wall Street Journal,* October 11, pp. B-1, B-4.

McCormack, Arlene. (1985) "The Sexual Harassment of Students by Teachers: The Case of Students in Science," *Sex Roles,* Vol. 13, Nos. 1, 2, pp. 21–32.

McKinney, Kathleen. (1990) "Sexual Harassment of University Faculty by Colleagues and Students," *Sex Roles,* Vol. 23, Nos. 7, 8, pp. 421–38.

MacKinnon, Catharine. (1979) *Sexual Harassment of Working Women,* New Haven: Yale University Press.

————. (1983) "Excerpts from MacKinnon/Schlafly Debate," *Law & Inequality,* Vol. 1, No. 2, pp. 341–53.

McQueen, Michel and Dorothy Gaither. (1991) "Clash Is Especially Sensitive for Blacks, Baring Legacy of Racism, Stereotypes," *Wall Street Journal,* October 14, p. A-6.

Malovich, Natalie, and Jayne Stake. (1990) "Sexual Harassment on Campus:

Individual Differences in Attitudes and Beliefs," *Psychology of Women Quarterly,* Vol. 14, pp. 63–81.

Mansfield, Phyllis Kernoff, Patricia Barthalow Koch, Julie Henderson, Judith Vicary, Margaret Cohn, and Elaine Young. (1991) "The Job Climate for Women in Traditionally Male Blue-Collar Occupations," *Sex Roles,* Vol. 25, Nos. 1, 2, pp. 63–79.

Marton, Kati. (1991) "An All Too Common Story," *Newsweek,* October 21, p. 8.

Maypole, Donald. (1986). "Sexual Harassment of Social Workers at Work: Injustice Within?" *Social Work,* Vol. 31, No. 1, pp. 29–34.

————, and Rosemarie Skaine. (1982) "Sexual Harassment of the Blue Collar Workers," *Journal of Sociology and Social Welfare,* Vol. 9, No. 4, pp. 682–95.

————, and ————. (1983). "Sexual Harassment in the Workplace," *Social Work,* Vol. 28, No. 5, pp. 385–90.

Middleton, Martha. (1980) "Sexual Harassment on Job: New Rules Issued," *ABA Journal,* June, Vol. 66, p. 703.

Mills, Trudy. (1981) "On the Use of Equal Employment Laws," *Pacific Sociological Review,* Vol. 24, p. 196.

Miramontes, David. (1984) *How to Deal with Sexual Harassment,* San Diego: Network Communications.

"A Moment of Truth." (1991) *Newsweek,* October 21, p. 24.

Montoya, Margaret, and B. Hobson Wildenthal. (1992) "Sexual Harassment in the Multicultural Work Place," *New Mexico Lawyer,* Vol. 4, No. 2, pp. 16–17.

Morlacci, Maria. (1987–1988) "Sexual Harassment Law and the Impact of *Vinson,*" *Employee Relations Law Journal,* Vol. 13, pp. 501–19.

Nacoste, Rupert Barnes. (1990) "Sources of Stigma: Analyzing the Psychology of Affirmative Action," *Law & Policy,* Vol. 12, No. 2, pp. 175–95.

Newsweek Poll, October 10–11, 1991. (1991a) (The *Newsweek* poll was conducted by the Gallup Organization and consisted of telephone interviews with 704 adults on October 10–11, 1991 and reported in the October 21, 1991, issue of *Newsweek* at pp. 28, 34, 38, 40, and 43. The information herein was compiled from information presented in the October 21, 1991, issue of *Newsweek.*)

Newsweek, October 21, 1991. (1991b).

Noah, Timothy, and Jackie Calmes. (1991) "Hill Passes Polygraph Test, Is Supported by Testimony," *Wall Street Journal,* October 14, p. A-6.

"Nude Photographs Sink Navy Captain: Officer Fired for Training Posters." (September 10, 1992) *Albuquerque Journal,* p. A5.

O'Connell, Lenahan. (1991) "Investigators at Work: How Bureaucratic and Legal Constraints Influence the Enforcement of Discrimination Law," *Public Administration Review,* Vol. 51, No. 2, pp. 123–70.

(O.T.A. Study). (1993) Congressional Office of Technology Assessment, *Scientific Validity of Polygraph Testing; A Research Review and Evaluation* (A Technical Memorandum), OTA-TM-H-15, 98th Cong., 1st Sess. 5.

Padgitt, Steven, and Janet Padgitt. (1986) "Cognitive Structure of Sexual Harassment: Implications for University Policy," *Journal of College Student Personnel,* Vol. 27, No. 1, pp. 34–39.

Painton, Priscilla, Michael Duffy, Julie Johnson, and Elizabeth Taylor. (1991) "Woman Power," *Time,* October 28, pp. 24–26.

Parker, J. Wilson. (1987) "The Uses of the Past: The Surprising History of

Terminable-at-Will Employment in North Carolina," 22 *Wake Forest L. Rev.* 167.

Paul, Ellen Frankel. (1991) "Bared Buttocks and Federal Cases," *Society,* Vol. 28, No. 4, pp. 4–7.

Podgers, James. (1981) "Male Clients Can Be a Trial for Women Lawyers," *ABA Journal,* Vol. 67, pp. 835–36.

Pollack, Wendy. (1990) "Sexual Harassment: Women's Experience vs. Legal Definitions," *Harvard Women's Law Journal,* Vol. 13, pp. 35–85.

Pollak, Richard. (1991) "Presumed Innocent?" *The Nation,* Nov. 11.

Pope, Kenneth. (1986) "Research and Laws Regarding Therapists-Patient Sexual Involvement: Implications for Therapists," *American Journal of Psychotherapy,* Vol. XL, No. 4, pp. 564–71.

————, Patricia Keith-Spiegel, and Barbara Tabachnick. (1986) "Sexual Attraction to Clients: The Human Therapist and the (Sometimes) Inhuman Training System," *American Psychologist,* Vol. 41, No. 2, pp. 147–58.

————, Hanna Levenson, and Leslie Schover. (1979) "Sexual Intimacy in Psychology Training: Results and Implications of a National Study," *American Psychologist,* Vol. 34, No. 8, pp. 682–89.

Popovich, Paula, and Betty Jo Licata. (1987) "A Role Model Approach to Sexual Harassment," *Journal of Management,* Vol. 13, p. 149.

Powell, Gary. (1986) "Effects of Sex Role Identity and Sex on Definitions of Sexual Harassment," *Sex Roles,* Vol. 14, Nos. 1, 2, pp. 9–19.

"A Problem for Clarence Thomas?" (1991) *Newsweek,* October 14, p. 56.

Pryor, John. (1985) "The Lay Person's Understanding of Sexual Harassment," *Sex Roles,* Vol. 13, Nos. 5, 6, pp. 273–86.

————. (1987) "Sexual Harassment Proclivities in Men," *Sex Roles,* Vol. 17, Nos. 5, 6, pp. 269–90.

————, and Jeanne Day. (1988) "Interpretations in Sexual Harassment: An Attributional Analysis," *Sex Roles,* Vol. 18, Nos. 7, 8, pp. 405–17.

Rabinowitz, Dorothy. (1991) "Senatorial Follies," *Wall Street Journal,* October 14, p. A-12.

A Redbook Questionnaire. (1976) "How Do You Handle Sex on the Job?" *Redbook,* Vol. 146, No. 3.

Redish, Martin (moderator), and Stephanie Goldberg (editor). (1992) "'What's the Alternative?' A Roundtable on the Confirmation Process," *ABA Journal,* Vol. 78, pp. 41–45.

Reid, Sue. (1987) *Criminal Justice: Procedures and Issues,* St. Paul, MN: West.

————. (1988) *Crime and Criminology* (5th ed.) New York: Holt, Rinehart and Winston.

Reidinger, Paul. (1991) "Drain the Swamp," *ABA Journal,* Vol. 77, December, p. 43.

Reilly, Mary Ellen, Bernice Lott, and Sheila Gallogly. (1986) "Sexual Harassment of University Students," *Sex Roles,* Vol. 15, Nos. 7, 8, pp. 333–58.

Reilly, Timothy, Sandra Carpenter, Valerie Dull, and Kim Bartlett. (1982) "The Factorial Survey Technique: An Approach to Defining Sexual Harassment on Campus," *Journal of Social Issues,* Vol. 38, No. 4, pp. 99–110.

Remick, Helen, Jan Salisbury, Donna Stringer, and Angela Ginorio. (1990) "Investigation of Sexual Harassment Complaints," *Women's Studies Quarterly,* Vol. 18, Nos. 1, 2, pp. 207–21.

A Report to the Congress: Joining Together to Fight Child Abuse. (1986) U.S. Department of Health and Human Services, Washington, D.C.

Research Symposium on Child Sexual Abuse, May 17–19, 1988. Children's Bureau, Administration for Children, Youth and Families, Office of Human Development Services, U.S. Department of Health and Human Services, Washington, D.C.

Reske, Henry. (1991) "Confirmation Hearings, Round II," *ABA Journal,* Vol. 77, pp. 14, 16.

Richardson, Laurel. (1988) *The Dynamics of Sex and Gender: A Sociological Perspective,* New York: Harper & Row.

Rizzo, Ann-Marie, and Dolores Brosnan. (1990) "Critical Theory and Communication Dysfunction: The Case of Sexually Ambiguous Behavior," *Administration & Society,* Vol. 22, No. 1, pp. 66–85.

Robertson, Claire, Constance Dyer, and D'Ann Campbell. (1988) "Campus Harassment: Sexual Harassment Policies and Procedures at Institutions of Higher Learning," *Journal of Women in Culture and Society,* Vol. 13, No. 2, pp. 792–812.

Robertson, Ian. (1987) *Sociology* (3rd ed.) New York: Worth.

Robinson, Robert, Delaney Kirk, James Powell. (1987) "Sexual Harassment: New Approaches for a Changed Environment," *SAM Advanced Management Journal,* Autumn, p. 15.

Roesler, John. (1989) "Public School Children — Tort and 'Constitutional Tort' Relief," *New Mexico Trial Lawyer,* Vol. 17, No. 5.

————. (1990) "Comment on Public School Liability Issues," 29 N.M.S.B.B. 4–7.

Rogers, David. (1991) "Bloc on Democratic Swing Votes May Decide Confirmation in Senate," *Wall Street Journal,* October 14, p. A-6.

Roscoe, Bruce, Megan Goodwin, Susan Repp, and Marshall Rose. (1987) "Sexual Harassment of University Students and Student-Employees: Findings and Implications," *College Student Journal,* Vol. 21, No. 3, pp. 254–73.

Rossi, Peter. (1982) "Defining Sexual Harassment on Campus: A Replication and Extension," *Journal of Social Issues,* Vol. 38, No. 4, pp. 111–20.

————, and Eleanor Weber-Burdin. (1983) "Sexual Harassment on the Campus," *Social Science Research,* Vol. 12, pp. 131–58.

Rubin, Alissa. (1991) "Behind the Decisions," *Congressional Quarterly,* Vol. 49, No. 42, p. 3027.

Rubin, Linda, and Sherry Borgers. (1990) "Sexual Harassment in Universities During the 1980s," *Sex Roles,* Vol. 23, Nos. 7, 8, pp. 397–411.

Rubinett, Lynn. (1986) "Sex and Economics: The Tie That Binds," *Law & Inequality,* Vol. 4, No. 2, pp. 245–93.

Saal, Frank, Catherine Johnson, and Nancy Weber. (1989) "Friendly or Sexy? It May Depend on Whom You Ask," *Psychology of Women Quarterly,* Vol. 13, pp. 263–76.

Safran, Claire. (1976) "What Men Do to Women on the Job: A Shocking Look at Sexual Harassment," *Redbook,* Vol. 148, No. 1, pp. 149, 217–18, 220, 222, 224.

Salholz, Eloise, Peter Annin, and Bob Cohn. (1991) "Thomas and Hill: Mentor or Tormentor?" *Newsweek,* October 21, p. 29.

Sandroff, Ronni. (1992) "Sexual Harassment: A Health Hazard," *Working Woman,* January, p. 11.

Sarat, Austin. (1990) "Off to Meet the Wizard: Beyond Validity and Reliability in the Search for a Post-Empiricist Sociology of Law," *Law and Social Inquiry,* Vol. 15, No. 1, pp. 155–70.

Scherer, Robert, James Brodzinski, and Frank Wiebe. (1990) "Entrepreneur Career Selection and Gender: A Socialization Approach," *Journal of Small Business Management,* Vol. 28, No. 2, pp. 37–44.

Schneider, Beth. (1982) "Consciousness About Sexual Harassment Among Heterosexual and Lesbian Women Workers," *Journal of Social Issues,* Vol. 38, No. 4, pp. 75–98.

_____. (1987) "Graduate Women, Sexual Harassment, and University Policy," *Journal of Higher Education,* Vol. 58, No. 1, pp. 46–65.

_____. (1991) "Put Up and Shut Up: Workplace Sexual Assaults," *Gender & Society,* Vol. 5, No. 4, pp. 533–48.

Schultz, Duane, and Sydney Ellen Schutz. (1986) *Psychology and Industry Today: An Introduction to Industrial and Organizational Psychology,* New York: Macmillan.

Segal, Jonathan. (1991) "The Sexlessness of Harassment," *HR Magazine,* Vol. 36, No. 8, pp. 71–73.

Shapiro, Laura, Linda Buckley, Karen Springen, Debra Rosenberg, Ginny Carroll, Sherry Keene-Osborn, Clara Bingham, and Katrin Snow. (1991) "Why Women Are Angry," *Newsweek,* October 21, pp. 41–44.

Shribman, David, and Michel McQueen. (1991) "Thomas and Senators Face Risky Decision at Dramatic Hearing," *Wall Street Journal,* October 11, p. A-1.

Siegel, Alexandra. (1992) "Washington Watch," *Working Woman,* March, p. 22.

Siegelman, Peter. *The Influence of Macroeconomic Conditions on Plaintiff Win Rates in Unpublished Federal Employment Discrimination Cases,* ABF Working Paper 9012.

Skaine, Rosemarie. (1990) *Sexual Harassment: Questions & Answers* (2d ed.) Cedar Falls, IA: Rosemarie Skaine.

Soehnel, Sonja. (1981) "Sex Discrimination in Law Enforcement and Corrections Employment," 53 A.L.R. Fed. 31.

Somers, Amy. (1982) "Sexual Harassment in Academe: Legal Issues and Definitions," *Journal of Social Issues,* Vol. 38, No. 4, pp. 23–32.

Sourcebook of Criminal Justice Statistics—1990. (1991) edited by Kathleen Maguire, Timothy Flanagan, et al., U.S. Department of Justice, Office of Justice Programs, Bureau of Justice Statistics.

Sourcebook of Criminal Justice Statistics—1991. (1992) edited by Timothy Flanagan, Kathleen Maguire, et al., U.S. Department of Justice, Office of Justice Programs, Bureau of Justice Statistics.

Spector, Malcom, and John Kitsuse. (1973) "Social Problems: A Reformulation," *Social Problems,* Vol. 21, No. 2, pp. 145–59.

The State of America's Children, 1991. (1991) Children's Defense Fund, Washington, D.C.

Stopping Sexual Harassment: An AFSCME Guide. (1988) American Federation of State, County and Municipal Employees, Washington, D.C.

Strauss, Marcy. (1990) "Sexist Speech in the Workplace," *Harvard Civil Rights— Civil Liberties Law Review,* Vol. 25, pp. 1–51.

Stringer, Donna, Helen Remick, Jan Salisbury, and Angela Ginorio. (1990) "The Power and Reasons Behind Sexual Harassment: An Employer's Guide to Solutions," *Public Personnel Management,* Vol. 19, No. 1, pp. 43–52.

Study Findings: National Study of the Incidence and Severity of Child Abuse and Neglect. (1981) U.S. Department of Health and Human Services, Washington, D.C., DHHS Publication No. OHDS 81-30325.

Summers, Russel. (1991) "Determinants of Judgments of and Responses to a Complaint of Sexual Harassment," *Sex Roles,* Vol. 25, pp. 379–92.

Tangri, Sandra, Martha Burt, and Leanor Johnson. (1982) "Sexual Harassment at Work: Three Explanatory Models," *Journal of Social Issues,* Vol. 38, No. 4, pp. 33–54.

Taylor, John. (1991) "Men on Trial II," *New York,* December 16, pp. 30–36.

Terpstra, David. (1986) "Organizational Costs of Sexual Harassment," *Journal of Employment Counseling,* Vol. 23, pp. 112–19.

————, and Douglas Baker. (1986) "Psychological and Demographic Correlates of Perceptions of Sexual Harassment," *Genetic, Social, and General Psychology Monographs,* Vol. 112, No. 4, pp. 461–78.

————, and ————. (1987) "A Hierarchy of Sexual Harassment," *Journal of Psychology,* Vol. 121, No. 6, pp. 599–605.

————, and ————. (1988) "Outcomes of Sexual Harassment Charges," *Academy of Management Journal,* Vol. 31, pp. 185–94.

————, and ————. (1989) "The Identification and Classification of Reactions to Sexual Harassment," *Journal of Organizational Behavior,* Vol. 10, pp. 1–14.

————, and ————. (1992) "Outcomes of Federal Court Decisions on Sexual Harassment," *Academy of Management Journal,* Vol. 35, No. 1, pp. 181–90.

Theberge, Nancy. (1990) "Gender, Work, and Power: The Case of Women in Coaching," *Canadian Journal of Sociology,* Vol. 15, No. 1, pp. 59–75.

Thomann, Daniel, and Richard Wiener. (1987) "Physical and Psychological Causality as Determinants of Culpability in Sexual Harassment Cases," *Sex Roles,* Vol. 17, Nos. 9, 10, pp. 573–91.

Thomas, Virginia. (1991) "Breaking Silence," *People Weekly,* November 11, pp. 108–12, 114, 116.

Thornton, Terry. (1986) "Sexual Harassment, 1: Discouraging It in the Workplace," *Personnel,* April, p. 18.

Tiner, Michael, and Daniel O'Grady. (1988) "Lie Detectors in Employment," 23 *Harvard Civil Rights–Civil Liberties Law Review* 85.

Toufexis, Anastasia, Ann Blackman, Barbara Dolan, and D. Blake Hallanan. (1991) "When Can Memories Be Trusted?" *Time,* October 28, pp. 86–88.

Townsend, Josephine. (1992) "Supervising Women in Policing," *Law and Order,* Vol. 40, No. 11, pp. 53–55.

Tracking Offenders: The Child Victim. (1984) U.S. Department of Justice, Washington, D.C.

Tucker, Robert. (1978) *The Marx-Engels Reader* (2d ed.), New York: W. W. Norton.

"Unemployment Compensation Benefits for the Victim of Work-Related Sexual Harassment." (1980) *Harvard Women's Law Journal,* Vol. 3, Spring.

USA Today Poll, October 14, 1991. (1991a) (A nationwide telephone poll by Gordon S. Black Corp. of 758 adults conducted 6–9 P.M. EDT Sunday. The poll has a margin of error of 3.5%. A total of 204 blacks were interviewed for comparisons between blacks and whites, with the poll weighted to accurately represent the percentage of blacks nationwide.)

U.S.G.A.O. (1988) *Equal Employment Opportunity: EEOC and State Agencies Do Not Fully Investigate Discrimination Charges,* U.S. General Accounting Office, Washington, D.C.: Government Printing Office.

U.S.M.S.P.B. (1981) "Sexual Harassment in the Workplace: Is It a Problem?" Office of Merit Systems Review and Studies.

_____. (1988) *Sexual Harassment in the Federal Government: An Update,* U.S. Merit Systems Protection Board, Office of Policy and Education, Washington, D.C.

Villamoare, Adelaide. (1990) "Politics and Research: Epistemological Moments," *Law and Social Inquiry,* Vol. 15, No. 1, pp. 149–54.

Wald, Sarah. (1982) "Alternatives to Title VII: State Statutory and Common-Law Remedies for Employment Discrimination," *Harvard Women's Law Journal,* Vol. 5, pp. 35–72.

Waters, Mary-Alice. (1971) "Are Feminism and Socialism Related?" *Feminism and Socialism,* New York: Pathfinder Press, pp, 18–26.

Weber-Burdin, Eleanor, and Peter Rossi. (1982) "Defining Sexual Harassment on Campus: A Replication and Extension," *Journal of Social Issues,* Vol. 38, No. 4, pp. 111–20.

Weeks, Elaine, Jacqueline Boles, Albeno Garbin, and John Blount. (1986) "The Transformation of Sexual Harassment from a Private Trouble into a Public Issue," *Sociological Inquiry,* Vol. 56, No. 4, pp. 432–55.

Weimer, Deborah. (1987) "Common Law Remedies of Employees Injured by Employer Use of Polygraph Testing," 22 *University of Richmond Law Review* 51.

Wertlieb, Ellen. (1991) "Individuals with Disabilities in the Criminal Justice System: A Review of the Literature," *Criminal Justice and Behavior,* Vol. 18, No. 3, pp. 332–50.

Whitcomb, Debra. (1985) *Prosecution of Child Sexual Abuse: Innovations in Practice,* U.S. Department of Justice, Washington, D.C.

_____. (1986) *Prosecuting Child Sexual Abuse—New Approaches,* U.S. Department of Justice, Washington, D.C.

White, Jack, Melissa Ludtke, and Don Winbush. (1991) "The Pain of Being Black," *Time,* September 16, pp. 24–27.

Williamson, John, David Karp, John Dalphin, Paul Gray, Stephen Barry, and Richard Dorr. (1982) *The Research Craft: An Introduction to Social Research Methods* (2d ed.), Glenview, IL: Scott, Foresman.

"Witnesses Paint Different Pictures." (1991) *Salt Lake Tribune,* October 14, pp. A-1, A-2.

Wolman, Benson. (1988) "Verbal Sexual Harassment on the Job as Intentional Infliction of Emotional Distress," *Capital University Law Review,* Vol. 17, pp. 245–72.

Wong, Molly. (1984) "Sexual Harassment at Work: Female Police Officers," Ph.D. diss., University of Pittsburgh.

"The Working Woman Survey." (1992) *Working Woman,* February, pp. 14–16.

Index